PICKING UP A PIN FOR THE LORD

PICKING UP A PIN FOR THE LORD:

ENGLISH PARTICULAR BAPTISTS FROM 1688 TO THE EARLY NINETEENTH CENTURY

Peter Naylor

Grace Publications

GRACE PUBLICATIONS TRUST
139 Grosvenor Avenue
London N5 2NH
England

Managing Editors
J. P. Arthur, M.A.
H. J. Appleby

ISBN 0 946462 25 9

Distributed by
EVANGELICAL PRESS
12 Wooler Street
Darlington
Co. Durham DL1 1RQ
England

Printed in Great Britain at the Bath Press, Avon

'If, therefore, the Lord command me to pick up a pin, it is as much my duty to comply, as it is to believe that Jesus Christ is the Son of God.'

So claimed William Buttfield, pastor of the Baptist church at Thorn, near Dunstable, in 1778.*

* See p. 110.

CONTENTS

LIST OF ILLUSTRATIONS

APOLOGIA AND ACKNOWLEDGEMENTS

There is a lawyer's maxim to the effect that assertion must be backed up by proof. No doubt this is, within wide limits, sound counsel. In a book such as this the axiom would have to fulfil itself in pages disfigured by tiny, superscribed numbers, numbers designed to guide the dedicated reader to pages of endnotes, and thence to scarce books in specialist libraries. This procedure might, hopefully, yield the needful 'proof'. In research theses the convention is, of course, essential. Here, the effect could be that you, the reader, become weary, lose interest, and put the unread volume to one side.

Nevertheless, the challenge of boredom has been accepted because of the nature of some of our material. Accuracy and readability had to be balanced nicely; in retrospect, the former seemed marginally more important. For example, we offer information about Strict Baptist origins which, as far as we know, has never been published. It followed that a failure to give the background references would have been irresponsible. Therefore, all necessary details, plus a bibliography, have been included for the sake of any readers who might wish to check up on what we have to say.

Essentially, this book is a development of a paper delivered to the Strict Baptist Historical Society in 1988. I would like to record my gratitude to the Society, to Grace Publications Trust and to other friends for their encouragement, and to the Tabernacle Baptist Church, Wellingborough, for generously enabling me to complete this project and for bearing with me patiently when enthusing at length about some of the eighteenth-century Particular Baptists. Thanks are due, too, to Regent's Park College, Oxford, for permission to study in the Angus Library, to the staffs of Dr Williams's Library and the Evangelical Library, to those churches which have allowed me access to their records, and to all who have offered helpful criticisms and other aid. My family has been patient with me.

The Authorised Version has been used throughout, one reason being that this was the Bible loved by the people of God in England in the eighteenth century. We cite from the texts which they read and from which their ministers expounded Jesus Christ.

The mistakes in the book are my own, as are any opinions which may be presented.

Peter Naylor

INTRODUCTION

For British Baptists the year 1887 was notable because it witnessed the outbreak of the 'Down-Grade' controversy. Although Dr E.A. Payne wrote more than seventy years later that 'there has been a general desire to say as little as possible about it, lest old wounds be re-opened',[1] it has not yet been forgotten. Nor will it be. When the storm broke, the man who was at the centre of it all, Charles Haddon Spurgeon (1834-92), wrote:

> We have had enough of *The Down-Grade* for ourselves ... Assuredly the New Theology can do no good towards God or man; it has no adaptation for it. ... Something will come of the struggle over *The Down-Grade*. The Lord has designs in connection with which his adversaries little dream of.[2]

One immediate consequence of the conflict was the hurt inflicted upon Spurgeon. In October, 1891, when standing on the platform at Herne Hill station on the way to Menton, in the south of France, where he died in the following year, Spurgeon confessed to his friends: 'The fight is killing me.'[3]

Less well-known might be the fact that Spurgeon then had opponents other than those within the Baptist Union. In the same year in which the controversy flared, William Jeyes Styles (1842-1914), pastor of a Baptist church which met in Keppel Street, near the British Museum, London, published a volume which, he claimed, was designed 'to ... advocate the tenets of the Strict and Particular Section of the Baptist Denomination'.[4] Styles remarked thus about Spurgeon:

> The Minister of the Metropolitan Tabernacle, our first Pastor, the President of the College to which we owe so much ... also claims a word. ... Some living preacher, whose sentiments are a present power, claimed our attention, and we felt bound to select the one we have. We beg that none will charge us with lack of love to him.[5]

One dead preacher mentioned by Styles was Andrew Fuller of Kettering (1754-1815), whom he considered to be 'perfectly uninfluential' by the 1880s. Styles proceeded to various criticisms of Spurgeon's views, such as a rebuttal of the latter's conviction, verbalised by Styles, that 'sinners must believe, to render the blood of Christ efficacious to their souls'.[6]

Time passes. Perhaps the volumes bequeathed by Spurgeon and others are now in some danger of standing unopened. While they are of abiding interest to many people, the truth is that, because of their age, they lack some of their earlier widespread appeal; they were not inspired. Nevertheless, their worth endures. This is because their authors were often controversialists, struggling in their times over issues which will occupy the energies of God's people for as long as the sun rises and sets. The fact is that most of the problems which confront the churches now are difficulties which existed in Styles's and Spurgeon's day, in Fuller's time, some eighty years earlier, and which were by no means unknown to the Baptists in the 1700s. For example, church registration by the state was an issue for the English Baptists both in the seventeenth century and in that which followed it. They would have sympathized with the assertion that 'we do not permit City authorities to meddle into our Church matters', made by a Christian in the Ukraine when writing to a member of the Wellingborough 'Tabernacle' in 1989.[7] Interference has always been a hazard for the Lord's people everywhere.

The truth is that a seeming lack of relevance of church history and historical theology for the generations which follow is illusory. Men will persist in trying to find out what others before them thought and did about various issues. Given time, children always develop the conviction that their fathers' doings (or misdoings) never lack significance for them, their offspring. So it is with church history. We go back to our predecessors because, contrary to Styles, they are by no means 'perfectly uninfluential'.

* * *

This book does not presume to be a history of the English Particular Baptists from 1688 through to the earlier part of the last century. Nor is it an attempt to trace accurately all major developments within the Baptist churches of the period. The purpose of these pages will be to look at some of the personalities, some of the churches, some of the emphases and some of the controversies in the denomination at that time. That is, we want to consider the period beginning at about the time of the 'Glorious Revolution' of 1688, when the population of England and Wales was estimated at five and a half millions, down to the early 1800s, when the population was more than ten millions.[8] We begin in the 1680s because it could be argued that the decade was one of the most decisive in English history, ranking with the 1530s (the opening ten years of the English Reformation), the 1640s (which witnessed Parliament's victory in the Civil War), and the 1940s (in which, according to Winston Churchill, occurred Britain's 'finest hour'[9]). The 1680s witnessed simultaneously the origins of our party-political system, confirmation that a non-Roman Anglican Church would for the indefinite future manage the established religion of England, and the defeat of Stuart trends towards a Continental-style absolutist government. On a wider horizon, the end of the 1700s saw the American Revolutionary War, the French Revolution, and the continuation of a second Hundred Years' War against France. This war lasted until the Battle of Waterloo in 1815 and, together with the Industrial Revolution at home, established both English commercial supremacy and the British Empire.[10]

We shall take our examination of the English Particular Baptists only as far as the early 1800s. At that time the extended literary debate within the constituency for and against restricted communion experienced something of a pause. Everything, it appears, that was worth saying had been said; boundaries had been prepared for the future.[11]

Times were cruel. The *Northampton Mercury*, which exercised an influence upon the young William Carey (1761-1834),[12] recorded in its edition for June 10, 1739, that Francis McDuff, a ten-year-old boy, would hang within the month, together with four others. He had been convicted for stealing threepence.[13] Notwithstanding the Evangelical Awakening, the 1700s were twilight years for the Baptists, then free to meet in their churches, yet effectively second-class citizens because of their faith. But the Lord blessed many of them; with other Dissenters they were steadily gaining in numbers, confidence and influence.

Certain matters, which we think important, will be discussed. We hope to show that the epithet 'strict baptist' was a derisory term applied by Paedobaptists, those who baptize babies, to restricted-communion Baptists in the late 1600s, some eighty or so years earlier than had been thought. That is to say, some of those who would in time be denominated as 'Strict Baptists' were known explicitly as such in the years immediately following the Revolution of 1688. Moreover, there is firm evidence to show that the people who were designated 'Strict Baptists' soon accepted the title; by 1750 at least they were referring to themselves as such.[14]

We shall try to demonstrate, too, that the term in its original usage by no means referred solely to 'high Calvinists'; it was ascribed to those Baptists who advocated the admission of baptized (for them, immersed) believers only to the Lord's table. Differences about the relation between the election of grace, justification and faith simply did not enter into the matter. Later interpretations of the doctrines of grace, as bequeathed by John Gill (1697-1771), for example, should not be thought to bear upon the issue. Andrew Fuller, no high Calvinist, was assuredly a 'Strict Baptist'.[15]

Two distinct issues which faced English Particular Baptists in this period will be examined: high Calvinism, particularly as systematized by John Gill, and ongoing arguments for and against restricted communion. A preliminary warning needs to be given concerning the way in which we shall try to handle our forefathers' arguments about restricted communion, lest the reader suspects that the presentation is unnecessarily repetitious. The fact seems to be that after 1688, although literary styles varied immensely, Baptists on both sides of the baptism-communion issue invariably echoed their predecessors; a second generation of antagonists took over where a first had left off, and anticipated a third. We wish to show that no substantially fresh arguments appeared either for or against restricted communion during the period under review. Further, we maintain that discussions from this period provide a complete education in the matter of who should approach the Lord's table; no relevant question was ignored. It can be shown, too, that during a period when Particular Baptists tended to split over the question of the terms of communion, 'Strict Baptists' normally found themselves under bitter and occasionally vitriolic attack; their relative mildness suggests that they were more sinned against than sinning. An application for our own times might be that those who adopt their position will find that they need to defend themselves in similar fashion.

These pages will build upon the apparent fact that during the eighteenth century, the first which offered toleration to Noncon-formity, 'General' and 'Particular' Baptists never identified as one coherent, national body of Baptist churches. This was because the 'General Baptists' were 'Arminians', people who tended to sub-scribe to the teaching of the Dutchman Arminius (1560-1609) and his followers. They held, among other matters, that Christ died to save all men in general (whence the term 'General Baptists'), and that it is possible for Christians to fall away from salvation.[16] Arminianism, even when immersed in water, as it were, upon a profession of faith in Christ, was seen by the Particular Baptists as a travesty of the gospel. These believed that Christ had died to secure the salvation of the elect in particular rather than all men in general (hence, 'Particular Baptists'). We believe that what Arminianism was then it remains today and forever. Perhaps there are important lessons here for the end of the millennium.

History, we shall suggest, shows that churches need to invest money and labour for training a well-equipped ministry. Now, as then, the people of God cannot and ought not to expect to rely upon the state. Nor should they look to seminaries which are reformed but not explicitly Baptist. Because both sound churchmanship and a competent ministry are essential for survival and growth, Particular Baptist churches should take their own business in hand. As we shall see, there are splendid eighteenth-century examples to encourage us.

CHAPTER I
THE ENGLISH PARTICULAR BAPTISTS: A SEPARATE DENOMINATION

The morning of Monday, November 5, 1688, was hazy, and the pilot of the ship carrying William, Prince of Orange, guided the Dutch fleet too far west beyond Torbay, where the Prince had planned to land. At Plymouth, meanwhile, a garrison had been posted by James II, King of England and the last of the Stuart monarchs, while the royal fleet had slipped out of the Thames in pursuit of William. The situation was unhopeful; an Anglican, Gilbert Burnet (1643-1715), sailing with William, was told by a friend that he might go to his prayers because all was over. In the event, the wind changed its direction, the mist dispersed, the sun shone and the vessels rounded Berry Head to ride safe in Torbay harbour. In London, James prepared to flee the country from before his Dutch son-in-law. Taking the Great Seal of England in his hand, he was rowed across the Thames, into which he cast the seal and from which it was dragged up accidentally some months later.[1]

In the country at large religious and political uncertainties were closely twined. Burnet, dispossessed by Charles II for rebuking his way of life, and then outlawed by James II, said later about the Baptists that they 'were generally men of virtue, and of an universal charity', and admitted that there is no precept given by the New Testament for the baptism of infants.[2] Like the vast majority of his fellow-countrymen, he remained in the doctrinally-blurred middle ground provided by the Church of England, a Church glad to see the back of King James. Soon after his settlement in 1689 as Bishop of Salisbury, Burnet claimed in a pastoral letter to his diocesan clergy that James's action seemed 'to imply this at least, That either he did not think of returning again, or that if he should return, that he would no more Govern by the shew of Law'. Indeed, this was why England had risen up against him: '*The Protestants of England ... are in*

divers kinds most intolerably vexed and oppressed by the *Popish*
Contrivances and Practices, covered with the pretences and name of
Authority.' So wrote certain of the English nobility to William
before ever he sailed from Holland and when James was still the
king.[3] In the event, James never came back to England, while the
revolution which confirmed Anglican Protestantism was glorious in
that it was bloodless, moderate and permanent.

William's first task was to exorcize from the minds of his people
the notion that he stood above the laws of the realm. Thus appeared
the Toleration Act of May, 1689. For the hitherto persecuted
Dissenters a new era was about to dawn. Burnet probably referred
to them when preaching at the Chapel of St James just before
Christmas, 1688, and before William had been crowned:

> It is to be hoped that we will study to be all of one mind; or, if
> we cannot arrive at so great a blessing, that at least we will love one
> another, and remember that we are Brethren, fellow Christians and
> fellow Protestants, that must have been destroyed together, and
> therefore must now support and bear with one another.[4]

* * *

This chapter considers the so-called 'Particular Baptists' in England
after the monumentally important Toleration Act. No reference will
be made to Baptists in Scotland because it is possible to regard them
as a movement with no essential connections with English Baptists.[5]

Why are we concerned with 'Particular Baptists' only, bearing
in mind that over the years, and certainly in the eighteenth century,
there have been many Baptists who chose to stand aside from
historic Calvinism? The short answer is that Calvinistic Baptists
always felt that there was a considerable, even impassable, gulf
between them and the General Baptists. Because this was reckoned
to be so, it follows that a study of 'Particular' and 'General' Baptists
under a common denominational title of 'Baptists' would appear to
be an unwarranted over-simplification. For example, according to
the London Particular Baptist minister William Kiffin (1616-1701),
as cited by the Baptist historian Joseph Ivimey (1773-1834), it
appears that before the time of the 1644 Particular Baptist confession, issued by seven London churches, there were 'many' members
of Dissenting groups in and around London who were immersed

William Kiffin (1616-1701); reproduced by courtesy of the
Evangelical Library

Benjamin Keach (1640-1704); a portrait reproduced by courtesy
of the Metropolitan Tabernacle, London.

upon their profession of faith in Christ as Lord. Among them, the doctrines of grace were divisive. Concerning the Arminian, or 'General', Baptists, Ivimey wrote: 'Admitting then that there were ministers of this description, it is not probable that Calvinists would repair to them for an administrator of baptism.'[6]

Because his writings will occur frequently in these pages Ivimey deserves an introduction. Born at Ringwood, Hampshire, he was the first of a family of eight children. A Calvinist, though not of the 'high' variety, and a convinced advocate of restricted communion, he added some eight hundred members to the Eagle Street, London, church during a pastorate which commenced in 1805, when he was twenty-three. Between 1811 and 1830 he published his indispensable four-volume work, *History of the English Baptists*, while in 1826 there appeared his *Pilgrims of the 19th Century*, a continuation of *The Pilgrim's Progress* by John Bunyan (1628-88), in which he attempted to follow up what he considered to have been Bunyan's train of thought. The inscription upon Ivimey's tomb in Bunhill Fields, London, read simply 'Grace reigns'.[7]

To return to the subject, Hercules Collins, who assumed the pastorate of John Spilsbury's London Particular Baptist church in 1677, whose congregation was scattered in 1684, and who died about the end of the century,[8] wrote in his book *Believers' baptism from heaven, and of divine institution: Infant Baptism from earth, and of human invention*, that English Baptists did not receive their baptism from John Smyth.[9] This is significant because John Smyth (about 1565-1612) finds his place in the history of the nation not only as one of the first Englishmen to demand full liberty of conscience, but also as the father of English General Baptists.[10] Evidently Spilsbury (about 1593-1668), his people and they who came after did not consider that a common renunciation of infant baptism was sufficient to unite believers who disagreed concerning predestination and election.

Thomas Crosby's thoughts on the matter are worth quoting, too. Son-in-law of Benjamin Keach (1640-1704), Crosby was a member of the Particular Baptist church which assembled in Goat Street, near St John's Church, Southwark. He died in or about 1751. His *History of the English Baptists* provides important source material for the period. Crosby wrote:

> It may be proper to observe here, that there have been two *parties* of the *English Baptists* in *England* ever since the beginning

of the reformation; those that have followed the *Calvinistical* scheme of doctrines ... And those that have professed the *Arminian* or remonstrant tenets; and have also from the chief of those doctrines, *universal redemption*, been called *General Baptists*.[11]

The ongoing reality of this fundamental distinction was indicated by the Calvinistic Baptist John Ryland junior (1753-1825), who some eighty years later wrote:

> The English Baptists have been usually divided into two distinct bodies, by their different views of the doctrines of grace. The *General Baptists* are so called, from their maintaining the sentiment of general redemption. Many of the old churches of this sort, have gone from general redemption to no redemption, and from Arminianism to Arianism and Socinianism.[12]

'Arianism' (after Arius of Alexandria, who died in A.D. 336) was a heresy which held that the Son of God was created rather than coeternal with the Father. 'Socinianism' (from the Italians Lelio Sozzini, 1525-62, and his nephew, Fausto, 1539-1604) was one of the forerunners of modern Unitarianism. 'Unitarianism', in turn, rejects both the doctrines of the Trinity and the essential deity of our Lord.

Crosby was less convinced about the rightness of this split among the Baptists. He had earlier expressed the view that those of the constituency who

> ... encourage such distinctions and divisions ... let them prepare to answer such unfaithfulness to the great shepherd of the flock, who has said, *that a house or kingdom divided against it self, cannot stand, but is brought to nought.*[13]

It ought, perhaps, to be said that Crosby's words should be assessed in terms of his character. In 1719 he left the Goat Street church, in company with John Gill and nearly two hundred others, after a dispute concerning Gill's ministerial appointment by the congregation. He returned to his old church, now meeting elsewhere, four years later, together with members of the Keach and Stinton families.[14] It might be that Crosby had been influenced by Gill's predecessor at Goat Street, Benjamin Stinton (1676-1718), ministerial successor to and another son-in-law of Benjamin Keach.

Stinton had tried hard, but failed, to bring together Particular and General Baptists in London.[15] It is possible that Crosby's somewhat unsettled disposition refuted his own convictions about what was for him the unhappy want of unity among Baptists of both 'General' and 'Particular' persuasions. He was never, it seems, an entirely stable man. In the view of W.T. Whitley, writing in 1916, 'his work has lost all authority.'[16]

We take issue with Crosby's approach. Differences between Calvinistic and Arminian Baptists cannot be smoothed over; a consensus about baptism will never overcome a disagreement about the relationship between conversion and the will of man. Such, at least, was the perception of our forefathers. Crosby ensured his place as an author, yet as a theologian he seems to have lacked discernment. This was a fault, however, which could not easily be attributed to the churches; they usually knew what they believed. At the time of the historic Salters' Hall controversy in 1719 attempts were made to close the gulf between the two sides.[17] The fact was that in the opening years of the century one London Baptist church only, that meeting in Paul's Alley in the Barbican, refused to adopt either of the opposing terms 'General' or 'Particular', ordering its preachers to remain silent on the points at issue. No other metropolitan church sought to stand aloof from either of the two Baptist bodies.[18]

Another illustration might be provided by the Baptist church at Wymeswold, Leicestershire. It seems that as early as 1712 the congregation was divided: 18 familes were characterized as 'Anabaptist universalists' and 7 as 'Anabaptist particulars'. In the same county Henry Coleman, when he had become pastor at Kilby, was charged in 1694 by Benjamin Winckles and a majority within the church with teaching that 'you Exhorted the Creature to do his part; and then no doubt but God would do his part'. Winckles was disconsolate and, with others, quit to worship at Arnesby, where he exercised a notably successful ministry in a growing church for more than thirty years.[19]

To digress for a moment, the Arnesby records reveal that the church, as such, first assembled in the village in 1702. Nevertheless, it seems that at that time there were members who lived far away. Church meetings, for the purposes of uniting at the Lord's table and for receiving new members, were sometimes held at Ramsey in Huntingdonshire, as well as at other places in the fen country, and

at Northampton and Coventry. Brethren from Leicestershire were
sent to attend these meetings.[20] This seems quite remarkable, bearing in mind that some sixty miles separate Coventry and Ramsey.
We should like to know why it was that Mr Winckles exercised such
a widespread ministry, and, particularly, why these scattered folk
were deemed to belong to one local church. It has been suggested,
indeed, that this was not a solitary phenomenon; it seems that other
churches developed in a similar fashion prior to the establishment
of Dissenting meeting-houses.[21]

David Bogue and James Bennett, in their *History of the Dissenters*, which traversed the years between 1688 and the time of writing,
1808, noted:

> As the two divisions of baptists differed from each other in
> religious sentiments, they were dissimilar in outward condition.
> Arminianism, among the dissenters has, in general, been a cold, dry
> and lifeless system, and its effects upon the heart have been
> commonly weak and spiritless. With the general baptists ... this was
> remarkably the effect. ... Among the particular baptists we are
> presented with a very different aspect of affairs. They were all
> calvinists, but from the want of an education for the ministry, many
> of them were not very judicious; and some of them abused the
> doctrine. An ignorant arminian preacher blunders through his
> system in a tolerable manner, but ignorance in a calvinist makes
> dreadful work.[22]

These Calvinists clearly had a long road to travel. The almost
undeniable suggestion remains, nevertheless, that, because of their
increasing numbers and because they stood apart from other
immersionists, it seems right to consider the Particular Baptists of
the eighteenth century as a quite distinct group worthy of its own
individual examination. It is upon this thesis that we shall proceed.

CHAPTER II
FROM REPRESSION TO PROTECTION: BEFORE AND AFTER THE REVOLUTION OF 1688

An outline of some of the principal events in the years surrounding 1688 will help us to understand the situation and prospects of the English Particular Baptists when William III became king in that year.

In 1633, according to Thomas Crosby, the Calvinistic Baptists, who hitherto had not formed their own churches, 'began now to separate themselves, and form distinct societies of their own persuasion'.[1] Crosby identified the congregation which he considered to have been the 'first': that established in Broad Street, Old Gravel Lane, in Wapping. Apparently, this church developed from an Independent (or, Congregationalist) group which had gathered in 1616 with Henry Jacob (1563-1624) as pastor. Jacob was followed by John Lathrop (or, Lathorp), who was in office in 1633 when discussion arose concerning baptism. Those who could not agree with the baptism of infants desired dismissal from the congregation in order to form their own church.[2]

Joseph Ivimey, however, was of the opinion that the idea that the origin of the baptized churches went back only as far as the 1630s was a 'common error', and suggested that such churches had existed since perhaps the reign of Edward VI (1547-53).[3] Be that as it may, Crosby cited William Kiffin's account of the formation of the Wapping church in its separation from the congregation under Lathrop:

> The church, considering that they were now grown very numerous, and so more than could in those times of persecution conveniently meet together, and believing also that those persons acted from a principle of conscience, and not obstinacy, agreed to allow them the liberty they desired, and that they should be constituted a distinct church; which was perform'd the 12th of *Sept.* 1633. And

as they believed that *baptism* was not rightly administred to *infants*, so they look'd upon the *baptism* they had receiv'd at that age as invalid: whereupon most or all of them received a new *baptism*. Their minister was Mr. *John Spilsbury*. What number they were is uncertain, because in the mentioning of the names of about twenty men and women, it is added *with divers others*.[4]

In his day Ivimey was not sure whether the church was composed entirely of baptized persons, although he thought that this was the 'most rational conjecture'. His record makes magnificent reading: by their conduct in the matter 'both parties ... bore testimony to the truth and sincerity of their professions'.[5] Personalities were not, it seems, attacked, and both sides agreed to differ in love and go their ways, perhaps reflecting the fact that the Calvinistic Baptists owed a considerable debt to their Paedobaptist brethren. Certainly, the first Particular Baptist confession of 1644 borrowed considerably from an earlier Separatist but non-Baptist confession which had appeared in 1596.[6] The confession of 1644 was issued in order to give protection from malicious slander and to distinguish the Particular Baptists from both the General Baptists and the earlier Continental Anabaptists, rather than to distance the constituency from Paedobaptists. Apparently, it served its purpose. Ivimey wrote that the confession 'being put into the hands of many of the members of parliament, produced such an effect, that some of their greatest adversaries ... were obliged to acknowledge, that excepting the articles against infant baptism, it was an orthodox confession'.[7] Several editions were printed at the time, one of them licensed by authority.[8]

We have seen that by 1644 there were at least seven such churches in London. As noted, the adjective 'particular' relates to the Calvinistic belief in an atonement confined in both its designed scope and its ultimate saving effect to the elect alone. Further, most Baptists practised what is often termed nowadays 'restricted communion'. At least, this appears to be the thrust of the 1646 reprint of the confession:

> Baptisme is an ordinance of the new Testament, given by Christ, to be dispensed upon persons professing faith, or that are made Disciples: who upon profession of faith, ought to be baptized, and after to partake of the Lord's supper.[9]

This was the sole reference to the Lord's table. The parent document of 1644 had, indeed, implied restricted communion, although without mentioning the table specifically; only baptized believers could join in the 'practical injoyment of the ordinances, commanded by Christ their head and King'.[10]

When the Civil War broke out in August, 1642, Dissenting groups were widespread. Parliament still subscribed to the idea of religious uniformity, while the Puritan clergy had no wish to enslave themselves to congregations of uneducated laymen. Nevertheless, Richard Baxter (1615-91), who was deprived of his living by the 1662 Act of Uniformity, and whose tongue usually caused his opponents to smart,[11] had to confess that sectarians and Independents were 'the soul of the army'.[12] Daniel Neal, an Independent, writing in the early 1700s, observed that in the 1640s the '*particular baptists* were strict *calvinists*', and 'were, for the most part, of the meanest of the people; their preachers were generally illiterate, and went about the country making proselytes of all who would submit to immersion'. 'Still', he conceded, 'there were among them some learned, and a great many sober and devout christians.'[13]

At that period a degree of intimate fellowship was known by some Calvinistic Baptist churches. For example, in 1653 a letter was sent by a member of the Baptist church in Dublin to the London congregations, seeking information about like-minded churches in England, Scotland and Wales. The exercise was designed to overcome the danger of 'receiving or refusing such as ought, or ought not to enjoy communion', 'communion' referring to inter-church fellowship.[14] The benefits of such fellowship were extolled in the letter: 'Oh, then let neither sea nor land, things present nor thing to come, separate us from a Christian correspondence, whereby we may knowingly mourn with those that mourn, and rejoice with those that rejoice.'[15] Apparently, this letter had a considerable effect upon some of the London churches, which sent a copy to their Welsh brethren seeking information about their state.

When Charles II's Act of Uniformity became law in 1662 there might have been about 130 Particular Baptist churches in England and Wales,[16] while among the 2,000 and more clergy, lecturers and others who were deprived of their livings between 1660 and 1662 there were no more than 19 Baptist ministers. Of these, 8 were English, and 11 Welsh. Of the 8 Englishmen, 7 advocated open communion, a practice not common to Baptists generally.[17] Perhaps

it was the ejected ministers' laxity in this crucial matter which led
them in the first place into the national Church. After the Act of
Uniformity 'we do not find that any person who rejected the baptism
of infants continued in the establishment', according to Ivimey.[18]

January, 1661 saw the Fifth-Monarchist rising led by a wine
cooper named Thomas Venner. The 'Fifth Monarchists' were so
called because they hoped to see the establishment of the earthly rule
of both Christ and the saints as successors to the Babylonian,
Persian, Greek and Roman empires. They regarded themselves as
these successors, people who were living in the end time which they
hoped to bring to its realization.[19] Accompanied by some fifty men,
Venner terrorized the city of London, killing twenty-two people. As
a result, a royal proclamation forbade all meetings of Anabaptists,
Quakers and Fifth-Monarchy men; within a matter of weeks over
four thousand Quakers found themselves in prison.[20] Some Baptists,
including Kiffin and Spilsbury, presented an address to Charles,
disassociating themselves from the affair.[21] Inevitably, perhaps,
Charles brought in the Corporation Act of 1661, by which membership of any municipal body was denied to Nonconformists. The Act
of Uniformity required submission to the Thirty-Nine Articles and
to the Prayer Book, a volume which became a standard of truth on
a level with the statute law of the kingdom. In 1664 the first
Conventicle Act decreed that no religious meetings of over five
persons could be conducted other than in accordance with the
liturgy of the Church of England. Then followed the Five Mile Act
in 1665, by which no Dissenting minister could come nearer than
five miles to a corporate borough unless, among other matters, he
vowed never to seek an alteration in both the government of Church
and State. These measures, known collectively as the 'Clarendon
Code', threatened Dissent with continuing impotence and probably
ultimate extinction.[22]

Then came Charles's Declaration of Indulgence in March, 1672.
This aroused the concern of the nation on two counts. First, it
seemed clear that the king was using his prerogative to bring to
nothing statute law, the effects of which would have been incalculable. Second, as a part-redemption of Charles's promise to Louis
XIV of France to declare himself a Roman Catholic, the Indulgence
was designed to re-introduce popery, a tactic suspected by not a few
Nonconformists at the time.

Because Parliament was even more jealous of its position as the legislature than were the people, the Declaration was cancelled. In March of the same year, 1673, came the first Test Act, accompanied by a bill for the 'Ease of Protestant Dissenters'. The latter, although passed by the Commons, was opposed successfully by the bishops. The Test Act was called 'An Act for preventing dangers which may happen from popish recusants', although it had long-term implications for Dissenters.[23] Nevertheless, the Independents, both Baptist and Paedobaptist, continued to spread rapidly. As early as 1641 Bishop Joseph Hall of Norwich had felt compelled to inform the Lords that in London and the suburbs there were not fewer than eighty congregations of sectaries, instructed by 'cobblers, tailors, felt-makers, and such like trash'.[24]

The 1673 act denied civil, naval and military employment to all who would not take the oaths of supremacy and allegiance, who would not receive communion under the Anglican rite, and who refused to declare disbelief in transubstantiation. In 1678 came the second Test Act, debarring all Catholics, apart from the Duke of York, later James II, from sitting in the House of Lords. Now, dissidents were excluded from any place in Parliament. They could not even take any action in the courts, be guardians to children, administer other people's business or receive legacies. The legislation remained on the statute books for many years; statesmen realised that any premature change in the status quo could release a flood of Tory fury, leading, perhaps, to the unsettling of the house of Hanover and a Stuart restoration. This nightmare also haunted the Dissenters and was one factor underlying their diffidence about pressing too hard for a repeal of the cruel legislation. Ivimey reported, in fact, that in 1745 it was likely that a circular letter sent by Dissenting leaders to the English churches led to the formation of armed associations of Nonconformists to resist the Pretender, Charles Stuart, when he invaded from Scotland.[25]

Loyalist Dissent was grudgingly tolerated by society rather than welcomed. Years later, when some Nonconformists were showing a certain sympathy for the French Revolution, George III (1760-1820) wrote in 1795 that the coronation oath implied that the crown should not assent to the repeal of the Test Acts, a repeal which would have favoured Roman Catholics.[26] This was important because, of necessity, Roman Catholic fortunes were linked intimately with those of the Dissenters, and had been ever since 1673; both Catholics and Nonconformists, albeit for very different reasons, had

placed themselves beyond the decreed bounds of established Protestantism. Even when the Test Acts finally disappeared, Nonconformists paid church rates until 1886, and until as recently as 1880
were obliged to employ the Book of Common Prayer at burial
services. Oxford and Cambridge were opened to them only in 1871.

Renewed persecution under Charles II, who died in 1685, made it
important for Baptists, Congregationalists and Presbyterians to show
a united front. As far as the Baptists were concerned, Quakerism
threatened the stability of some of their churches,[27] those of the General
Baptists more, perhaps, than the Particular Baptists. Among the former
there circulated a belief in the possibility of direct inspiration by the
Holy Spirit, a belief which led to some, perhaps many, going over to the
Quakers.[28] Meanwhile, in the West of England, Thomas Collier, a
leader among the Particular Baptists, had modified his early Calvinism.
All in all, it was desirable, even essential, for Particular Baptists to
indicate where they stood. This necessity was illustrated by a voluminous tome from the pen of one Matthias Maurice, not to be confused
with the later Matthias Maurice who ministered to the Independent
church at Rothwell, Northamptonshire, in the early eighteenth century.[29] The earlier Maurice wrote in 1682 concerning recent heresies
'started up' by the devil that they included 'the *Swenkfeldians,
Anabaptists, Mennonists, The Family of Love, Quakers, Ranters*, and
the rest of the Modern Sects'.[30] Wrote Crosby concerning the Calvinistic Baptists of the period: 'They judged it necessary to join together
in giving a testimony to the world of their firm adhering to those
wholesome principles, by the publication of this.'[31] 'This' was, in fact,
a quite new statement of faith. The Particular Baptists employed the
Westminster Confession, the 1646 statement of Presbyterianism, as a
basis for their confession, which appeared in 1677. No names were
attached, and it was recommended subsequently to their general
assembly in 1689 at a time when Baptists could meet without fear,
publish the minutes of their proceedings and affix their names to their
resolutions.[32]

At that period there were other confessions. Crosby wrote:

> The great increase of the *Baptists*, and the many converts gained
> by the force of their arguments and the exemplariness of their lives,
> brought upon them many clamours and defamations; the chiefs were
> represented as Jesuits, Hereticks, and what not; many books were
> published, misrepresenting them.

This necessitated them to publish many Confessions of Faith; some in vindication of particular churches, others of particular persons.[33]

Of all the confessions, it was that of 1689 which achieved pre-eminence. Crosby observed that in his day it was 'still generally received by all those congregations, that hold the doctrine of personal election, and the certainty of the saints' final perseverance'.[34] Indeed, the preface to the published version stated that 'many others have since embraced the same truth which is owned therein'.[35] Further editions appeared over the years, although the era of confession-making passed away as Baptists discovered a larger degree of toleration than they had ever known before.[36]

* * *

Until 1688 there had been a few Dissenting ministers with university traditions, including just a handful of Baptists such as the Irishman Thomas Delaune. Henceforth, there would be none. Delaune spent his earlier years in a friary near Cork, but later came to know the Lord. Afterwards he travelled to London. When, in 1683, Benjamin Calamy, Rector of St. Lawrence Jewry, invited Nonconformists to consider their position carefully, Delaune printed his *Plea for the Nonconformists*, justifying separation from the Church of England. For this he was sent to Newgate prison, together with his wife and two small children. He died there after fifteen months' confinement. Daniel Defoe (1661-1731), participant in the ill-fated Monmouth rebellion, unsuccessful business man, and author of *Robinson Crusoe*, wrote about Delaune's *Plea*: 'If any man ask what we can say why the dissenters differ from the church of England, and what they can plead for it; I can recommend no better reply than this.'[37] In practice, exclusion from the professions and government offices set up a considerable social road-block for the Particular Baptists.

The sufferings of the Nonconformists were unspeakable. Defoe recorded that 'near *eight thousand* protestant dissenters ... perished in prison in the days of that merciful prince King Charles ii, and that merely for dissenting from the church'.[38] Nevertheless, there was a swing in favour of the Dissenters. Charles's Indulgence of March, 1672, by which the monarch asserted his absolute power, led to more than thirty-five hundred licenses being issued to Nonconformist preachers in the following ten months. Ivimey recorded that 'many of our ministers availed themselves of the privilege of obtaining a license from the King ... and be left at liberty to preach the gospel of Christ without interruption'.[39] John Bunyan was released after twelve years' imprisonment in Bedford, only to be sent back in 1676.

When James II became king in 1685 he issued a declaration putting into effect the penal laws against all separatists from the Church of England. To quote Hercules Collins concerning the Monmouth rebellion of that year:

> Many good men of most persuasions, of the church of England, Presbyterians, Independants, and Baptists, were zealously concerned in the Duke of Monmouth's time, and many fell. ... [There were] no better men in the world than some who fell in the Duke's cause, in the west; yet by the hands of one of the most debauched armies that ever was in the world.[40]

William Kiffin lost two grandsons, William and Benjamin, aged nineteen and twenty-two years respectively. They were hanged, the younger at Lyme Regis, and the elder at Taunton, for their part in the revolt. Just before his execution the teenager was heard to say: 'Oh, now my joy and comfort is that I have a Christ to go to.'[41] Benjamin, two hours before his end, concluded a final letter to his mother with the prayer that the Lord might carry her 'through this vale of tears with a resigning submissive spirit; and at last bring you to himself in glory; where I question not but you will meet your dying son'.[42] Their grandfather later stated: 'For myself it was a great comfort to me, and is to observe what testimony they left behind of that blessed interest they had in the Lord Jesus, and their humble and holy confidence of their eternal happiness.'[43]

James's cruelty was shown, too, in the condemnation of Elizabeth Gaunt, according to Bishop Burnet 'an Anabaptist, who spent a great part of her life in acts of charity'.[44] She was burnt alive at Tyburn late in 1685 for harbouring a fugitive from the Monmouth revolt. The king was as devious as he was vicious. When he issued his own Indulgence in 1687 in order to humble the Anglican clergy, many, although not all, Dissenters again feared the return of Catholicism as the established religion. Ivimey recorded that 'Baptists in London were divided in opinion on this matter.'[45] Kiffin wrote:

> I thought it my duty to do all I could to prevent those dissenters of my acquaintance from having any hand therein. But from the sense

they had of their former sufferings, and the hopes of finding all things as was promised, I could not prevail.[46]

* * *

The number of meeting-houses possessed by the Particular Baptists at the time is not known. In London they generally procured licenses and maintained numerous public gatherings.[47] Following the Indulgence, it appears that they also often rented city halls belonging to the different companies of liverymen. This meant, as Ivimey noted, that 'they were subject to the will of those companies'.[48] Because tenancies were of limited duration and subsequent rent increases were exorbitant congregations took the short-term view and tended to move to other halls rather than seeking to provide their own costly buildings for worship. There was, for example, the congregation, one of the oldest Particular Baptist churches in London, which met originally at Joiners' Hall. The people removed in 1708 to Pinners' Hall, moving thence in 1724 to premises in Devonshire Square, which they occupied alternately with others in mornings and afternoons until their own church-state came to an end.[49] One reason, Ivimey suggested, for the dissolution of this church, apart from the high Calvinism of Clendon Dawkes in mid-century,[50] was the fact that the people had no settled place of worship. Had they not had to move around, 'the church at Joiners'-Hall would have been perpetuated.'[51]

* * *

In short, although the Dissenters were tolerated by the law of the land, they were heartily disliked by most Churchmen. Thomas Bennett, an Anglican, wrote in 1702:

> Tho' the Act of Toleration did really free all the Dissenters in *England* from all that obligation to join with the Established Church, which the Acts of Uniformity did formerly lay upon them; yet all the Dissenters in *England* are Schismatics notwithstanding.[52]

It was recognised that, although the ascendancy of William III meant that the old Tudor despotism and the more recent pretensions of the Stuarts had vanished, concord might not prevail. The power of the Church was such that public peace required the goodwill of the bishops and clergy towards the government, a goodwill which would never be given without a price. So, when the Toleration Act, the Magna Carta of Dissent, was passed in 1689, enacting the first legal toleration which England had ever known, it gave freedom of worship, though nothing else, to the Dissenters. The act stereotyped the division of the nation into Anglicans and others. Nevertheless, there were compensations. For the first time ever, Nonconformists were relieved of all penalties for separating from the Church of England. In an address entitled 'Of the Temptations of the Present Age', the Baptist and high-Calvinist John Brine (1703-65) wrote:

> We enjoy our liberties as men and Christians. Separation from the Establishment is not deemed by our laws criminal, nor are we on that account subject *now* to any penalties ... we suffer no such hardships *as our forefathers underwent*, to preserve a good conscience.[53]

Brine italicized the little word 'now'.

Dissenters were still obliged to take the oath of allegiance and to subscribe to most of the articles of the Church of England. Nonconformist meeting-houses had to be unlocked when in use and there was no exemption from tithes and other parochial dues. Those who did not swear and subscribe were subject to the penalties of the Act of Uniformity of 1662, still unrepealed, and those of the Conventicle and the Five Mile Acts. All laws compelling attendance at public worship were to be enforced against absentees. No Dissenting place of worship could be used until it had been licensed by the diocesan bishop, his archdeacon or a justice of the peace.

In effect, the Toleration Act deprived those who chose to think for themselves of a portion of their civil privileges; England expressed her solemn and deliberate judgment that such men could not be trusted. The statesmen of the Revolution sacrificed the Dissenters, who constituted no less than 6 per cent of the population of England and Wales at that time,[54] to appease the jealousies and the fears of the lower orders of the clergy. Further, the act failed to make clear the legal position of Dissenting schools and academies, so that Nonconformists could still be prosecuted in both civil and ecclesiastical courts for teaching without an episcopal licence. As late as 1733 the Chancellor of Peterborough prosecuted the Independent minister Philip Doddridge (1702-51) for conducting his Northampton academy without such a licence. The matter was vastly unpopular even among Anglicans, so much so that the churchwarden in whose name the prosecution went forward told Doddridge that he was considering whether he could with safety to himself refuse to sign the legal documentation. Happily, the Northampton pastor won the case.[55] It seems that the king, George II (1727-60), when he heard of the pressures under which Doddridge laboured, exercised his prerogative, declaring that '*there should be no Persecution for Conscience sake*' during his reign.[56] It was not until 1779 that Dissenters were to be relieved of the necessity of subscription to most of the Thirty-Nine Articles.

Baptists themselves took no part in the 1688 settlement of William and Mary; it appears that all public spirit among them had been suppressed by earlier persecutions. Nevertheless, a thaw was on the way. In 1696, following the failure of an assassination attempt on William, Joseph Stennett, pastor of the Seventh-Day congregation meeting at Pinners' Hall,[57] London, from 1690 until his death in 1713, composed an address of congratulation to William in which he applauded the 'benign influences' of his government.[58] The Baptists, as others, knew where their interests lay, although, under William, not a single penal act was ever repealed or amended; all that was possible was exemption from penalties if a man would take certain oaths. Every position of vantage was retained for the Anglican. On the other hand, no licence was needed for the Nonconformist preacher. He was entitled to make certain declarations and take certain oaths, to have the facts recorded in court, and to claim a copy of the record. A man was entitled to register any building which he controlled as a Dissenting place of worship, while no bench of bishops had any power to refuse such applications. The Dissenters were made free by the Toleration Act of 1689, although remaining in a position of distinct social disadvantage.

That this legislation rankled with Nonconformists is shown by the reaction in hindsight of Robert Robinson (1735-90).[59] Converted in his youth under the ministry of George Whitefield (1714-70), the celebrated but in some important respects doctrinally unorthodox Robinson settled at the age of twenty-three as pastor of the Particular Baptist church which met at Stone Yard, Cambridge. When he began his labours there were a mere thirty-four members who could just afford a quarterly stipend of £3.6s.0d. In 1774 Robinson was able to number a thousand souls in his congregation, including children and servants. One of his daughters, Julia, passed away in 1787 at the age of seventeen, while six other children of the family of ten were baptized by Robinson at Christmas in the same year. Two years later he, too, was gone. In 1774 Robinson recorded an

approach which had been made to him in 1765, some seven years
after his settlement, by Dr Ewen, a justice of the peace, who had
advised him and some other Dissenting ministers in the area to
qualify in accordance with the terms of the Act of Toleration. The
advice, offered, it seems, in a friendly fashion, was designed to
preserve all concerned from trouble on account of the omission.
Accordingly, the Baptist pastor went to the shire hall at the next
sessions and 'took the oaths of allegiance, and supremacy, and also
the oath of abjuration, subscribing our names as the act directs'. His
note commented wistfully:

> Had I seen things in the light I now do, 1774, I might have
> thanked Dr. EWEN for his advice, but would have run all hazards
> rather than have qualified thus. Blessed be God for an High-Priest,
> who can have compassion on the IGNORANT, and on them that are
> OUT OF THE WAY.[60]

Men such as Robinson loathed having to go to the king's servants
to obtain permission to preach the gospel. To jump ahead for a moment,
it is sad to read Ivimey's remark that, such was the magnitude of
Robinson's errors concerning the Trinity, it was necessary to suppose
that he had been 'evidently insane' when he died.[61]

In 1702 the vindictive High-Churchman Henry Sacheverell,
himself the son of an ejected Presbyterian minister, in a notable
sermon preached at Oxford, referred to Dissenters as enemies of the
commonwealth and state. They were, he believed, '*greater Mon-
sters than Jews, Mahometans, Socinians, and Papists*'.[62] Popular
opinions were sharply divided. For example, an anonymous collection of 'poems' for and against Sacheverell was published in 1710,
including a ditty, obviously composed with the Dissenters in mind.
Here is one verse:

> The grand Incendiaries of the Age,
> Dare boldly with the Truth engage;
> Despise Authorities, and charge
> Their own curs'd Principles, at large
> On th' *Church of England*, and derive
> Their Guilt on it; and so contrive
> If possible, its Dissolution,
> And infringe our Constitution.[63]

On the other hand, a lengthy 'Low-Church Litany' commenced with the following prayer:

> Preserve our Queen, the Church and State;
> Let none but honest Men be Great;
> The haughty Clergy's Pride abate.
> > *We pray Thee*
> Let them a good Example give,
> And Preach what they themselves believe,
> And not the Ignorant deceive.
> > *We, &c.*[64]

In 1703 Defoe met Sacheverell's furious denunciation of Dissent by a satire so delicate that for a while it deceived the High-Church party into the belief that it had been written by one of their own side. Entitled *The Shortest Way with the Dissenters: Or, Proposals for the Establishment of the Church*, it took the form of a grave political tract, and was circulated with eager zeal by partisans of the establishment. It asserted:

> It is now near Fourteen Years [since the Toleration Act, 1689] that the Glory and Peace of the purest and most flourishing Church in the World has been Eclips'd, Buffetted, and Disturb'd, by a sort of Men, who God in his Providence has suffer'd to insult over her, and bring her down.[65]

What, then, should be done to the Dissenters? Defoe had the remedy:

> I answer, 'TIS Cruelty to kill a Snake or a Toad in cold Blood, but the Poyson of their Nature makes it Charity to our Neighbours, to destroy those Creatures not for any personal Injury receiv'd, but for Prevention; not for the Evil they have done, but for the Evil they may do.[66]

When it became clear that these words had been penned by a Dissenter to expose the designs of the High-Church party, the author was soon denounced as a malignant slanderer. A state prosecution was commenced immediately. Defoe, who admitted authorship, was fined two hundred marks, equivalent to over three hundred pounds, a huge sum at the time, was made to stand three times in the pillory, and was imprisoned at the Queen's pleasure. The sentence

showed that Defoe's satire had not at all libelled the Church of
England.[67]

Hot on Sacheverell's heels came Samuel Wesley, the son and
grandson of ejected ministers, and father of John (1703-91) and
Charles (1707-88). Samuel attacked the Dissenting academies as
immoral in character and disloyal in their tendency. In so doing he
was merely following the fashion set by the throne; Queen Anne
(1702-14) herself despised those who would not conform. A consequence was that in 1714 a bill was introduced to ensure that all
schoolmasters would be Anglicans, and another to the effect that
Dissenters should lose their vote at elections. This was, of course,
resented bitterly by the dissidents. Amid the flood of literature a
pamphlet of some sixteen pages appeared in 1714 in defence of the
Nonconformist academies. It claimed:

> The Act of Toleration grants the Dissenters the just Liberty of
> Worshipping God according to their Consciences, under the con-
> duct of *Preachers* and *Teachers* of their own Chusing. Since they
> are allow'd the Benefit of a *Ministry* in their Religious Assemblies,
> it seems highly reasonable that they shou'd be permitted to Educate
> a sufficient Number of Scholars for the *Ministry*. The same Law that
> grants the *End*, must be suppos'd to consent to the *Necessary Means*
> also, without which the End cannot be attain'd.[68]

The anonymous writer commented that he had known Dissenting academies for some thirty years past, and had never been aware
of 'Republican Doctrines' being taught in them. Cleverly, he cited
Samuel Wesley in support of his assertion.[69]

Feelings were running high. In that same year, 1714, Mr
Benjamin Read was baptized at Exeter upon profession of faith, so
provoking the publication of an anonymous pamphlet on behalf of
the establishment. This condemned rebaptism for a number of
reasons. One was that it denied Charles I, beheaded in 1649, 'to be
a Christian', while another was that 'this new Doctrine is an Affront
to her present *Majesty*, and arraigns Her Conduct'. Worst of all,
rebaptism 'renders every Man's Christianity precarious, and absolutely uncertain'.[70] Quite so.

In the event, on the day in 1714 when the Schism Act was due to
become law, Anne died. And yet the new bill, now ineffective, had
demonstrated the real feelings of the Church of England, an
enormously powerful enemy of Dissent. The fact was that although

a measure of liberty for Nonconformists was often assumed after the Toleration Act, this could not in practice be taken for granted. So, because of the scandal of Anglican clergy marrying couples in the Fleet prison without notice, an act passed in 1753 compelled all English marriages, except those of Quakers and Jews, to be celebrated in parish churches.[71]

With respect to civil offices, opened only as late as 1828 to Dissenters, the notorious case of Allen Evans indicated the mood of the time. Evans was a deacon until 1756 in the Particular Baptist church in Little Wild Street. Later, he transferred to the Barbican church, perhaps because his wife and others of his family were members there, 'whom the church in Little Wild-street refused to admit to their communion'. This refusal was, according to Evans, because of a 'want of charity'.[72] In 1754 he was elected to the position of sheriff to the city of London. A necessary qualification for office was communicant worship with the Church of England, heavy fines being payable by an elected man if this requirement was not met. This was virtual blackmail, a form of extortion which was said to have raised over fifteen thousand pounds from conscientious Dissenters. Evans took the matter to court, whence it was transferred to the House of Lords in 1767, thirteen years later. Evans, aged eighty-two and a dying man, won the day. Lord Mansfield, the Chancellor, declared in the upper house concerning the Toleration Act:

> It is now no crime for a man, who is within the description of that act, to say that he is a dissenter; nor is it a crime for him not to take the sacrament according to the rites of the Church of England: nay, the crime is, if he does it contrary to the dictates of his conscience.[73]

* * *

Joseph Ivimey remarked that, in his opinion, many Dissenters at that particular time tended to overrate the degradation which attached to exclusion from civil office, as also the advantages which possession would have conferred.[74] This sense of depression among the Nonconformists was totally understandable; they felt shut out. Monsieur de la Roque, a government official in Hanover, writing to an English opposite number, Mr Warre, at Whitehall in November, 1689, expressed well the universal, deep-rooted and ongoing dislike of Nonconformity:

I have always regarded what the English Church is now doing towards the nonconformists more as the result of true Christian charity, which tolerates the weaknesses of its brethren, than as any token of blemish in its own belief. There are few foreigners who have laboured more than I, to instruct themselves in the differences which have parted the English Church and the nonconformists; and for that reason, I impute all the wrong to the latter, who refuse to submit to an established discipline, and who join a society that they themselves avow is pure.[75]

Discrimination against Dissent remained alive and well; as late as 1790, and influenced by the American War and the French Revolution, a bill for the repeal of the Test and the Corporation Acts was rejected in the Commons by a massive 294 votes against to 105 in favour.[76] Even at that later date Dissenters had to reckon upon being protected but never encouraged by the crown and its servants.

CHAPTER III
THE EARLY 1700s

Now that the Dissenters had been relieved of all pains and penalties for separating from the Church of England, it appears that the Baptists, in Ivimey's words, took 'immediate steps to improve their privileges by enquiring into the state of the churches, and to have adopted means to promote their prosperity'.[1] He recorded that an assembly of 'Pastors, Messengers, and ministering Brethren' from English and Welsh churches, 'owning the doctrine of personal election and final perseverence', was held in London in September, 1689.[2] Significantly, invitations were not sent to those 'Seventh-Day' churches which met on Saturdays, or to the Barbican, London, church, which included both Arminian and Calvinistic Baptists in its membership.[3]

In the event, more than one hundred congregations sent representatives to consider, among other matters, the low state of the churches and the problem of ministerial scarcity. It was resolved to pray to God for the gift of 'true, broken, and penitent hearts for all our iniquities, and the sins of his people', for cleansing from sin, for an outpouring of the Holy Spirit, for a greater understanding of Scripture 'that we may understand whereabouts we are, in respect of the latter time, and what he is doing', for God's blessing upon the churches, for love among believers, for the new king, William III, and for the conversion of the Jews, that they with the Gentiles might submit to the 'one Shepherd Jesus Christ'. The confession which had been issued in 1677 was brought to the attention of the brethren. Their introductory statement indicated that the churches involved denied Arminianism, and 'thought meet, for the satisfaction of all other Christians, that differ from us in the point of *baptism*, to recommend to their perusal the *confession of our faith*, which confession we own'.[4] In a sense, then, the re-issue of the 1677 confession was tactical; the assembly felt it important to show that their churches were and would remain within the mainstream of the English Calvinistic tradition. For this reason the confession may be assessed as something less than a Baptist creed, if by 'creed' is meant a comprehensive and enduring statement of what must be believed.[5]

In 1688 a letter extolling the necessity of maintaining a separated ministry had been written by Hanserd Knollys (1599-1691), William Kiffin and others, even before William of Orange had landed on English soil. The assembly followed this up by debating 'whether it is the duty of every church of Christ, to maintain such ministers as are set apart by them, by allowing them a comfortable maintenance, according to their ability', later writing to the constituent churches to the effect that lack of ministerial support was 'a great evil, and neglect of duty in churches'.[6]

The initial momentum of this first assembly waned. The 1692 assembly decided that the churches should divide themselves into two groups, one to meet henceforth in Bristol and the other in London. The London meetings soon declined. Realistically, the Bristol assembly of 1693 noted that a knowledge of biblical languages is not essential for the appointment of a man as a minister of the gospel. Not essential, perhaps, yet highly desirable. Edward Terrill (1635-86) seems to have had no doubts about it.[7] In 1679 most of his estate had been willed to the Broadmead church in Bristol to finance the settlement of a minister. The man concerned was to be skilled in Hebrew and Greek, and would devote three half-days a week to teaching these disciplines to not more than twelve young men, all to be members of baptized churches in the area, for up to two years. Thus was conceived the Bristol academy. Bernard Foskett (1685-1758) was the first minister of note who served under Terrill's arrangement; he held office from 1720 until his death, some sixty-four students studying under him.[8] He was said by John Rippon (1750-1836) to have been 'strenuous for what he apprehended to be the truth, yet was he fond of no extreme'.[9]

Terrill's bequest showed that Nonconformity had come of age; some Baptists at least, although suffering severe social disabilities, were determined to show that within their own ranks there were resources sufficient for the needs of their churches.[10] Further afield, the question of ministerial support was not, however, resolved so quickly, as is shown, perhaps, in a 1733 sermon by Samuel Wilson.

Wilson was the first minister of the congregation which left the Broad Street, Wapping, church in 1730 to meet in Little Prescott Street, Goodman's Fields, London, possibly because of some disagreement about whether or not to build a new place of worship.[11] He died in 1750 at the end of a notably successful pastorate, many eminent men, including Benjamin Beddome (1717-98), going from that church into the ministry during his time.[12] Mr Wilson entertained convinced opinions:

> And as to such as leave their secular callings, as it is, or ought to be, by the advice and desire of the church, so when that is the case, it becomes unrighteous, as well as ungrateful, not to allow them a competency for the maintenance and the support of their families.[13]

It appears, indeed, that most Baptist ministers at the time were expected by their people to eke out their stipends by undertaking other work; the lot of the Baptist pastor was not, from the financial point of view, altogether a happy one.[14] Ivimey took the view that those who were wealthy and who failed to contribute realistically to establishing a fund for ministerial education thereby gave a negative example to poorer members. He believed, too, that the 'covetousness' of affluent Baptists was the real reason for the 'destruction of the Assembly itself'.[15] With respect to its démise, Ivimey remarked:

> It is mortifying to find, that their well-meant efforts to unite the churches in a compact body, by means of an annual general assembly ... proved abortive, and that it was so soon relinquished. ... our history seems to warrant the conclusion, that our independent principles will always prevent any general union of the churches, and render nugatory any concentrated plan of co-operation.[16]

This conclusion is capable of challenge. Perhaps the major reason for the success of the Bristol academy, for over one hundred years the only Baptist venture into the field of ministerial education, apart from noble efforts by John Fawcett (1740-1817) at Hebden Bridge in Yorkshire and John Sutcliff (1752-1814) at Olney, Buckinghamshire, was that two churches at the most, the Broadmead and Pithay Baptist churches in Bristol, were involved; with no central authority called in or needed to superintend the work, the project went ahead.[17] There might be a lesson here for present times.

Although there were no further assemblies, association life

persisted. Minutes and circulars from the Abingdon, Midland, Northern and Western associations for the opening decades of the eighteenth century give a vivid picture of activity in the churches.[18] Nevertheless, it is usually held that, following the Toleration Act, there was a general spiritual decline among the Dissenters. On the other hand, meeting-houses sprang up in most of the towns and many of the villages of England and Wales, visible reminders of the failure of the Church of England either to extinguish or absorb Dissent.

The wave of tolerance under William III was followed by a trough of intolerance under Queen Anne, who declined to respond to a loyal address presented to her upon her accession by London Dissenting ministers. Following Marlborough's victory at Blenheim in 1704, a written transcript of a congratulatory address by Joseph Stennett (1663-1713) pleased the Queen exceedingly. Not knowing that it came from a Baptist, who, for his part, did not realise that it had been presented to her, the monarch ordered a gratuity to be paid to the preacher out of the privy purse. Thomas Bradbury (1677-1759), tempestuous minister of the Fetter Lane, London, Congregational church, who later involved himself in the 'Modern Question',[19] in August, 1714 noticed in the gallery of his church building a messenger from Bishop Burnet. The envoy had come to the service to signal by dropping a handkerchief the death earlier that day of Queen Anne, and thereby the probable breakdown of the notorious Schism Act. After his sermon Bradbury engaged in prayer for the new king, George I (1714-27), and not long after preached on the words 'Go, see now this cursed woman, and bury her: for she is a king's daughter' (2 Kings 9:34). His opposition to Anne's persecuting measures had been such that it was in vain that the monarch tried to buy Bradbury off with a bishopric.[20] Benjamin Stinton observed that, but for 'kind Providence', Anne would have effectively destroyed the civil and religious liberties of all Dissenters.[21]

The Joseph Stennett who pleased the Queen so much was the son of Edward Stennett, who died about 1690, and the father of Joseph the younger, who lived until 1758, and grandfather of Samuel, who survived until 1795. All four were Baptist ministers of distinction. Edward ministered to his own Particular Baptist congregation in Wallingford Castle, near Oxford, which, as a royal residence, was free from search. Joseph senior, pastor to the Sabbatarian congregation near Devonshire Square, London, was one of the earliest Baptist hymn-writers whose hymns were printed. His son, too, was an eloquent preacher, and in December, 1745 delivered a memorable sermon entitled 'Rabshakeh's Retreat', 'Rabshakeh' (2 Kings 19:8) being Charles Stuart, who in the same month retreated from Derby back to Scotland. Ivimey, citing Stennett at some length, observed that the address was 'far superior to, the most able military harangues (most of them composed for them by others after the battle was over) that are attributed to the famous generals of Carthage or of Rome'.[22]

Concerning the Rome of his day, Stennett entertained no doubts whatever. His sermon posed the following question about the Pretender: 'What can you expect, my brethren, and fellow-subjects, from an invader bred up in the policy of *France*, and the religion of *Rome*? fired with revenge, for what he is taught by the *father of lies*, and the *mother of harlots*.'[23] Apparently, the effect upon Stennett's congregation at Little Wild Street was dramatic. To cite Ivimey, the men unsheathed their swords, and the meeting-house, in earlier days a Roman Catholic chapel, was converted for 'training men to military discipline, who were determined to shed their blood, if that were necessary, to defend a British king, and a protestant government, against French ambition, and popish tyranny'.[24] Joseph later baptized his son Samuel, who, according to Dr Joseph Jenkins when preaching at the latter's funeral, 'desired no higher honour upon earth, than to be an useful Baptist Minister'.[25]

* * *

The fortunes of the church at Little Wild Street, Holborn, London, and its minister, John Piggott, reveal tensions which existed sometimes among the Particular Baptists.[26] Piggott had settled originally as pastor with the Hart Street, Covent Garden, church in 1691, a church established in that year by the fellowship meeting in Rupert Street, Goodman's Fields, and one of the five churches in London established upon the six principles of Hebrews 6:2. Such congregations always had among them many who were strictly Arminian, and Arminianism would lead to problems for Piggott. By 1699 a difference of opinion had emerged between the pastor and some of his people with respect to personal election and final perseverance, a difference which led to some fierce debates. It was not that Piggott was a high Calvinist, as might be illustrated by his remarks to the unconverted during his funeral sermon for Thomas Harrison. Harrison had been the minister at Lorimer's Hall, by Basinghall Street, until his premature death in 1702 at the age of thirty-five:

> O adore the Patience and Long-suffering of God, that you are yet alive, and have one Call more from this Pulpit, and another very Awful one from the Grave of that Person that us'd to fill it. His Death calls upon you to repent, and turn to close with Christ, and make sure of Heaven. ... receive him as offer'd in the Gospel; submitting to his Scepter, as well as depending on his Sacrifice; that you may eternally be lodg'd in the Bosom of his Love.[27]

In the sermon delivered by Joseph Stennett following the death of Piggott in 1713 it was noted that during his final illness

> ... he order'd many persons to be sent for, whom either the Ties of Friendship and Acquaintance best endear'd to him, or whom he had observ'd to attend his Ministry, without knowing what Effect it had upon their Souls, or those with whom he knew God had intrusted considerable talents, that he might earnestly recommend to them the Improvement of Time, in order to their eternal Felicity.[28]

This man was surely a good and faithful pastor to his sheep. In earlier days, however, the church in Hart Street requested Mr Piggott to be as 'inoffensive in his preaching as he could on those points of controversy, and that he would desire those ministers that preached for him to be as inoffensive as they could'.[29] Feelings ran high and Piggott and his supporters removed to Little Wild Street, where they hired the chapel erected by a former Spanish ambassador. The church became fashionable and was attended by, among others, Daniel Defoe.

Thomas Harrison's son of the same name followed Piggott in the pastorate, but, by 1729, complained that the state of his health would not permit him to preach twice on the Lord's day. Assistance was provided for him without any reduction in his salary. After a while, Harrison's absence on Sunday mornings was found to be because he was attending established worship at Tunbridge Wells. He resigned the pastorate and later obtained ordination in the Church of England.[30]

The Little Wild Street church then called Andrew Gifford (1700-84). Gifford's father, Emmanuel, had suffered much for his Dissent-

ing principles, while his grandfather, Andrew, pastor of the Pithay
Baptist church, Bristol, had been imprisoned four times. After assisting
at a church in Nottingham and then at the Bristol academy under
Bernard Foskett, Gifford accepted the call to Little Wild Street.
Unhappily, in 1731 there was internal controversy, some seeking to
eject the pastor from his office. A majority of the members declined to
receive the charges brought against Gifford, yet the society of London
ministers, to which Gifford belonged, excluded him precipitately from
their fellowship.[31] He removed, with his adherents, to found a new
church in Eagle Street, Holborn, in 1735-6, the newly-erected building
possessing three galleries and able to seat some four hundred worshippers. At the opening service Gifford preached from Isaiah 63:16,
'Doubtless thou art our father, though Abraham be ignorant of us, and
Israel acknowledge us not: thou, O Lord, art our father, our redeemer;
thy name is from everlasting.'

The text seems to have been chosen with regard to the 'opprobrium'
(Ivimey's word) under which pastor and people had laboured when
establishing a separate church.[32] Here, Gifford preached with great
success. He saw eight men sent into the ministry, the building enlarged
and a baptistery installed. The father of three children who all died in
infancy, he became an assistant librarian at the British Museum. In
Ivimey's words, he was 'a pathetic, and yet powerful preacher ... a
Calvinist of the old school'.[33] On one occasion, when visiting the
Tottenham Court Chapel to hear George Whitefield preach, he said that
he would light his 'farthing rushlight' at the Anglican's 'flaming
torch'.[34] Probably because he had in the 1720s been an assistant to
Bernard Foskett, he left various books and manuscripts to the Bristol
institution. This handsome legacy was estimated at one thousand
pounds, according to a letter sent by Robert Robinson to his fellow
open-communionist Daniel Turner at Abingdon, Oxfordshire, in
1781.[35] Early associations led to life-long attachments and loyalties.

* * *

The Salters' Hall discussions of 1719, though not concerned directly
with Particular Baptist issues, were a watershed event for the constituency. The shock of non-subscription by many Paedobaptists as well as
General Baptists to a trinitarian declaration of faith served to move the
Calvinistic Baptists towards a separate denominational structure.

This conference developed from a controversy which flared

initially in 1718-19 among the three Presbyterian congregations in
Exeter, Devon. There, two of the ministers declined to affirm the
usual interpretation of the doctrine of the Trinity in the Westminster
Assembly's Catechism. The Exeter Presbyterians sought from
London the advice of the general body of ministers of the three
Dissenting denominations. In effect, the latter resolved, albeit by a
slender majority, to endorse the first of the Thirty-Nine Articles of
the Church of England and the fifth and sixth of the Westminster
Confession.[36] This did not settle the matter; controversy continued.
Later the same year some of the ministers subscribed their names to
a trinitarian declaration. This act led to the two sides being designated as 'Subscribers' and 'Non-subscribers'. An anonymous publication in 1719 perceived the matter thus:

> The Ministers on one hand apprehended a Subscription of such
> *Humane Words* as might most directly meet with and convict the
> Erroneous was, in the present State of Things, a necessary Method
> to obviate the Danger: The other Ministers thought a Declaration in
> the Strongest and clearest *Words of Scripture*, would be at once
> more safe, and more effective for that Purpose.[37]

The 'Non-subscribers' surely anticipated the comment of Dr F.W.
Gotch, when chairing the Baptist Union's autumn meeting in 1868: 'If
the creed put forth or recognized by any church is proveable by the
scriptures, what greater power has it than the scriptures on which it
rests?'[38] On the other hand, a recognized creed, although admittedly
without 'power', might well be necessary for bringing into focus that
which the churches believe. Conversely, a failure by churches to
commit themselves to a creed could imply that, like the priests and the
elders, when questioned about an important issue (Matthew 21:27),
they 'cannot tell' because they will not. Definition is often indispensable; the people of God have always needed good men to explain matters
to them. This happened, for example, at the time of the Jews' return
from Babylon (Nehemiah 8:8).

It is significant that, of the 78 Dissenting ministers known to
have been Subscribers at Salters' Hall, 14 were Particular Baptists,
and 1 only a General Baptist. Of the 73 Non-subscribers, 14 were
General Baptists, and just 2 Particular Baptists. The Arminians
declined to commit themselves. One of the most zealous Non-
subscribers was Dr John Gale, assistant minister at Paul's Alley, in
the Barbican, London. He might have been the target of the taunt of

some at the conference who wished to know whether or not they 'came thither to be contradicted by Anabaptist teachers'. To which it was replied that, because 'Anabaptism' means re-baptism, there were no Anabaptists present, but only Baptist ministers.[39] Concerning the matter at issue at the Salters' Hall conference, within a century most Presbyterian and many General Baptist churches connected with the discussions had become unitarian. On the other hand, the Congregational and Particular Baptist churches not only remained trinitarian, but continued to honour the theology of John Calvin.[40]

Like their metropolitan brethren, the Particular Baptist churches in the West of England were not reluctant to define their faith. The association which met at Tiverton, Devon, in 1721 prepared rules for assembly proceedings and a paper was presented to the 1722 association which gathered at Frome, Somerset. While subscriptions to specific forms of words were not required, it was intimated strongly that churches should express themselves 'in such terms as should prove them to be sound in the faith of the equal Persons in the Unity of the Godhead'.[41]

It is possible that diversions such as these, important though they might well have been, had caused Particular as well as General Baptists to react rather negatively to opportunities for growth and expansion. Thus, albeit in earlier years, the Bristol assembly of 1694 wrote to London to complain of the latter's lack of interest in the country as a whole.[42] In London so many building schemes were being promoted that both pastors and laymen grew weary of the continuous begging for money. According to Whitley, writing in 1932, a study of surviving documents from the early 1700s reveals that in many cases the erection of a meeting-house meant the shrinkage of the local church: because the pastor now lived near the building his out-services diminished. While the total number of Dissenting places of worship licensed in the two years from 1688 to 1690 was nearly 1,000, the number avowedly belonging to Baptists was only 16. The figures speak for themselves.[43]

* * *

Between 1715 and 1729 records were made of every Dissenting congregation in both England and Wales by Daniel Neal, the Congregationalist, and Dr John Evans, a Presbyterian. According to their figures, worked over and checked recently, it appears that by about 1715-18 there were some 206 Particular Baptist and 122 General Baptist congregations, the Particular Baptists constituting just 11 per cent of the Dissenting congregations in England and Wales and somewhat less than 1 per cent of the total population. The latter figure escalated quite remarkably to over 5 per cent in Bedfordshire because, possibly, of Bunyan's influence, and in parts of Wales.[44]

In 1704 an attempt was made by thirteen metropolitan Particular Baptist churches to revive the London Association, the first meeting being at Lorimer's Hall. According to Ivimey's record, the assembly was concerned about 'persons of an unsettled mind' who would easily neglect their own places of worship in order to hear Dissenting ministers of note, such people being described by Ivimey in the words of the Anglican John Newton (1725-1807) as 'the flying camp'. Accordingly, the assembly resolved

> ... that the members of each church ought ordinarily to attend the worship of God in the church to which they stand related: and that to make a common practice of deserting the assemblies to which they belong, is a great discouragement to the ministers of those churches; that it occasions the neglect of the poor among them; and that the continuance of such a practice has a tendency to weaken, and will perhaps, in time, issue in the dissolution of some churches.[45]

The effort at reviving assembly-life was short-lived, due partly to involvement by churches with Arminian and Seventh-Day convictions. Ten years later Benjamin Stinton tried to draw together all the London Baptist ministers, General and Particular, by establishing a ministerial society which would meet at the Hanover Coffee House in Finch Lane. This well-meant effort eventually failed. Fearing Arianism and Socinianism, the Particular Baptists separated to found in 1724 their own society, the Baptist Board. Consulted frequently by ministers in the provinces who required guidance, its influence extended far beyond London.[46] There were many considerable needs. For example, the low financial state of the churches is indicated by the fact that in 1715 the Baptists of Pennsylvania opened a correspondence with the London ministers, requesting help. A supply of books from London was denied on the grounds that there were inadequate funds for domestic needs, the letter sent to America taking refuge in confession:

As to a fund for the support of the ministry, we have not yet been able to raise any such thing for the benefit of the churches in *England*; tho' our interest has suffered very much in some parts of this kingdom for want of it; so that there cannot, at present, be any thing of this nature expected.[47]

Facilities for the churches were few and far between; the London congregations had hitherto conducted most of their baptisms down-river at Battersea, Lambeth or Bow. So it was that in 1716 a quite resplendent baptistery was completed at a cost of some six hundred pounds at the Barbican meeting-house, the wealthy Hollis brothers, whose father had come to London from Rotherham, Yorkshire, meeting most of the bill. According to Ivimey, it seems that it was made available to 'all the congregations which should be admitted by the Messrs. Hollis to that privilege'.[48] Baptismal candidates were charged two shillings each for the use of the baptistery. (We ask: would Paul, who could not remember how many he had baptized — 1 Corinthians 1:16 — have invoiced his converts for water and words?) The pool was installed in front of the pulpit, with sides and bottom of polished stone, and with a marble kerb around the top, the whole surrounded by an iron rail. Water was pumped in from a well, into which the baptistery drained. There were three changing-rooms, one each for male and female candidates, and the other for the minister.[49]

After the Great Fire of London in 1666 the entrepreneurial Hollis family had acquired a long lease of the Glass House, built by some Huguenot refugees in the time of Elizabeth, and had renamed it Pinners' Hall. Because the people to whom it properly belonged occupied it only on Sunday mornings, Thomas, one of the lessees, made money rapidly by subletting it five days a week for business purposes. On Sundays it was made available by him to two churches and on Saturdays to yet another.[50] It appears that the family acted on a neutral basis as between Paedobaptists and Baptists; they seem never to have attempted to instal a baptistery in the building.[51] Their lease expired in 1778. Thomas Hollis died in 1730 at the age of seventy-two, having donated generously to, among other causes, Harvard College in America.

Another, less grand, pool was enlarged and repaired at Horsleydown, Fair Street, Southwark, in 1717, at an estimated cost of some one hundred and thirty pounds, and was made available for all the Baptist churches.[52] A letter sent to their own congregations by

Nathaniel Foxwell, John Noble and other ministers explained the rules governing the use of the baptistery and, recorded Ivimey, contained 'some oblique allusions to what they considered an improper management' of the more impressive Barbican pool:

> It is designed, that the propriety of this place shall not be lodged in any single person, or in any one community, but that every congregation that shall advance £10 towards the charge of its reparation, shall have a propriety therein equal with others ... and that every congregation who shall advance any less sum, shall be entitled to the free use thereof.[53]

Contributions from ten London churches to the cost of the baptistery amounted to £118.10s.0d., three churches, those at Fair Street, Goat Street and Flower-de-luce-court, giving twenty pounds each. The baptistery continued in use for about sixty years.[54] Nevertheless, most baptisms were out of doors, sometimes in wintry conditions. Referring to the fact that in 1694 John Cropper had been baptized in the open when there was a hard frost and deep snow, the Fenstanton, Cambridgeshire, General Baptist church record urged that 'none be afraid to venture into the water when the season is cold, lest they be laid in their graves before the weather be warm'.[55]

The year 1717 was notable for the Particular Baptists in that it saw the setting up of the London Fund, which continued as the Particular Baptist Fund, for supporting both students for the ministry and poorer pastors.[56] Many ministers fell into the latter category and were obliged to look to themselves. They often kept schools or wrote or translated for booksellers. Crosby observed that English baptized churches had difficulty in maintaining 'the public worship of God with any tolerable reputation', and noted 'the great want of able and qualified persons to defend the truth, and to supply those churches that are in want of ministers'.[57] A circular letter sent in 1719 by some London Baptist ministers to various churches asserted that

> ... we have too much reason to fear that there are many in the churches who are shamefully deficient in their duty of contributing to the maintenance of their ministers; some through a covetous disposition of mind, and others from their having imbibed some mistaken principle.

The former was then said to have been usually the case.[58] The first meeting of the fund was attended by elders and messengers from six churches, which proposed to raise together over nine hundred pounds, the largest contribution, two hundred pounds, coming from the Little Wild Street church.[59] There was a little improvement in the overall situation, and in 1724-5 John Gill received £17.10s.0d. from this source, probably for the purchase of Hebrew books from the collection of John Skepp (about 1670-1721), who had been one of the ministers present at the initial meeting.[60] As a matter of policy, the fund refused to co-operate with Arminians, an issue which gave rise to considerable discussion at the time.[61] Benjamin Stinton, balancing as usual on the fence, argued that the establishment of the fund along narrow lines would weaken its chances for success and that such a restriction would lead to endless debates among the managers. In the end, he agreed to the expediency of such a measure.[62]

It would appear that a fund serving the interests of Particular Baptists only marked a turning point in the fortunes of their London churches, and this for three reasons. First, the move dealt a death blow to any hope that the meetings of General and Particular Baptist ministers at the Hanover Coffee House would lead eventually to a closer union between the two groups. Second, the fund was instrumental in promoting and then maintaining doctrinal stability at a time when trinitarianism was being attacked, as later it was at Salters' Hall. That debate could only have confirmed the London Particular Baptists in their policy of not aligning themselves further with the General Baptists.[63] Finally, the fund gave the London Calvinistic Baptists their second permanent denominational structure, the Baptist Board having been instituted already.[64] All this was of great importance; at a time of doctrinal uncertainty among the General Baptists, to name only one Dissenting group, the Particular Baptists in the metropolis defined their faith and their responsibilities, laying down a sound foundation for future days.

So it was that the fund turned down subscriptions from the wealthy Barbican Baptist church on account of its Arian tendencies, and also from the prosperous church at Pinners' Hall, which, most unusually, retained an open membership. After the rebuff to the Barbican church Pinners' Hall did not make formal application to support the fund. Thus emerged the curious spectacle of the managers of the fund meeting in the hall, for them somewhat strange territory, and accepting two hundred pounds from the afore-mentioned brothers Hollis, members of this church.[65] When John Hollis died in the 1730s he left to the poor of several London churches eleven hundred pounds and some annuities to be held in trust by his son, Isaac. One thousand pounds were to be invested, and of the remaining hundred, three pounds a year were to be given to the 'Ministers and Messengers of the Particular Baptist Fund', 'to be spent by you in a dinner, every year'![66] According to Joseph Ivimey, by the middle of the century the fund

> ... had now begun to produce a happy influence upon the state of the denomination, in offering pecuniary assistance to those ministers whose churches could not support them. Many young ministers, too, had received literary help, principally at Bristol.[67]

By these means, continued Ivimey,

> ... evangelical principles were thus maintained; a holy discipline was in some good degree preserved; some pious people were constantly added to the churches; and God heard their fervent and united prayers.[68]

* * *

By the late 1730s there were some thirty-three Baptist churches in London, more than in any other Dissenting communion. These churches were generally smaller than those of the Presbyterians and the Independents. Elsewhere, it appears that the majority of Dissenters were to be found in the cities, boroughs or market towns, and that a tendency to gather in towns increased as the age of toleration gave rise to an ordered devotional life. Their attitude to the establishment may be illustrated by the fluctuating fortunes of the Particular Baptist church at Arnesby. For more than fifty years the church automatically excommunicated both those members who married unbelievers and those who married in the parish church. The result was that by 1751 this once-flourishing fellowship was reduced to about thirty members, mostly aged. A regular income due from letting a property bequeathed to the church by the affluent Winckles family was denied them by an unscrupulous trustee. They bemoaned the fact that 'our number is but few and circumstances low'.[69] When Robert Hall senior (1728-91) settled in the church in 1753, he recorded that 'they were a poor, plain people', yet 'pressed him much to abide with them'. Life was difficult for Robert. The father of fourteen children, most of whom were either stillborn or

Robert Hall, senior (1728-91); reproduced by courtesy of the
Evangelical Library.

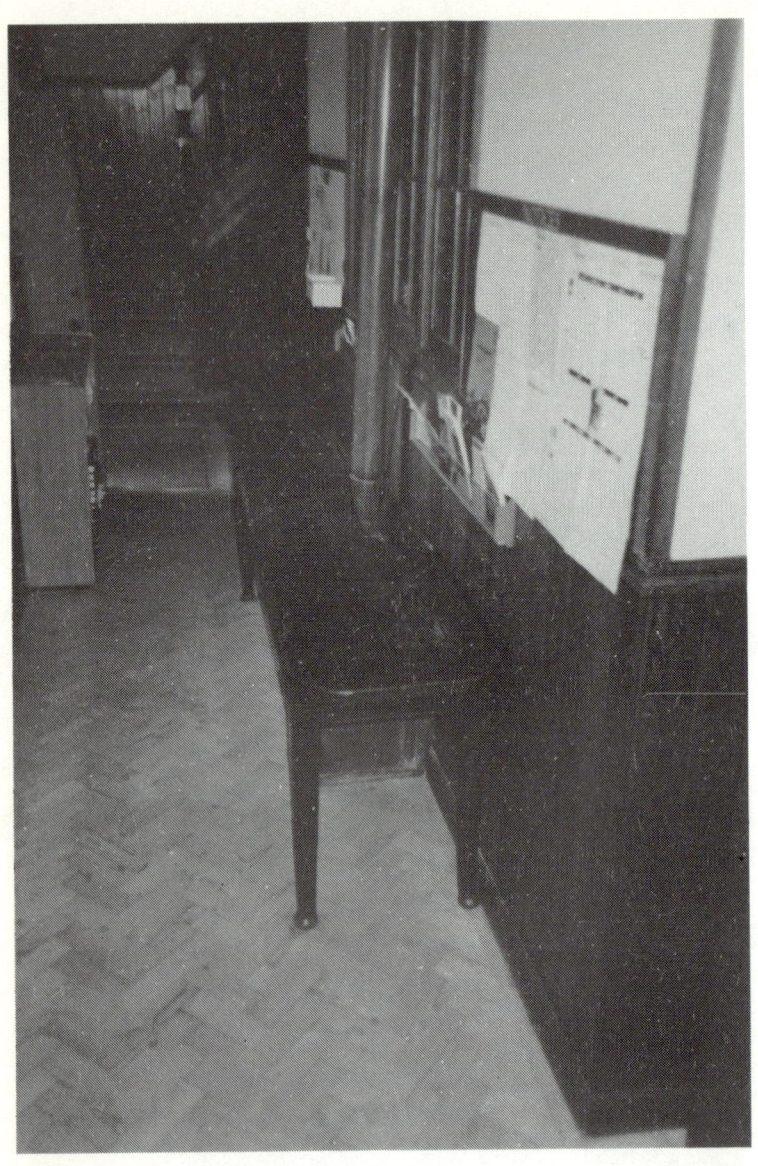

The original communion table at Arnesby. It included a semi-circular flap which could be lowered so that Robert Hall senior, a sick man, could administer the elements. The photograph is reproduced by courtesy of Arnesby Baptist Church.

who died in infancy, he ministered during the earlier years at Arnesby with a stipend of never more than fifteen pounds annually. Happily, this figure was raised in time to thirty-two pounds.[70] Hall wrote: 'I found my heart so united to the people, that I never durst leave them, though I often thought I must.'[71]

Discipline was generally severe. Bankruptcy, for example, was regarded as a clear infringement of Paul's command to 'owe no man any thing' (Romans 13:8). The Baptist church at Carlton, Bedfordshire, founded in 1688, felt obliged in 1732 to consider the case of one of their members. The church book records that

> ... Richard Green was sent unto by the church, being Assembled together at our church meeting, and was examined about his contracting debts and taking no regard to pay them, this being proved was admonished for this immorality.[72]

Sometimes attempts were made to distinguish between church members who were financially irresponsible and those who, through no fault of their own, had fallen upon hard times. In other ways, too, discipline was tempered by humanity. The move by the church at Abingdon in 1721 to appoint Benjamin Tompkins as an elder was resisted by another member, brother W. Butler, because it appeared that Benjamin was inclined to fall asleep in the meetings. Butler insisted that if the nominee could not control himself he ought not to be asked to govern in the house of God. When asked to give an account, Benjamin confessed candidly that this was a personal infirmity, for which he was sorry. In the event, brother Butler's reservation was ignored and Tompkins accepted the call.[73]

In 1732 both lay and ministerial representatives of the Independent, Baptist and Presbyterian churches in London formed the Board of Dissenting Deputies in order to protect their people. Their records, for example, show that in 1746 they succeeded in quashing an ecclesiastical prosecution against 'one *Greenwood*, for living in Fornication with his own Wife; because he had not been married according to the rites of the Church of *England*, but in the Congregation of Protestant Dissenters, of which he was a Member'.[74]

* * *

We come now to the vexed question of singing in the churches. Although this might seem strange to us, congregational singing was a major issue. Indeed, it had long been a controverted matter.

In the year of Cromwell's death, 1658, Robert Steed and Abraham Cheare, members of the Particular Baptist church at Tiverton, wrote concerning Israelite singing in Moses' 'shadowy dispensation', that 'there were added Musical Instruments, and Singers specially appointed to attend that service'. Steed and Cheare claimed that instruments and choirs 'are done away in Christ'. Nevertheless, the Tiverton people denied the accusation of Richard Bellamy, a defector from the Baptists to St Peter's Church, a hundred yards away, and a man who described himself as 'a leper cleansed', that they rejected the unaccompanied singing of psalms, hymns and spiritual songs.[75]

In the churches generally such music and singing as there were faded out after Charles II came to the throne in 1660; the people could not afford detection. The situation was restored only in 1689 when the Toleration Act made it safe for churches to advertise their presence. Then, singing came into its own, although, again, not always without protest. Indeed, a furious debate on the issue had been raging among the Particular Baptists in London since 1690. Hanserd Knollys had favoured singing, while William Kiffin was not so enamoured, possibly, it has been suggested, because he might have thought that it would prejudice restricted communion.[76] Clearly, if men of the stature of Knollys and Kiffin did not agree about this there were severe problems ahead. This was no storm in a teacup; the matter threatened to split the churches. It seems that virtually the entire leadership of the London Baptist Calvinistic community was involved.[77]

Many Baptists would undoubtedly have agreed with the Northampton Quaker, John Mulliner, who wrote way back in 1677 that 'it is true I love this Musick, but what good can these sounds do when my Soul wants Peace with God; and this doth but stir up Laughter, and Lightness of Spirit, to make me forget my Maker'.[78]

At Olney, William Walker surrendered the pastorate of the Baptist church in 1752, twenty-three years before John Sutcliff was transferred there as member and minister from Wainsgate, near Halifax. Walker quit, 'chusing as he said rather to commit himself to providence than to labour in the fires at Olney'.[79] Part of the difficulty was that before the pastor's settlement there had been no congregational singing. It was agreed by the people that Mr Walker 'should have his liberty to act according to his conscience'. At first, the 'antisingers' agreed but, following the pastor's settlement, they stated that, although remaining in their places in the congregation, they would not sing.[80] One can well imagine that the 'antisingers' contributed to the aggravation which led Walker to leave for London after eleven years in Buckinghamshire.

In the dedicatory epistle to the articles of faith of the Horsleydown church, the pastor, Benjamin Keach, wrote concerning like-minded churches which, nevertheless, did not agree with him concerning the 'singing of God's praise'. He indicated that Horsleydown should 'not refuse Communion with them'.[81] In fact, Keach succeeded in persuading many, both within his own church and elsewhere, to accept his views. Sadly, some of his people remained truculent; a number left to set up their own congregation at Maze Pond, 'founded on the same principles, *singing only excepted*, which, through time, and the succession of pastors, is now become a credible church', according to Crosby in 1740.[82]

The conservative bent of many Particular Baptists in this respect might be illustrated by an experience of John Gill. A godly woman in his London pastorate was troubled about the two new tunes which had been introduced to the congregation in the space of some three years. While the younger folk liked the tunes, the woman could hardly bear with so much innovation and so spoke to the pastor. Gill asked her if she understood singing. The lady confessed that, just like her aged father, she could only manage the Old Hundredth, but that she would like to hear David's tunes. Gill suggested gently that if she could, perchance, get them, the church would try to sing them.[83]

* * *

A striking feature of Dissenting congregations of the time was the high proportion of tradesmen and workpeople.[84] This might have been because Dissent appealed to those who were economically self-reliant and who depended neither on the crown nor its ministers for social and political advancement, nor yet on the squire or the parson for their daily bread. On the other hand, for members of the aristocracy and gentry, association with a Dissenting conventicle was totally incompatible with their social standing and political ambitions. It transpired that, in the main, Dissenters were outcasts from polite society because they would not conform to the establishment. This was particularly the case for Baptists owing to their position on baptism; their consciences were always sensitive to the issue of a notional Christian commonwealth. These people, more than other Nonconformists, remained an inferior social group.

According to Joseph Ivimey, the condition of the churches at the end of the reign of George I in 1727 is not easy to state exactly. He wrote that Christians generally 'were at ease in Zion' and that Dissenters appeared to show no desire whatever to extend the 'kingdom of Christ in the world'. According to him, the Particular Baptists, being left quiet from earlier persecution, had sunk largely into a state of 'inanity and supineness'.[85] He added that their churches desired simply to assemble for worship 'undisturbed by the sons of Belial who were without, or by the ministry of the pastor within'.[86] Thankfully, all was not lost. The breakaway Maze Pond church, to which we have just referred, numbered 6 men and 13 women in the original church covenant of 1694. By 1726 no less than 89 men and 145 women were signatories, an astounding twelvefold increase in thirty years and in a church which, originally, did not favour music.[87]

It appears that Particular Baptists were on occasion perceived to be arrogant in their isolation. If this was true they would not, of course, have served their own best interests. Ann Dutton of Northampton, London and then Great Gransden, near Cambridge, was an oft-quoted example.[88] She, after becoming the pastor's wife at Gransden in 1732, aspired to be a matriarchal figure within her own denomination, and spent the next thirty years in discharging a flood of largely biographical and critical pamphlets, often signed by some such phrase as 'one who has tasted that the Lord is gracious'. In her defence it should be said that her surviving correspondence shows that she loved the doctrines of grace and that she was ready to acclaim those who preached them, certain well-known Anglicans featuring prominently among her addressees. She also wrote that, in her view, 'as to *national Churches*, of the purest *Form*, I humbly think, there are none of Christ's Appointment under the *Gospel*.'[89]

This was fair comment for a Baptist, yet we question why, upon this view of things, she felt able to maintain ongoing contacts with those who served in the Church of England. Certainly, George Whitefield used to reply to her letters with an invariable caution; he was always sympathetic but equally non-committal. His first letter to her, sent from Philadelphia in 1739, began with ominous raillery: 'I owe you several letters ... have patience with me and I will pay you all.' Whitefield had chosen his text, Matthew 18:26, carefully. James Hervey (1713-58), the well-known Rector of Weston Favell, near Northampton, wrote to his friend, the Particular Baptist John Collett Ryland (1723-92), in 1755, recording that he had received a long letter from Mrs Dutton; he had decided to ignore it.[90]

In 1750 John Gill wrote:

Faithful and painful ministers are few. There are scarcely any that naturally care for the estate and souls of men, and who are heartily concerned for their spiritual welfare: all comparatively seek their own things.[91]

* * *

The Particular Baptists were, nevertheless, not without their shining lights. One such was Benjamin Beddome, a Calvinist who remained in his country pastorate at Bourton-on-the-Water, Gloucestershire, for some fifty-four years until his death.[92] A son of John Beddome, one of the pastors of the Pithay church, Bristol, he had been baptized at Little Prescott Street, London, at the age of twenty-two, and was called by that church to the work of the pastoral ministry. He studied under Bernard Foskett at Bristol, and afterwards, for a time, at the Independent academy, Mile End, London, after which he assumed the pastorate at Bourton. According to William Newman (1773-1835), the first president of the Stepney Baptist college, in his memoirs of John Collett Ryland, there was in 1741 'a great awakening in Beddome's congregation at Bourton. Forty persons were brought to repentance at the same time, and Mr. Ryland was among them'.[93] In 1744 the young Ryland, recently accepted at the Bristol academy, wrote thus in his diary concerning his twenty-seven-year-old pastor:

> Surely Mr. Benj. Beddome is an instance of the existence of God and the Truth of the Christian Religion. Wt [= what] Could Change his Heart, and induce him to leave his Profession or Trade — which was much more Profitable ... what is it yt [= that] moves him to preach, Pray, and be so active? is it not ye Delight he finds in ye Work — Tis plain that tis not Worldly Interest.[94]

A preacher until the end of his days, his ministry was exercised for the most part in his own church; he was not easily prevailed upon to visit elsewhere, let alone transfer to larger churches. For children he produced a widely-popular catechism. Never without sorrows, he lost three sons prematurely, John at the age of fifteen, Foskett, at the age of twenty-six, and Benjamin, a doctor, in 1778 at twenty-five.

Selections from his sermons were published after his death. They are, for any minister who would take the trouble to obtain them, models of the preaching art, displaying as they do a lively understanding both of Scripture and of the soul of man. Benjamin Beddome was the embodiment of his own words:

All that ministers can do is to persuade; God must do the rest.
Without his efficacious influence, all the force of reasoning, and all the
charms of eloquence will be lost. Paul may plant, and Apollos water;
but it is God that giveth the increase.[95]

In his earlier years Beddome honoured the traditional practice of
restricted communion. This is borne out quite clearly by his exposition
of the Baptist catechism; the proper subjects of the ordinance of
communion are 'they who have been baptized upon a personal
Profession of their Faith in Jesus Christ and Repentance from Dead
Works'.[96] It seems that later on he shifted his position to allow improper
subjects to attend. His assistant, William Wilkins, appointed in 1777,
introduced to the Lord's table, when it was possible, some who had
been sprinkled as babies. Furthermore, together with Ryland at Northampton, Daniel Turner at Abingdon and Robert Robinson at Cambridge, Beddome tended to favour 'open' membership.[97]

Impetus towards this development came from other quarters, too.
Isaac Watts (1674-1748), the hymnist and friend of Richard Cromwell,
son of Oliver, was a link in time between the later Puritans and the
founders of Methodism. According to John Gill, he was also a
'Sabellian'. Sabellianism was a third-century heresy which considered
the three persons of the Trinity as equivalent manifestations of the one
God. Perhaps Gill was rather too severe. Alfred Light, who worked his
way through most of the extensive literature available to him, claimed
in 1913 that Watts, while erring sadly about some fundamental
doctrines, was no Unitarian.[98] Isaac did like to tamper; at one stage he
was concerned about visible unity among Dissenters and intended
seriously to try to bring the Baptists and the Independents into one
body, given that their principal point of disagreement was baptism. He
considered that Baptists should surrender their insistence upon immersion and that Independents should give up the baptism of infants. In the
event, as might have been predicted with some certainty, his denominational horse-trading never saw the light of day.[99]

* * *

An issue of vital importance to the Particular Baptists was the practice
of taking Anglican communion in order to qualify for civil office, a
practice described by Daniel Defoe as 'a kind of playing Bo-peep with
God Almighty'.[100]

A bill for the prohibition of the abuse, repugnant also to many

Anglicans, was first introduced by the two members for the universities in 1702, and was eventually passed in 1711, only to be repealed in part in 1718. This allowed the continuation of occasional conformity. The practice was unknown in the London Particular Baptist churches until 1742, when a Mr Baskerville was elected to the office of common-council man for London; he proceeded to qualify by taking Anglican communion. For this he was censured by his church, that at Unicorn Yard, Southwark. Baskerville maintained the right of conscience to do as he saw fit. For its part, the church approached the Baptist Board of Ministers through their own minister, Mr Flower. The reply from the Board stated that

> ... they could not hesitate one moment in their refusal of communion with a church [the Church of England], the very frame of which is contrary to the appointment of our great Lord and his apostles, — a church that owes its constitution, its officers, its discipline, and many of its modes of worship, merely to human policy and power; — a church that assumes to itself an arbitrary right of imposing its prescriptions on the consciences of men; — in a word, a church that has almost universally departed from many of those articles of its own faith ... and that indulges in its bosom multitudes of people of the most corrupt principles, and the most immoral and profligate lives.[101]

Baskerville remained unrepentant, and in 1743 it was decided that he should no longer be considered a member of his church. Ivimey observed that most Particular Baptist churches had been preserved from such a disgraceful compromise by their people.[102] Nevertheless, the problem lingered. As late as 1786, Jonathan Turner was excluded from the Norwich church pastored by Joseph Kinghorn (1766-1832), his fault being that he had submitted to the Test Acts by receiving the Lord's supper according to the rites of the Church of England. He did this so that he could qualify for a government appointment.[103]

* * *

The history of the Unicorn Yard, Horsleydown, Southwark, church might give a further snapshot of life among the Particular Baptists of the time.[104] The church, originally meeting in Goat Street, Horsleydown, had been composed of part of the congregation of

Benjamin Keach. He was succeeded by the thirty-year-old
Benjamin Stinton. Stinton, lacking education, placed himself under
tuition following his induction. Unfortunately, he died at the early
age of forty-three. A dispute arose about his successor. Some of the
people called John Gill of Kettering to office, while others, compris-
ing the older and more wealthy element in the church, were
dissatisfied about the manner in which the election of the new pastor
had taken place. Discontent persisted, perhaps because some of the
people were happier with the rather more bland Calvinism of their
former minister and had hoped for a similar man to replace him.[105]
Reference was made to the society of ministers meeting at the
Hanover Coffee House, who advised that Gill should preach as a
probationer for one part of each Lord's day and that the dissenting
voices should provide the ministry for the other part. Afterwards,
Gill and his friends withdrew from the place in Goat Street and
rented Thomas Crosby's schoolroom for worship. Crosby, it might
be noted, was a man of parts, a schoolmaster as well as an aspiring
Baptist historian. The Goat Street people stayed on in their building
until the lease ran out in 1720, at which time Gill with his supporters
returned, paying the departing congregation ten pounds for the pews
which had been erected. They discovered that the place was sadly
in need of repair, and had to meet a bill of £128.3s.5$^{1/2}d$.[106]

Matters were not always easy for Gill. In 1720 his wife Elizabeth
miscarried, and for some seven months considered herself an
invalid. She was so treated by her husband. Some women in the
church, including Susannah Keach, widow of Benjamin and
mother-in-law of Crosby, then a deacon in the church, advised her
to pull herself together. She seems to have ignored this counsel, for
which her husband was taken to task by Crosby at a private meeting
at the Ram's Head Tavern. In the event, the Keach-Stinton tradition
which Gill had inherited might have been too much for the young
minister; he probably concluded that Crosby would have to go. He
chose his time well and, in due course, declined to stand by Crosby
when the latter was excommunicated by the church.[107]

That the situations which arose in church life were not altogether
different from present-day issues might be further illustrated by the
case of Hannah Cooper. In 1720 Hannah desired to be baptized and
admitted to membership in Gill's congregation. The minutes record
that several members, including 'Bro. Crosby', were appointed to

hear Hannah's account of her 'Faith and Repentance, she being not able through Bashfulness to speak before the whole Church'.[108]

A new meeting-place in Unicorn Yard was opened by the anti-Gill faction in the same year, 1720, with seating for some five hundred people, and with the man of their choice, William Arnold, in charge of the destitute congregation of a hundred or more members. Mr Arnold served usefully until he died in 1734. Eventually, the church issued a call to Thomas Flower junior, whose father was the pastor at Bourton-on-the-Water until his death in 1740. The son, who had trained at Bristol under Bernard Foskett, accepted, and was ordained at Unicorn Yard in 1736, John Gill taking part in prayer. It is good to observe that Gill was not reluctant to meet a congregation which, sixteen years earlier, had not favoured him. After some eight years Thomas Flower junior resigned from the pastorate, never to take charge of any other church. He went back to secular business, only preaching occasionally. 'It should seem,' wrote Ivimey, 'his true character was that of a tradesman, as he was distinguished by the appellation of "worldly-minded Flower".'[109]

* * *

The scruples then entertained by Particular Baptists about the Church of England can be brought into relief by George Whitefield's attitude towards Dissent. This very remarkable man of God preached his first open-air sermon near Bristol in 1739, and died as a clergyman entirely loyal to his Church and its articles in 1770, shortly before the decease of the equally sincere but differently endowed John Gill. Whitefield was opposed fiercely by many within his own communion:

> Is Whitefield landed on our British Isle?
> Does Heaven seem upon our Foe to smile?
> Why did the winds assist him on his Way?
> Or Spanish Robbers miss so just a Prey?

So wrote Thomas Gurney in 1741, anticipating Whitefield's return from the Americas.[110]

Whitefield himself, writing in May, 1742 to a minister in Leominster, stated:

> If the LORD gives us a true Catholic spirit, free from a party sectarian zeal, we shall do well. .... I hope that dear Mr. O— will be kept free, and not fall into disputing about *Baptism* or other non-essentials.[111]

Already in 1739 he had written to a Revd Kinchin to persuade
him not to separate from the Established Church:

> My being a minister of the Church of England, and preaching its
> articles, is a means, under God, of drawing so many after me. As for
> objecting about habits, robes, etc., good God! I thought we long
> since knew that the kingdom of God did not consist in any externals,
> but in righteousness, and peace, and joy in the Holy Ghost.[112]

He might have included in his inventory of the furnishings of the
Kingdom of Heaven full civil liberties under the Crown of England,
such as the possibility of a university education enjoyed by both
John Wesley and him but, among others, denied to the eminently
suitable John Gill. One could speculate about the comments which
the Unicorn Yard church might have passed had they ever read the
pragmatic Whitefield's youthful and eloquent eulogy of the establishment. Perhaps we are still able at this distance in time to perceive
the force behind Philip Doddridge's cutting remark: 'I take him to
be a very honest, though a very weak man. Who can wonder if so
much popularity has a little intoxicated him? He certainly does
much good, and I am afraid some harm.'[113]

These were early years; the passage of time was to mellow the
travelling preacher. In 1742 the Welshman Howell Harris (1714-
73) wrote to Whitefield:

> One cries to us, we are the most Orthodox, and the other cries,
> we are in the right, and we are the only rightly founded Gospel
> Church; but God speaks plainly for each of them, in Scotland He
> owns Presbytery, in America Independency, here and in Wales
> Episcopacy.[114]

Or, was it that God simply spoke for the gospel?

This perception might be borne out by a 1762 excerpt from
Harris's journal, in which he noted that 'a great work' was being
done by, among others, 'Mr. Rowland' in Northampton.[115] With
respect to Anglican evangelicals such as Harris and Whitefield, it
should not be forgotten that these men had, and undoubtedly knew
that they had, a potential constituency many times larger than that
of the Dissenting communities. So they stayed where they were.

'Mr. Rowland' was, in fact, none other than John Collett Ryland,
who, as we have seen, turned to Christ during the ministry of

Benjamin Beddome's home at Bourton-on-the-Water,
Gloucestershire; photograph reproduced by courtesy of
The Old Manse Hotel, Bourton-on-the-Water.

John Ryland junior (1753-1825)

Benjamin Beddome, pastor after Thomas Flower senior at Bourton-on-the-Water. Without Ryland knowing what was happening, his pastor arranged with Bernard Foskett for the young man to go to the Bristol academy to prepare for the ministry. Ryland's praise of Beddome has already been mentioned. Separated to the work of the gospel by the Bourton church in 1746, he was ordained at the Particular Baptist church at Warwick in 1750, John Brine giving the charge. The pastorate proved to be of moderate length, Ryland transferring eventually to Northampton. William Newman remarked concerning the Warwick ministry: 'It is highly probable that his differing with his people respecting terms of communion was the chief cause of his leaving them, and of the coldness they evinced, not only towards him, but to the people at Northampton also.' The letter of dismission from the Warwick church recorded wryly: 'Mr. John Ryland ... as far as we know, has not acted altogether inconsistent with the grace of God, and the profession he made amongst us.'[116] So, in 1759 Ryland moved to his new church, where, after seven years in that pastorate, he could claim that he had seen nearly 130 souls added to the membership. A professing Baptist who admitted 'other good men to the Lord's table, though in his opinion they are unbaptized',[117] he exerted a considerable influence among Particular Baptists, as did his son after him. The father was a man of strong views. For example, he could or would not tolerate bad singing; on one occasion, offended by the hideous noise made by a congregation, he told them that he wondered that some of the angels did not come down and wring their necks off.[118] In 1764 Ryland noted concerning his boy of eleven years: 'John ... has read Genesis in Hebrew five times through; he read through the Greek Testament before nine years old. He can read Horace and Virgil. He has read through Telemachus in French.'[119] It seems that there were giants, albeit temperamental specimens, in the land in those days. Ryland senior's warmth of temper apparently led him into indiscretions. In his defence, John Rippon observed that 'a small speck in scarlet is more visible than a great stain in russet'.[120]

During this period the Particular Baptists do not give the appearance of being uniformly bigoted. The evidence shows that these people were only too glad to recognize good when they saw it; for them, the Church of Christ extended beyond the boundaries of their own constituency. So it was that in 1772 Samuel Stennett wrote about both Baptists and the Lord's people in general:

Most of the productions from the pens of Baptists are answers
to the writings of Paedobaptists: So that they [the Baptists] are
scarce ever to be considered as aggressors ... it affords me infinitely
greater joy to hear, that a man is become a sincere disciple of Christ,
than that in a frenzy of party-zeal, he has thrown down the gauntlet,
and declared himself a Champion in the cause of Baptism.[121]

Such charity was not untypical. Nevertheless, the Particular
Baptists maintained a stubbornly negative attitude towards the
Evangelical Awakening; in addition to their views about the Church
of England, they would not digest the Arminianism of the Wesleys.
John Rippon cited an unnamed eighteenth-century writer:

That which appeared in Mr. John Wesley the most censurable
part of his conduct, was his very unfair statement of the arguments
of his Calvinistic adversaries, which, in a man of his acuteness of
intellect, will hardly admit the plea of unintentional mistake.[122]

Over the years Whitefield showed himself infinitely less of a
bigot than Wesley and was often received with gladness by Dissenters in Britain and by Independents in America. Rippon felt free to
cite the same commentator concerning Whitefield: 'Perhaps no man
since the days of St. Paul, nor even Luther himself, was ever
personally blest to the call and conversion of so many souls from
darkness to light.'[123] This was appreciated by some Baptists at the
time. Dr Andrew Gifford was one of Whitefield's most intimate
friends, as well as being an eminent 'favourite', to use the historian
Skeats's word, of other evangelical Anglicans such as William
Romaine (1714-95) and Augustus Montague Toplady (1740-78).
This information depresses; who wants to be someone else's favourite?[124] For the most part, Particular Baptists seem staunchly to
have kept their distance.

                              *   *   *

John Collett Ryland wrote in 1753 an account of the Baptist
churches in London. His estimates, modified by Ivimey, suggest
that altogether there might have been some 11 Particular Baptist
churches in the metropolis, with a total membership of about 1,000.
Ryland himself reckoned that in England and Wales together there
were some 121 churches, with nearly 5,000 members, the total

number of hearers being less than 20,000.[125] With regard to the numbers of the churches in 1760, when George III ascended the throne, Ivimey compiled a list taken from records retained by the managers of the London Baptist Fund in 1763, from John Ryland's 1753 records, which Ivimey believed to have been somewhat incorrect, and from other sources. Not mentioning Wales, Ivimey calculated that there might have been some 200 churches in England. The historian reckoned that at that time memberships were small, 'probably not fifty upon an average'.[126] We bear in mind that there were then no Sunday schools, no home or foreign missions, no itinerant village preaching by Baptists, no tract and Bible societies; there were only the London and Bristol Baptist Funds for helping poor ministers.[127]

Nevertheless, there was ground for optimism. Ivimey tells us that during the reign of George II 'there was a goodly number of ministers ... that maintained the doctrines of the gospel, and aimed to promote pure and undefiled religion among their people'.[128] On the other hand, writing in 1823 about Particular Baptist spirituality and numbers in the mid-1700s, Ivimey observed:

> Our churches were far more prosperous and numerous at the Revolution in 1688, than at this period, sixty-five years afterwards; so that prosperity had indeed slain more than the sword.[129]

Freedom had not been without its price.

CHAPTER IV
'STRICT BAPTIST' ORIGINS

We come now to a fascinating question. When was it that Particular Baptists, or at least some of them, came to be called 'Strict Baptists'? By 'Strict Baptists' we mean those Christians who, faithful to their Baptist principles, held that immersed believers only should unite as a church and participate together at the Lord's table. For such people baptism has been a necessary condition both for church membership and attendance at communion. In the eighteenth century the Particular Baptists usually reckoned the Lord's table as an element of church life; for them, therefore, church members only could break bread. Effectively, the basic issue was that of the terms of church membership.

Evidence suggests that 'Strict Baptists' came to be known as such at least as early as 1696, that is, only seven years after the Act of Toleration. However, the people and churches so described are not known, with the exception of the Baptist group which was meeting in the very early 1700s at Walgrave, near Kettering in Northamptonshire.

In 1700 an anonymous member of the Church of England published in London a slim volume, *An Account of the Doctrine and Discipline of Mr. Richard Davis, of Rothwell, in the County of Northampton, and those of his Separation.* Richard Davis, though by no means a Baptist, requires an introduction. From 1689 until his death in 1714 he was the pastor of the thriving Independent church at Rothwell, a village only a few miles from both Kettering and Walgrave. In earlier years he had been a teacher at an academy at Nettlebed in Oxfordshire, where Samuel Wesley, father of John and Charles, was one of his pupils.[1] When he transferred to Rothwell, the fiery Welsh evangelist started a movement which had repercussions far beyond his village and, in so doing, antagonised many within his

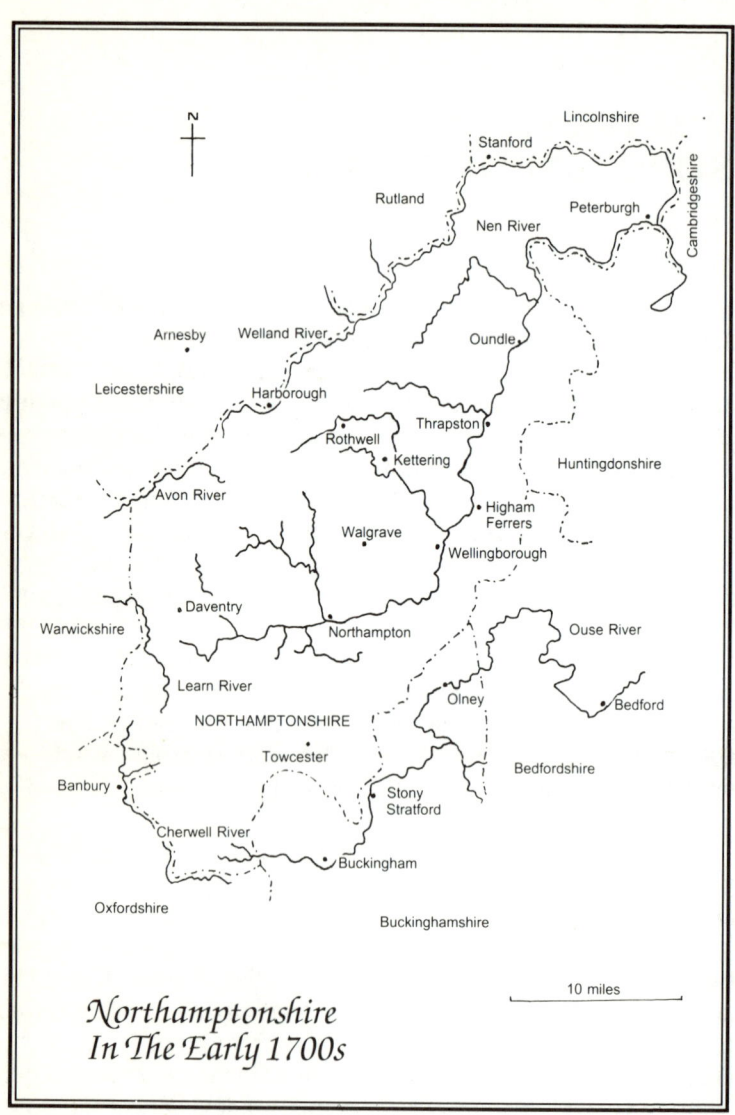

N

Lincolnshire

Stanford

Rutland

Nen River

Peterburgh

Cambridgeshire

Arnesby

Welland River

Oundle

Leicestershire

Harborough

Thrapston

Rothwell

Kettering

Huntingdonshire

Avon River

Walgrave

Higham
Ferrers

Wellingborough

Daventry

Warwickshire

Northampton

Ouse River

Learn River

Olney

Bedford

NORTHAMPTONSHIRE

Bedfordshire

Towcester

Banbury

Stony
Stratford

Cherwell River

Buckingham

Oxfordshire

Buckinghamshire

10 miles

*Northamptonshire
In The Early 1700s*

John Bunyan (1628-88)

own denomination; even Joseph Hussey, the equally high-Calvinist Independent pastor at Cambridge, opposed him at first.[2] John King, minister of the Congregational church in Wellingborough, in the same county as Rothwell, was Davis's most virulent enemy, and under a *nom de plume* issued a condemnation of Davis for the latter's alleged divisiveness, unsoundness and Antinomianism. Feelings ran high, so much so that local followers of Davis started a cause of their own in Wellingborough rather than join the society of which King was minister.[3] The anonymous friend of the Established Church who published in 1700 his account of Davis's tenets reckoned that 'there are about Thirteen gathered Congregations of this Separation under settled Pastors, the members whereof are computed to be between two and three Thousand'.[4] If numbers, then, are a measure of success and influence, Davis was both successful and influential.

The point to be made is that in the 1700 publication outlining Davis's views there was an explicit reference to 'Strict Baptists'. The Anglican entered into print because he reckoned the Rothwell Independents, among others, to be enemies of the establishment and sought to encourage his own Church to attract the separatists back into its bosom.[5] This issue does not concern us. What is relevant is that the writer made the following affirmation concerning Davis's immediate congregation at Rothwell, going back to the year 1696, four years before publication. He insisted that his record was accurate:[6]

> If any Member plead Conscience for leaving them, and desire a discharge, and offer his Reasons in publick; they will not give him a discharge, unless it be with a Testimonial recommending him to some Congregation they approve of. If he refuse to joyn with such a congregation as they approve of, and withdraw himself from them, they cut him off as an Apostate. No pretence of Conscience will prevail with them to allow any to joyn with the church of *England,* or the Presbyterians, or Quakers, or the strict Baptists. They plead they cannot discharge them, because those Churches they desire to joyn with, do not walk according to the Rule of God's Word; saying, should we suffer you, we should comply with you in Sin.[7]

Several observations might be made.

First, the Rothwell Independent church was nearly, if not totally, high-Calvinist.[8] Therefore, the denominator 'strict Baptists', apparently in vogue at Rothwell, would appear to have had no essential connection with high-Calvinist views. In other words, 'strict' does not appear to have been understood as a parallel to 'particular'; it was not at that time taken as relating in some way to the Particular Baptists' interpretations of the doctrines of grace. As we shall see, this limitation in meaning is verified by the use of the word 'strict' by both restricted-communion Baptists and their opponents later in the eighteenth century.[9] Indeed, we might surmise that the baptismal issue rather than Calvinism would appear to have been the most striking point of difference between the Rothwell Independents and local 'strict Baptists'; apart from this there would have been considerable common ground between them.

Second, the reference to 'strict Baptists' does not appear to contradict the rule-of-thumb definition which we have given, namely, that Strict Baptists were understood originally to have been those who restricted the Lord's table (and church membership) to immersed believers only. There is no evidence whatever to suggest that the word 'strict', as employed by Baptists later in the century, ever did shift its frame of reference. What it came to mean for both advocates and opponents of restricted communion in the mid-1700s, when controversy flared, it seems to have meant for North-amptonshire Independents (and the somewhat irascible Anglican) back in 1700.

Third, the 1700 volume was published in London. This might be taken to imply not only that Davis's influence had attracted attention as far away as the metropolis, but that the 'strict Baptists', too, were reckoned not only at Rothwell village but also by the Anglican writer to have been a recognizable group of churches in their own right, and a constituency of perhaps more than local proportions. 'Strict Baptists' were grouped with the Quakers, Presbyterians and the establishment, bodies which were, of course, of national dimensions. Davis's Anglican expositor has left posterity the impression that 'strict Baptists', just like the other denominated bodies, would not have been unknown at that time by interested city folk. Further, he referred to each grouping, 'strict Baptists' included, as a 'Church'. All this might even suggest that by 1696 Anglicans nationally had to reckon with a 'strict Baptist' Church or, as the people at Rothwell (and Walgrave) might well have put it, with 'strict Baptist' churches.

Fourth, the writer closed his pamphlet with the remark that 'this was the state of the Separation, at *Rothwell*, about the Year 1696, which, as I understand, has receiv'd no considerable alteration since that time'.[10] He implied that 'strict Baptists', just like the Quakers, the Presbyterians and, of course, the establishment, had been a recognizable body for some years. We might surmise that other Independents and Anglicans, no doubt, were then busily levelling the nickname 'strict Baptist' at restricted-communion Baptist churches; the Rothwell people do not seem to have devised the expression.

Finally, there is no evidence in the booklet to suggest that the 'strict Baptists' had then accepted the title as descriptive of their position; the words appear simply as an epithet which in time past had apparently originated elsewhere. As Daniel Mayo, the Presbyterian, put it in 1713, the advocates of immersion as the only valid mode of baptism 'therefore like not the name of *Anabaptist,* but call themselves *Baptists*'.[11] He did not say that they called themselves 'strict Baptists'.

* * *

Evidence from the Rothwell Independent church itself confirms the account published in 1700. It seems that for some little while Richard Davis had been vexed by local Baptists; his church articles refer disparagingly to them as 'Antipaedobaptists'.[12] It comes as no surprise, then, to find that Davis was troubled when, apparently, at least one of his flock, sister Chapman, attached herself to such people. We have not been told if she was baptized by them as a believer. All that is revealed by the Rothwell church book is that in 1706-7 Davis felt obliged to deal with this difficult lady member. The record states that at the time it was observed that

> ... Sister Chapman ... was in Conscience for walking with Strickt Baptists; And was offended, that it should be preached that the covenant made with Abraham ran from his naturall seed; And that many Godly Parents should see many of their children in Heaven that they did not ixpect.[13]

To be 'in conscience' meant to live according to principles. Thus, the lady believed that she should identify with local 'Strickt Baptists'. In reality, matters were not quite so simple; pastoral problems seldom are. The problem for the Rothwell church did not lie solely in what she both believed and did not believe. To repeat, it transpired that sister Chapman (whether wife, widow or spinster is undisclosed), by then a long-standing member at Rothwell, was covertly identifying with a Baptist community at Walgrave, just a few miles away. She was not prepared to make an open change. The Walgrave people were the 'Strickt Baptists' mentioned in the church book. It might well be that at that time this village group was small; earlier, in 1676, the population of Walgrave numbered 1 Roman Catholic, 8 Nonconformists (whether Baptists or Independents is not known) and 456 Conformists.[14] These figures, of course, refer to the state of things before the Toleration Act in 1689, after which the proportion of Nonconformists could well have enlarged. Even so, given the influx to Rothwell Independent church, the 'Strickt Baptist' congregation might not have flourished. At any rate, in 1706-7 sister Chapman was admonished twice 'for Schism and lying' and, to quote the church book again, because she refused to hear the Rothwell church, 'she was actually ex-communicated.' In fact, the lady herself had long been in trouble with Mr Davis and his flock. As far back as 1694, twelve years earlier, no less, she had been admonished by the church for going to the 'publick', that is, to the Church of England, and had relented, promising to be more watchful.[15] As time passed, however, she appears to have been unwilling to sever her links with the Independents while remaining a consistent wanderer; she learned little. When she lied about the 'Strickt Baptists' the Rothwell church apparently concluded that enough was enough.

The fact of the matter is that, consistent with the Anglican publication of 1700, six years later the somewhat triumphal Independents at Rothwell dealt severely with one of their people who was more or less attached to the Walgrave 'Strickt Baptists'. Further, the record is capable of being taken to imply that the epithet was already in circulation; it might seem that churches so denominated by others were reckoned to have been no recent phenomenon. In short, the Rothwell church book indicates quite clearly that only a few years after the Toleration Act of 1689 and the Particular Baptist confession of the same year, some Baptists were being characterized, in Northamptonshire at least, as Strict Baptists. We might infer with some certainty that this had to do with immersion as a term of communion.

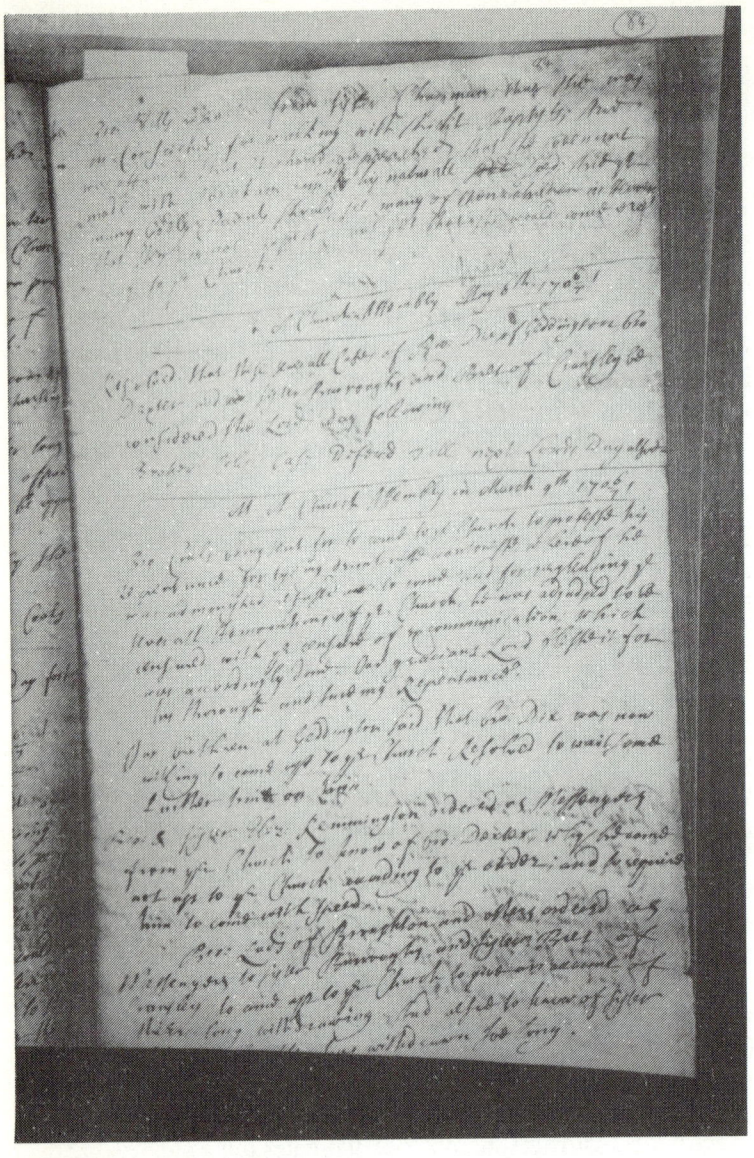

A page from the first church book of the Independent Church, Rothwell; reproduced by courtesy of Rothwell United Reformed Church. The date is 1706-7; 'Strickt Baptists' are mentioned in the second line from the top.

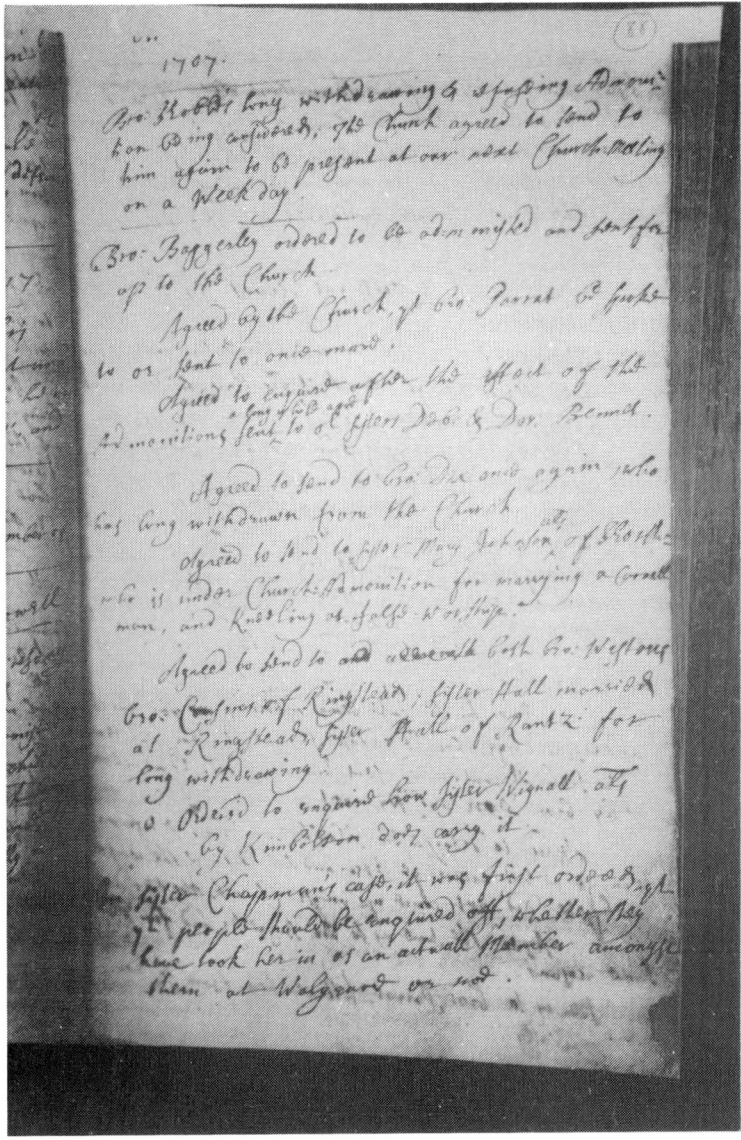

Another page from the same church book, noting (at the bottom of the page) that inquiries will be made about sister Chapman's possible reception into membership by the Walgrave 'Strickt Baptists'.

To repeat, at this period Baptist churches almost always accepted baptized believers only to membership and to the Lord's table. Unusually, John Bunyan did not insist upon immersion when receiving folk to his Bedford church. It was just because of this point that he parted company with the restricted-communion Baptists; Bunyan would never accept that baptism was a 'church ordinance'.[16]

* * *

As was perhaps inevitable, the nickname 'strict baptist' was gradually acknowledged by the churches thus labelled. John Brown of Kettering wrote in 1777, seventy years later, about those who 'have adopted and go by the name of strict Baptists',[17] while Abraham Booth (1734-1806) in the following year, 1778, approved, indeed almost welcomed, the term:

> If by the epithet *strict*, they mean *exact, accurate, conscientiously nice;* their candour deserves commendation. In that sense of the term we are not ashamed to be called STRICT *Baptists:* we cheerfully adopt the character.[18]

Then came a qualification:

> But if, on the contrary, our brethren mean by the epithet, that we are *bigoted, unnecessarily exact, unscripturally confined;* their forwardness to give us a name calls for our censure. In the former sense, I will venture to affirm, every Baptist *ought* to be a *strict* one, or else to renounce the name. In the latter use of the term, we reject the distinguishing epithet, and require our opponents to prove — I say to *prove,* not to surmise, that it justly belongs to us.[19]

On balance, Booth was more than happy to employ the expression as a denominator:

> Our character, then, is fixd. Their own pens have engrossed it. And, be it known to all men, we are STRICT BAPTISTS. To this character, as before explained, we subscribe with hand and heart.[20]

It should not escape our notice that Booth wrote on behalf of the 'Baptists', and not 'Strict Baptists'. The title implies clearly that, as he saw it, in his day the vast majority of Baptists practised restricted communion.

Significantly, Abraham Booth was not the first Baptist to endorse the use of an epithet which, as a term of abuse, was in circulation in Northamptonshire at least some seventy or more years earlier. There is, in fact, firm evidence which shows that the title had been adopted by some Baptists as early as the 1750s.

It is certain that Dissenters outside the Baptist fold looked askance at the practice of restricted communion, a disapproval which helps us to see how and why the epithet 'strict baptist' came into being. In 1749 Thomas Bradbury, the London Independent pastor who could not keep himself out of controversy about high Calvinism (or anything else, for that matter),[21] wrote about baptism in general and the Baptists in particular:

> Ye are baptized *into Christ,* not into this or that Denomination of his People. It's pity that we are known among men by meer Circumstances: The Name should not be taken from the Quantity of Water that is used; for God never did by the Church, as he had done by the Earth, *founded it upon the Seas and established it upon the Floods.*[22]

John Brine, better known for his high Calvinism,[23] came into print in 1756 on the subject of the connection between baptism and the Lord's table with his *The Baptists vindicated from some Groundless Charges brought against them by Mr. Eltringham.* Eltringham was called to the ministry by the Kettering Baptists in 1753, but in 1757 he was removed by the people. He disagreed with restricted communion.[24] So, he wrote a pamphlet entitled *The Baptist against the Baptist Or, a Display of Antipaedo-Baptist Self-Inconsistency; In Answer to Several Letters from a Baptist-Brother.*[25] It was this which Brine sought to confute. We introduce Eltringham's complaints and Brine's rejoinder here rather than in the chapter which deals with eighteenth-century controversy about closed communion because they relate to the emergence of the term 'strict baptist'.

In fact, William Eltringham had already ventured into print in 1754 with a slim pamphlet entitled *The Doctrine of Believer's Baptism by Immersion for Justification, Exploded, and proved to be Antiscriptural.* At least, the copy retained by the Northampton Central Library displays the name of William Eltringham as the author written in ink on the front cover. The main purpose of the book was to condemn John Gill, an intimate friend of Brine, for teaching allegedly that immersion in water is essential to salvation.[26] Eltringham was really coming round to the conclusion that because baptism is not a term of salvation, it ought not to be made a term of communion. In defence of Gill, it needs to be said that he denied strenuously that baptism is a condition of salvation. For example, he proclaimed at one of his baptismal services that baptism 'is a way of duty, but not of life and salvation'.[27] Eltringham, if he was the author of the 1754 booklet, wrote trenchantly about immersion as a harmful barrier between Christians:

> For my Part, I am sure Christ's Body is but one; and that separating, dividing Spirit, on the Account of a Mode or Ceremony, cannot be the meek and lowly Spirit of Jesus; and they who separate upon that Consideration only, are self-condemned.[28]

Eltringham's *The Baptist against the Baptist* of 1755 developed his earlier objections to immersion as a necessary pre-condition for communion. John Gill was taken to task frequently. So, 'your Doctor shuts out them whom he owns Christ has received; therefore in this he follows his own sensual spirit, and not Christ.'[29] Eltringham, daringly, was comparing Gill to those censured by Jude 19.[30] Further, it is clear that Eltringham, when he penned these pages, had in front of him both John Bunyan's *Confession* and 1673 *Differences in Judgment about Water-Baptism no Bar to Communion,*[31] he cited exactly from both works, deploying Bunyan's arguments against restricted communion. John Bunyan's ghost had been called up to anathematize John Gill.

In his *The Baptist against the Baptist* Eltringham wrote to an unidentified 'Baptist-Brother':

> Now brother observe; *Mr. Bunyan* calls this practice of strict communion which *Dr. Gill* and many others plead for, scriptureless light, — wordless opinion, — froward notion, — carnality, — babes that do it — to make laws where God has made none — you do it by a spirit of persecution.[32]

Notice that Eltringham conceded that there were 'many' Baptists in his day who 'plead' for what he termed 'strict communion'. Further, he implied that John Bunyan employed the same expression. The reality is that neither in his *Confession,* nor in his *Differences in Judgment about Water-Baptism,* nor in his slightly later

Peacable Principles and true: Or, a brief Answer to Mr. Danvers and Mr. Paul's Book against my Confession of Faith, and Differences in Judgment about Baptism no Bar to Communion, did Bunyan employ the expression 'strict communion'. The conclusion to be reached is that by the 1750s 'strict communion' was an epithet being hurled against the majority of Particular Baptists and that, by Eltringham at least, Bunyan's prestigious name was being brought into the conflict retrospectively.

It is now that we discover 'strict-communion' Baptists (to take up Eltringham's words) endorsing the title 'Strict Baptist'. In 1756 John Brine referred repeatedly and favourably to 'Strict Baptists' in a way which suggests that the expression had been current among a number of Baptist churches for some time at least. His name, of course, would have enhanced the prestige and acceptability of the epithet. Not missing the opportunity to take John Bunyan to task because 'he was not eminently qualified for polemical writing', Brine asserted:

> There is no Disagreement, between the strict Baptists, and others, who differ from them, respecting the Subject and Mode of Baptism, in this Matter; for both make Baptism a Term of Communion.

The 'others' mentioned by Brine were Paedobaptists.[33] The true issue, wrote Brine, related to 'Communion, *mixt,* or *strict, viz.* Whether Persons for, and against Baptism, infant, and adult, may lawfully unite in Christian Fellowship'.[34] Brine then asked his opponents to 'let it be proved to the *strict* Baptists, that Baptism is not an initiating Ordinance, into the Church'.[35]

* * *

It is important for the present argument concerning Strict Baptist origins that we take note of Brine's antithesis between 'mixt' and 'strict' communion. By 1756 Brine seemed to be aware of the jargon current in discussions both among Baptists and between Baptists and others concerning terms of communion; some were for 'mixt', while others were for 'strict' communion. We ask: when did such terms arise among the Baptists, or, at least, when were restricted-communion Baptists aware that they needed to defend themselves as 'Strict Baptists'? That some Baptists were being called such at the beginning of the century is, as we have shown, certain.

With respect to the expression 'mixt communion', we can go

back as far as John Bunyan. He wrote in his *Peacable Principles,* in answer to Henry Danvers: '*You tell us, you meddle not with Presbyterians, Independents, mixt communionists* (a new name) *but are for liberty for all according to their Light.*'[36] Henry Danvers (or, D'Anvers), born about 1620, had at one time been a colonel in the Parliamentary army and died a fugitive in exile in Holland about 1686-7, a year or so before Bunyan. When governor of Stafford in the mid-1650s he had already embraced Baptist principles. Later on he became increasingly associated with the Fifth Monarchists.

Neither was 'mixt' a new adjective nor 'mixt communionists' 'a new name'; Bunyan himself had used the latter expression. Further, it might be that Danvers, having come across it in reading Bunyan's writings, had decided cleverly to employ it against Bunyan, who, we might infer, responded to the ploy.

In his somewhat earlier *Confession* Bunyan had written that 'Mixed Communion polluteth the Ordinances of God',[37] 'Mixed Communion' being understood as a communion service to which are admitted 'them that profess not Faith and Holiness; or that are not visible saints by calling'.[38] Whether or not Danvers was indeed lifting the expression from Bunyan, his intention was quite certainly to show that the Lord's table, when attended by 'visible saints by calling', yet saints who had not been immersed, would be tantamount to Bunyan's 'Mixed Communion' and, as such, would be a pollution of the ordinance. Via an association of terms, he was in effect criticising Bunyan's practice in the strongest possible manner.

John Bunyan described his Baptist opponents thus:

> Those of the rigid way of our Brethren, the Baptists *so called,* whose Principles will neither allow them to admit TO Communion, *The Saint that differeth from them about Baptism*'.[39]

Indeed, Bunyan employed the adverb 'strictly' only in connection with an open table:

> *I am bold* (say I) *to have Communion with visible Saints as before, because God hath Communion with them, whose example in the case we are strictly commanded to follow.*[40]

By the 1670s, then, there were 'rigid Baptists' who opposed 'mixt' communion, their definition of 'mixt' communion being other than that of Bunyan. By the 1750s arguments were reappearing for and against 'mixt' communion as understood by Baptists of Bunyan's way of thinking. Restricted-communion Baptists were by this time coming to acknowledge that they were, indeed, 'Strict Baptists'. By the middle of the eighteenth century we hear much less about 'rigid Baptists'; it seems that the adjective 'rigid' had for a number of years been dropping away in favour of 'strict'.

*   *   *

During the 1720s, half-way between Bunyan's and Brine's polemics on the subject, controversy about 'mixt' communion had already flared up. In 1726 there was published in London an anonymous pamphlet, *The Manner of Baptizing with Water Cleared up from the Word of God and Right Reason*, presenting a debate between an advocate of immersion, 'Mr J.P.', and an advocate of pouring or sprinkling, 'Mr B.W.' John Gill, however, in a volume which appeared in 1727, suggested that the true author of this work 'appears to be Mr. *Matthias Maurice of Rowell* in *Northamptonshire*'.[41] Matthias Maurice, who had previously spent some eighteen months at the 'Upper Meeting' at Olney, was recommended to the people at Rothwell by no less a person than Isaac Watts.[42] Maurice, as successor to Davis and committed, of course, to infant baptism, moved to his new charge in 1714 to remain there until his death in 1738.

Maurice must have been aware of the note in his church book about sister Chapman and the Walgrave 'Strickt Baptists'. So, forewarned and forearmed by relatively recent events in his church, in his anonymous publication of 1726 the Congregational minister allowed 'Mr B.W.' victory in the dialogue. The latter was made to stress in conclusion

> ... the equity and necessity of communion with saints as saints, without making difference in judgment about water baptism, a bar unto evangelical church fellowship. God has received them, and we should be *followers of God as dear children*; we are commanded to receive one another.[43]

It would seem that 'Mr B.W.' was not unaware of Bunyan's writings on the subject; the expression 'communion with saints as saints' echoed precisely the mind of the Bedfordshire pastor.[44]

Who, exactly, were Messrs 'J.P.' and 'B.W.'? If Gill was correct in attributing the writing to Matthias Maurice — and there is little likelihood that he was wrong; Gill knew the Northamptonshire scene well — then it seems possible (but only just) that Maurice, the Independent, was proceeding upon the thesis that to divide is to conquer, doing so in what seems to have been a quite regrettable fashion. According to Whitley's *Baptist Bibliography*, it appears that 'Mr B. W.' was none other than Benjamin Wallin (1711-82),[45] about whom a word must be said. Concerning 'Mr J.P.', nothing is known.

With the encouragement of, among others, John Gill and John Brine, Benjamin Wallin became pastor at the Maze Pond, London, Baptist church in 1741, where his father, Edward, had been minister until his decease in 1733. Benjamin, too, remained in office until he died.[46] By 1726 Wallin junior, of course, was no more than fifteen years of age; he was just recovering from treatment for a nearly incurable lameness incurred in infancy.[47]

If Whitley is correct in his identification of 'Mr B.W.' — and here we depend upon the accuracy of the reference in the *Baptist Bibliography*, a publication which began to appear in 1916 — we arrive at a bizarre conclusion.[48] It seems that in order to bolster his argument for free communion Maurice introduced somewhat surreptitiously the name of the frail, teenage son of the eminent Edward Wallin, a close friend of John Gill.[49] We know that Gill soon remarked upon the fact that Maurice brought out this publication in favour of free communion without putting his name to it.[50] Gill, no doubt, would have expressed himself in the strongest possible terms had he realised that Maurice was making the son of a well-loved Baptist family speak for 'mixt' communion. If he did, indeed, do this, the ruse does not reflect well upon the Independent pastor, to say the least. It also seems particularly strange in the light of Benjamin's own stated views. In 1758 he asked about Christ and his people: 'And, what is his Church, but his Disciples joined in Communion, and walking together in his Ordinances, to whom alone they are each Subjected as their King, in the Affair of Religion, which includes Divine Worship?'[51] He declared: 'I am persuaded that a conscientious Conformity to Gospel-Institutions, will be found of greater Consequence at the Judgment-Seat than seems generally thought of by the Hearers of the Day.'[52] Four years later Wallin published a sermon on Romans 14:19, in which Paul urges his readers to 'follow after the things which make for peace', a biblical context always a favourite platform for free-communionists. The Baptist pastor stated: 'The Truth before us is plainly this, namely, that it becomes the Faithful united in a Church-State, to follow the Things which make for Peace, and Things wherewith one may edify another.'[53] All in all, it is obvious that Wallin reckoned baptism to be indispensable for 'a Church-State', and that, for him, the 'things which make for peace' by no means included a neglect of the ordinance.

The suspicion is unavoidable that Whitley erred in his identification of 'Mr B.W.' Maurice, surely, would have been neither so unscrupulous nor so unwise. The matter is mentioned simply because Whitley does introduce the teenager as the advocate of affusion and sprinkling as valid modes of baptism.

Maurice's 1726 pamphlet was answered in the same year by John Gill's third publication, *The Antient Mode of Baptizing by Immersion, Plunging, or Dipping into Water*.[54] The cover of Gill's book promised that comment would be made about 'the Author's Reasons for the Practice of a *free* or mixt Communion in Churches.' The 'author' referred to was, as far as Gill was concerned, the Independent minister Matthias Maurice. We shall not detail the arguments produced by Gill in refutation of Maurice's thesis that saints as saints should join at the Lord's table. Our concern is solely about discussions among Particular Baptists.

It is important to observe that Gill attacked 'the Practice of a *free* or mixt Communion in Churches', anticipating the terminology of his very good friend John Brine thirty years later, in 1756, in the latter's defence of 'Strict Baptists'. This implies that Gill was aware of the word 'strict', the antithesis to 'mixt', although it is true that the pages of the slim volume do not actually employ it. Gill came from Kettering, three miles from Rothwell. In his boyhood he had known Richard Davis personally; Gill's recommendatory preface to the seventh edition of Davis's hymns in 1748 stated that 'his memory has always been precious to me'.[55] Further, we decline to believe that Gill, always an advocate of restricted communion, had never heard of 'Strict Baptists' in the area. We know, too, that John Brine, also from Kettering, in 1756 referred to 'Strict Baptists' in a manner which suggests that the epithet had been accepted by restricted-communion Baptists for some considerable time. So, why did Gill mention the Strict Baptists as such neither in his 1726 *The Antient Mode*, nor in the follow-up which appeared in 1727, *A Defence of the Book intitled, The Ancient Mode of Baptizing*?

We suggest the following scenario. To repeat the point, Gill must have been well aware that the epithet 'strict baptist' was current, at least in his home county, Northamptonshire, in the 1710s and 1720s. Now this man was, *par excellence*, a theologian; even in his earlier years he would have sensed instinctively that free (or 'mixt') communion was opposed diametrically to the Baptist concept of the gathered church; he must have realised that, by definition, a church admitting non-immersed Christians to the Lord's supper was simply not a Baptist church. At a deeper level Gill would surely have taken the view that 'mixt' communion was contrary to both the precepts and practices of the New Testament. Therefore, for him the soubriquet 'strict baptist' must have been an annoying irrelevance; he could not have felt that he needed to introduce the term any more than he would have defended the odious denominator 'Anabaptist'. So, while he attacked what he called 'free' or 'mixt' communion, we infer a reluctance on his part to deploy the adjective 'strict'. For Gill, the issue was between Baptists on the one hand and, on the other, immersed mixed-communionists who could not, strictly speaking, be reckoned as 'Baptists'.

Gill's *Antient Mode* was answered in the same year, 1727, by Maurice in his *Plunging into Water No Scriptural Mode of Baptizing: Or, Mr. Gill fairly answered, and Baptizing with Water defended*. Maurice considered Gill ungracious:

> Thro' grace, there are hundreds who are constantly under the conduct of a different and more agreeable Spirit: But that any of those that are called the ministers of Christ, especially under a more strict and separate consideration, should allow themselves the liberty of rank injustice, burlesque, and banter, is and must be grieving unto those who delight to walk with God.[56]

Notice that Maurice informed Gill that the latter was 'strict' and did so with respect to Gill's link between immersion in water and admission to the Lord's table. Because Maurice described John Gill, a Baptist, as 'strict', he was only one tiny step away from calling Gill a 'Strict Baptist'.

Here we might have come across the earliest known example of the adjective 'strict' being levelled point-blank at a Baptist because of his view of the terms of admission to the Lord's table. The date, again, is 1727. Even though, back in 1706-7, Mr Maurice's predecessor, Richard Davis, no doubt discussed with his elders the case of the unfortunate 'Strickt Baptist', sister Chapman, and might conceivably have told her to her face that she was such, it is John Gill who seems to emerge as the first identifiable target of such abuse.

*   *   *

In process of time the adjective 'strict' slipped into denominational terminology. For example, Joseph Burroughs (1685-1761), minister at Paul's Alley, in the Barbican, from 1717, and a 'Non-subscriber' at the Salters' Hall discussions, was described by Joseph Ivimey retrospectively as a 'strict Baptist'. Further, both Ivimey and Walter Wilson, whose *History and Antiquities of Dissenting Churches* began to appear in 1808, reported that Burroughs ranked with the 'General Baptists'.[57] With regard to Burroughs's Arminianism, we might ask how it was that he became minister at Paul's Alley, bearing in mind that, notwithstanding earlier hesitations about Calvinism, the church joined the association of Particular Baptist churches in 1706. In spite of this move it was never, it seems, a church with convinced views, which is no doubt why Burroughs was allowed as his assistant Dr John Gale, another 'Non-subscriber' and, moreover, a professed Unitarian. Gale died prematurely in 1721. The church, once the largest Baptist community in London, declined. In 1768, seven years after Burroughs's death, it dissolved itself.[58]

The fact is that Burroughs's theology and churchmanship demonstrate convincingly that neither at that time nor for many years later were essential connections drawn between 'strict' communion and Calvinism, let alone a Calvinism of the 'high' variety. This is significant. According to Wilson, Burroughs held that no particular terms of church communion are laid down by Scripture, yet believed (quoting Wilson) 'that churches formed upon the principle of the Baptists, should admit none to their communion but those who had been baptized at years of maturity'.[59] We note that Wilson published these remarks about fifty years after Burroughs's death. Ivimey, relying upon Wilson as a source when the former wrote in 1830, described Wilson as Burroughs's 'biographer' and claimed that Wilson actually wrote that Burroughs had been 'a strict Baptist', citing Wilson directly.[60] This was not quite true. In point of fact, Wilson did not describe Burroughs explicitly as a 'strict Baptist'. Ivimey must have known this. So, deliberately embroidering, he put the words into Wilson's mouth.

For all this, Ivimey's inaccurate imputation of the expression 'strict Baptist' to Burroughs (via Wilson) is revealing. It proves that Ivimey, normally a precise enough historiographer, reckoned Wilson to have thought quite genuinely that Burroughs, the Arminian, had also been a 'strict Baptist'. There is no reason to believe that Ivimey was wrong in his assessment of either Wilson or Burroughs. Perhaps it would be better to go back to Burroughs's own words. He wrote in 1746:

I had rather persuade my unbaptized brethren to communicate with such societies as believe them baptized, than run the risque of breaking to pieces those societies, where the greatest part believe immersion in water on profession of faith to be necessary to the constitution of a Christian church; or contribute to the intire loss of the practice of Christian baptism, which mixt communion, in this great city, would effectually do.[61]

We see, then, that, by 1746, Burroughs, a non-Calvinist and pragmatically, although not perhaps ideologically, a Strict Baptist, was inveighing against 'mixt' communion. This he did in much the same fashion as did John Brine, a committed Strict Baptist and a high Calvinist, ten years later. It might even be said that Burroughs was, to coin a phrase, a 'Strict-and-General' Baptist.

* * *

To conclude. In the early 1670s John Bunyan was aware of so-called 'rigid' Baptists opposed to Christians such as he who were quite prepared to break bread with unbaptized believers. William Eltringham, writing in 1755, asserted that Bunyan had written against 'strict communion', although there is no evidence to show that Bunyan had employed the expression.

As early as 1696 the adjective 'strict' was being ascribed to some unspecified Baptists by Richard Davis and his people at the Independent church, Rothwell, Northamptonshire. This information is given by an anonymous London publication which appeared in 1700. In 1706-7 the same congregation in its church book referred to 'Strickt Baptists' in their area, specifically at Walgrave, between Rothwell and Kettering. In 1727 the identical epithet, 'strict', was levelled by Davis's successor at Rothwell against the youthful Baptist pastor John Gill, then quite recently settled in London. Matthias Maurice did this almost certainly because of Gill's views on the terms of communion. In sum, the evidence shows that, while restricted communion had been practised by English Baptists for many years,[62] the epithet 'strict baptist' was known in the English East Midlands in the late seventeenth century. The evidence suggests, but does not prove, that the expression originated in this area.

In time, the nickname passed into more widespread use. A generation later, John Brine, another Northamptonshire man, appeared as the first Baptist to acknowledge the term 'strict baptist', yet only by way of concession. This was in the 1750s. In Brine's situation the term possessed an expediency, even an appropriateness, which it probably did not have for Gill back in the 1720s. Brine introduced the expression with a certain reserve because he knew that it had been thrust upon the constituency. There is no evidence that at that period it had been accepted widely as a denominator by all or even many restricted-communion Baptist churches. Even Abraham Booth, as late as 1778, needed to qualify the term carefully before he was prepared to approve it.

Joseph Ivimey observed that it was in the time of Abraham Booth that ministers and churches which admitted immersed believers only to the Lord's table 'were now first designated "Strict Baptists"'.[63] This assertion, we believe, was inaccurate; the designation was a good deal older. 'Strict Baptists' as such were an element within English Dissent almost since William III's introduction of religious toleration in 1689. Further research might even establish that they had been described in such a way in earlier years. In those times the expression had no essential connection with Calvinism; there was no generic relation.

CHAPTER V
RESTRICTED-COMMUNION BAPTISTS AND CONTROVERSY ABOUT COMMUNION IN THE LATE 1600s

It is certain that by the very late 1600s some Baptists were known explicitly as 'Strict Baptists'. In all probability this was because of their insistence upon baptism as a term of Christian profession and hence as a term of communion. There were also some who, although holding to immersion as the only valid method of baptism, rejected strict communion quite emphatically. In this chapter, and the two which follow, we shall attempt to trace the arguments presented by Particular Baptists on both sides of the issue from about the time of the 'Glorious Revolution' in 1688 to the earlier part of the nineteenth century.

The first stage in the ongoing controversy would appear to have been the confrontation in the late seventeenth century between, on the one hand, Henry Danvers and William Kiffin and, on the other, John Bunyan. Not surprisingly, they were unable to settle the matter to the permanent satisfaction of all. The second principal bout occurred in the 1770s, involving, among others, Abraham Booth and the two men who styled themselves 'Candidus' and 'Pacificus'. The third and final episode was the battle of books between Joseph Kinghorn and Robert Hall junior (1764-1831) in the opening decades of the nineteenth century. As has been mentioned, the arguments which both sides produced were repetitive; although personal styles varied considerably, Booth and his opponents elaborated points made by Kiffin and Bunyan and anticipated the lengthier works of Kinghorn and Hall.

Over the years, the advocates of restricted communion were one with their opponents in holding that baptism is not essential for salvation; all were quick to point out that they baptized believers solely upon a personal profession of faith. The restricted communionists held that the teaching of Christ and the unvarying practice of his apostles demand that only baptized believers be admitted to the Lord's table. When challenged about their approach, all they could do, and felt that they needed to do, was to cite the precepts and practices of the New Testament.

Open communionists usually claimed that the New Testament never demands as a term of admission to the Lord's table anything which is confessedly not a condition of salvation. They maintained steadfastly that for this reason Scripture does not present immersion as a term of communion; they claimed that they had been quite unable to discover chapter and verse which clearly teach restricted communion. When challenged about their practice, all they could do, and felt that they needed to do, was to turn back to what they believed to be the teaching, both explicit and implicit, of the New Testament.

In short, neither side would admit that it was contravening the Word of God.

*   *   *

An important point needs to be given focus. It appears that, since their emergence in the early 1600s, the majority of English Baptists, both 'General' and 'Particular', favoured the practice of inviting to the Lord's table those alone who had been immersed upon profession of faith;[1] all were, in effect, Strict Baptists. The reason for this was that these people took the New Testament at face value; neither did they split hairs about baptism not being a term of salvation and therefore not of communion, nor did they concede that infant baptism, even when maintained by Bible-loving Christians, could be right.

Abraham Booth, in his *An Apology for the Baptists*, claimed that restricted communion was practically the universal custom 'till about the middle of the last century here in England; when some few of the Baptists began to call it in question, and practically to deny it'.[2] He was referring to the 1650s onwards and, principally, to John Bunyan.

The conviction underlying restricted communion was the notion that, as expressed by the anti-Calvinistic *Short Confession* of John Smyth, issued in 1610, baptism was the essential hallmark of a Christian church. So, ran the confession, 'baptism is the external sign of the remission of sins', while 'the Lord's Supper is the external sign of the communion of Christ, and of the faithful amongst themselves by faith and love.'[3] The 1644 Particular Baptist confession, the first confession to identify immersion as the proper mode of baptism and, writes William Lumpkin, a confession which 'served Baptists all over the country at a time when the Particular Baptist stream was becoming the major stream of Baptist life',[4] was to insist that the church is

> ... a company of visible Saints, called & separated from the world
> ... to the visible profession of the faith of the Gospel, being baptized
> into that faith, and joyned to ... eachother ... in the practical injoyment
> of the Ordinances, commanded by Christ their head and King.[5]

A further confession was issued in 1656 in the West Country. Attempting to effect something of a reconciliation between Particular and General Baptists, it declared that 'it is the duty of every man and woman, that have repented from dead works, and have faith toward God, to be baptized', and that such people 'do walk together in communion in all the commandments of Jesus', one of these commandments being 'BREAKING of bread (I Cor.11:23,24)'.[6] The 1677 Particular Baptist confession, designed to exhibit the substantial agreements of Calvinistic Baptists with the Congregationalists and Presbyterians, was silent concerning the terms of communion, a silence which was tactical rather than ideological. So, the appendix to the confession declared pragmatically that for the sake of peace it omitted all reference to differences of opinion between those who were prepared to commune with baptized believers only and those who had 'a greater liberty and freedom'.[7] The logic of restricted communion was not to be tested at that time.[8]

A General Baptist confession issued in 1678 affirmed that 'no unbaptized, unbelieving, or open profane, or wicked heretical persons, ought to be admitted to this ordinance to profane it'.[9] The 1689 Particular Baptist assembly, in noting that there were some present who did not maintain closed communion, chose to be less dogmatic. It declared:

> In those things wherein one church differs from another church in
> their principles or practices, in point of communion, that we cannot,
> shall not impose upon any particular church therein, but leave every
> church to their own liberty to walk together as they have received from
> the Lord.[10]

We ask: have churches received liberty in this most sensitive area? In practice, the vast majority of Baptists were in complete agreement; most were what the Independent church at Rothwell in 1707 termed 'Strickt Baptists'. Their common-sense approach was illustrated by a slim volume published in 1690 by Philip Carey of Dartmouth, Devon, who died about 1710. His book was entitled *A Solemn Call, or a Discourse concerning Baptism*, and included a preface signed by, among others, the Calvinists William Kiffin and Benjamin Keach. They wrote that

> ... *God has been pleased to raise up many Learned Men ... who have Learnedly, and with much clearness and strength of Argument made it appear, that a true Gospel visible Church, is to consist only of such as are Saints by Profession, and who give themselves up to the Lord, and to one another by Solemn Agreement, to practise the Ordinances of* Christ.[11]

Ivimey observed that the 1692 assembly included neither all the English Baptist churches nor even all those which were traditionally Calvinistic. Concerning the latter, he mentioned as absentees those 'many' congregations in Bedfordshire founded largely by the activities of John Bunyan. The absence of all but two of the churches of this county was due, Ivimey reckoned, to 'difference of sentiment on the subject of communion at the Lord's table, as these latter did *not make baptism on a profession of faith essential to church fellowship*, which the former did'. Or, as the members of the Carlton Baptist church, just a few miles from Bedford, expressed the matter in 1703:

> It is agreed that if any members have any light into the baptizing of believers that they may have it administred to them but if they have no light in it to receive them as saints.[12]

We can infer that there must have been at the time a developing polarisation among the Particular Baptists in the adjacent counties of Bedfordshire and Northamptonshire. The boycotting of the 1692 assembly by most of the former occurred just four years before restricted-communion Baptists at Walgrave, no more than twenty or so miles away from Bedford, were termed 'strict Baptists'. Perhaps the epithet was employed, even generated, among some churches in Bunyan's territory who looked askance at their stricter neighbours.

*   *   *

John Bunyan was always most careful about wearing a denominational label. In Bedford, the church which he pastored, and which became known as the 'Bunyan Meeting', contained members who queried the validity of infant baptism, yet at the time it did not doubt that it was a Congregational church.[13] All this is consistent with the fact that Bunyan was reluctant to side openly with the Baptists, although in his *The Heavenly Footman* he did confess, perhaps illogically, that he went under the name of 'Anabaptist'.[14] For him, baptism was an essentially personal matter and had little to do with church organisation. He exposed his heart in his *Peaceable Principles* when he wrote: 'Titles of *Anabaptists, Independents, Presbyterians*, or the like ... came ... from *Hell* and *Babylon*; for they naturally tend to divisions.'[15] Anabaptist or not, his 1673 treatise written in response to Thomas Paul and William Kiffin,[16] *Differences in Judgment About Water-Baptism, No Bar to Communion: OR, To Communicate with Saints, as Saints, proved lawful*, attacked bitterly the idea of restricted communion:

> As for our not suffering those who you plead for to preach in our Assemblies, the Reason is, because we cannot yet prevail with them, to repent of their Church-renting Principles.[17]

This appears to mean that they who were in time denominated as 'Strict Baptists' were being shunned by the great man and his disciples. *The Pilgrim's Progress*, written by Bunyan during a second, brief imprisonment in Bedford town jail and published in 1678, 'chalketh out before thine eyes the man that seeks the everlasting prize', according to the author's *Apology*.[18] Neither Christian nor any other character in the allegory was, it appears, baptized. Bunyan, in his *Grace Abounding to the Chief of Sinners*, declared that in his own ministry he

> ... never cared to meddle with things that were controverted, and in dispute among the saints, especially things of the lowest nature; yet it pleased me much to contend with great earnestness for the word of faith, and the remission of sins by the death and sufferings of Jesus: but I say, as to other things, I should let them alone, because I saw they engendered strife; and because that they neither in doing, nor in leaving undone, did commend us to God to be His: besides, I saw my work before me did run into another channel, even to carry an awakening word; to that therefore did I stick and adhere.[19]

Although Bunyan did not specify baptism as one of those 'things of the lowest nature', the allusion to immersion seems probable.

Bunyan was by no means the first to question the necessity of

baptism as a precondition for church fellowship and attendance at
the Lord's table; he did no more than adopt the position held by John
Gifford, first pastor of the Bedford church, who wrote just before his
death in 1655 that *'UNION with Christ is the foundation of all
saints' communion'*.[20] The saintly Henry Jessey (1601-63), born
near Cleveland in the West Riding, converted when studying at St
John's College, Cambridge, and later deprived of his living in
Yorkshire because of Nonconformity, was immersed in 1645 by
Hanserd Knollys. Eight years earlier he had taken pastoral charge of
the Independent church in London formed in 1616 by Henry Jacob.
He 'blamed those that made their particular opinion about baptism
the boundary of church communion', according to Ivimey.[21] In the
closing pages of Bunyan's attack upon restricted communion,
Differences in Judgment About Water-Baptism, Jessey's words
concerning Romans 14 were cited:

> The most that I think can be said is, That we have no Gospel-
> Example for receiving without Baptism, or rejecting any for want
> of it: Therefore it is desired, that what hath been said, may be
> considered, lest while we look for an example, we do not overlook
> a Command upon a mistake, supposing that they were all in Church-
> fellowship before, whereas the Text saith not so, but *Him that is
> weak in the Faith receive you, or unto you.*[22]

This looks peculiarly like a suggestion that the New Testament
keeps its silence upon terms of communion. Bearing in mind that
Jessey died twenty-five years before Bunyan, when the Bedfordshire man was thirty-five years of age, it seems certain that Bunyan
did not feel that his own opinions were an innovation; no doubt he
was relieved to be able to cite Jessey. Bunyan showed no compunc-
tion whatever in attacking those 'Brethren of the Baptized-way', as
he described them, who welcomed baptized believers only to the
Lord's table:[23]

> Is it not a wicked thing to make *bars* to communion, where *God*
> hath made *none*? Is it not a wickedness, to make that a Wall of
> Division betwixt us, which God never commanded to be so?[24]

He asserted, with respect to William Kiffin's understanding of
the matter, that 'in my simple opinion, your *rigid* and Church-
disquieting Principles are not fit for any Age and state of the

Church'.[25] Although Bunyan allowed that there were those 'of the Baptized-way ... *more moderate than some*',[26] he proceeded to lump all such with Diotrephes (3 John 9-10): 'I am for Communion with Saints: I shut none of the Brethren out of the Churches, nor forbid them that would receive them.'[27] It seems that tempers had arrived at flash point!

*   *   *

Because of the Bedfordshire pastor's widespread influence we note his principal arguments in favour of opening church membership and the table to non-immersed believers.

He held that baptism is not included among those 'laws' which should be observed by the church; it is not a 'Church Ordinance'.[28] This being so, it does not give 'being, nor well-being to a Church, neither is any part of that Instituted Worship of God, that the Church, as such, should be found in the practice of'.[29] Further, baptism was never required by the earliest churches as a condition for fellowship. So, for example, on the day of Pentecost, Acts 2, there were probably unbaptized converts who were 'received into the Church'.[30]

Christ has given his word to all believers who hold the keys of the kingdom of heaven, whether or not they have been baptized.[31] It cannot be shown, for example, that all the Corinthians were baptized, even though they did call upon the name of the Lord and were reckoned by Paul as 'saints' (1 Corinthians 1:2).[32] Therefore, baptism is not essential to church fellowship.

Restricted communion implies the intolerable notion that unbaptized believers should be unchurched.[33] In practice, reception to church fellowship should be upon the basis of '*Faith, and a Life becoming the Law of the Ten Commandments*', and this because '*Baptism makes no man a visible Saint*'. A man may know the grace of God in his heart without possessing 'the signification thereof'.[34]

Scripture does not say explicitly that '*No Unbaptized Person Shall enter, no Unbaptized Person Shall eat of the Supper*'.[35] Therefore, unbaptized believers are to be received. Water-baptism is not to be 'the Rule, the Door, the Bolt, the Bar, the Wall of Division between the Righteous, and the Righteous'.[36]

In the wilderness Israel was uncircumcised but, nevertheless, ate the Passover. Therefore, unbaptized believers should be allowed to participate at the Lord's table.[37]

In general, because Christ receives unbaptized saints we should receive them too.[38]

Insistence upon baptism as a necessary pre-condition to church fellowship will 'make rents and divisions among Brethren!' How can communion be refused to those concerning whom Baptists are convinced that 'they have communion with God' and who have been 'admitted through his Grace to as many Promises as you'?[39] In reality, baptism is a matter of conscience only and 'hath nothing to do with Church-membership', nor is a 'Character of my visible Saintship to the Church'.[40] That is, baptism, unlike the Lord's table, was given by Christ solely for the personal benefit of the believer and not with regard to his involvement in church life.

On the basis of Romans 14:1-15:7, they who are relatively weak in the faith because they 'want Light in Baptism' should nevertheless be received to communion.[41]

The 'Great Commission' (Matthew 28:18-20) does not prohibit ministers instructing those 'that have not Light in Baptism'.[42] Christ, not baptism, is the foundation of the Church.[43]

Paul's statement in Galatians 3:27 that 'for as many of you as have been baptized into Christ have put on Christ' does not mean that, for Paul, the Galatians were known to be believers because they had been baptized. Love, rather than baptism, is the true mark of discipleship.[44]

* * *

The response to Bunyan was swift. Henry Danvers, by then joint-elder in a baptized congregation in Houndsditch, near Aldgate, London,[45] published in 1673 *A Treatise of Baptism: Wherein That of Believers and that of Infants is examined by the Scriptures*, a second edition of which appeared in 1674 and which was given approval by, among others, Hanserd Knollys and William Kiffin. Danvers perceived that there is an intimate connection between baptism and communion:

> How consonant (by the way) and agreeable both to Rule, Reason and Righteousness, doth it appear to be, to admit men upon *Profession of Faith*, to both Ordinances, keeping thereby the right *Subjects*, as well as the *due Order*.[46]

At the end of the first edition Danvers noted that he had just read through Bunyan's *Differences in Judgment About Water-Baptism, No Bar to Communion*, which had appeared earlier that year. Danvers listed what he considered to be John Bunyan's '*Fundamental Mistakes*' in not allowing baptism to be a condition for church membership and communion. For some reason these criticisms were not repeated in the 1674 edition.

Bunyan was taken to task because he had insisted that a principle not taught by Scripture should be a practice for worship,[47] had maintained a discipline which was contrary to that of the Acts of the Apostles,[48] had assumed that ignorance concerning the nature of baptism absolved the ignorant from sins of omission and commission,[49] had trampled upon Christ's instituted worship,[50] had asserted that the New Testament churches were not all baptized and, finally, had declared that baptism is not a church ordinance.[51] Sadly, it may be that the usefulness of this excellent book was prejudiced by the author's Fifth-Monarchy views; his later career was perceived, perhaps, to have contradicted his writings.[52]

In the same year, 1673, there appeared a pocket-sized volume of some sixty-one pages entitled *Some Serious Reflections On that Part of Mr. Bunion's Confession of Faith: Touching ... Communion With Unbaptized Persons*.[53] This was a response to an earlier volume by Bunyan published in 1672. The author's preface, addressed to the reader, is initialled 'W.K.', although Kiffin's full name does not appear anywhere. The body of the book is addressed directly to Bunyan. We assume that the author was William Kiffin, notwithstanding the fact that Thomas Crosby in 1740 knew of one published work only by Kiffin, his *A Sober Discourse of Right to Church Communion*, which appeared in 1681. Joseph Ivimey, some eighty years after Crosby, took the latter's view.[54]

Kiffin argued powerfully in favour of restricted communion. Principally, the admission of unbaptized persons to communion was a doctrine unknown 'in the first Gospel Churches',[55] while infant baptism, being invalid, should not be reckoned a term of admission to the Lord's table.[56] The 'Rules given by our great Lord' take precedence over a proper desire to commune with all saints.[57]

Baptism is not 'the Inlet' to 'perticuler Churches'. Yet it does prepare Christians 'for Reception'. Consent only makes a man a member of a 'perticuler Church, and not Faith and Baptism'.[58] So, baptism is part of the Christian's expression of obedience to the

Lawgiver, without which no profession of holiness can be convincing.[59]

The New Testament letters were written to baptized believers only.[60] This implies conclusively that Scripture does not admit that there should be unbaptized Christians within the churches. Because it is an ordinance of Christ baptism is not a 'Pest and a Plague', and can never divide Christians.[61] The 'one baptism' mentioned by Ephesians 4 is baptism in water, as is the baptism referred to in 1 Corinthians 12. Therefore, all Christians should be baptized.[62]

John Bunyan should not 'pretend' to be a 'Minister of the Gospel'. Should he, Kiffin asked boldly, have dared to 'disparage Gospel truths ... to discharge men of their obedience to them?' Christ, said Kiffin, 'will not take this well at your hands'. Bunyan should not have divided between Christ and his precepts.[63]

With regard to the Paedobaptists, Kiffin reckoned that they were in error concerning the administration of baptism, concerning those who should be baptized, concerning the mode of baptism and, finally, concerning the purpose of baptism. Thus, they were 'enemies' to 'these Essentials of Gospel-Baptism' and should not be admitted to communion.[64]

Romans 14-15, which concern mutual reception by believers, are irrelevant to the controversy because these chapters are addressed to those who had been baptized and who were already in 'Church-Communion'. The disagreements mentioned by Paul focus upon indifferent matters.[65]

The fact that God receives unbaptized people does not mean that the churches should admit such to communion. We were all received by God before we were baptized, yet we had to be baptized.[66] In practice, outward conformity to the expressed will of Christ is important.[67]

Love for unbaptized Christians by no means demands that they be received at the Lord's table. Indeed, it is an act of love not to receive them.[68] Returning to Scripture, Kiffin claimed that Matthew 28 shows that baptism should precede admission to the church.[69] The New Testament indicates both by precept and by practice that believers ought to be baptized.[70] Galatians 3:26-9 demonstrate that, as far as the apostle Paul was concerned, those who were unbaptized were not reckoned by him to have visibly or obviously put on Christ;[71] they yet stood apart. Baptism is the hallmark of oneness in Christ.

Negatively, indifference about baptism could act as a precedent for neglecting the Lord's table. In that event, the churches would be composed of 'visible Sinners' rather than 'visible Saints'.[72]

Penetratingly, Kiffin observed that the New Testament says more about baptism than about the supper. Should, then, baptism be downgraded?[73] Basically, it was with Christian baptism as it had been with the baptism of John: they who were immersed by the forerunner justified God by their act (Luke 7:29).[74] So now.

Kiffin then proceeded to direct some embarrassing personal questions to John Bunyan. For example, he wished to know whether or not Bunyan's attack on restricted communion was due to a desire for 'popilarity, and applause of variety of professors',[75] or whether he was imitating Diotrephes in attempting to 'keep out all the Brethren that are not of your mind in this matter, from having any entertainment in the Churches, or meetings to which you belong'.[76] Diotrephes, we note, found ready employment by both parties. Kiffin's diatribe against Bunyan leaves us with the impression that, at the time, some baptized Calvinists were perceived to have been splitting away because of the issue, those in Bunyan's open-communion circle taking the lead.

This defence (or attack) was followed up in 1681 by Kiffin's more extensive *A Sober Discourse of Right to Church Communion*. Kiffin did not name Bunyan, and it might be that he had others in mind. With regard to the Devonshire Square, Bishopsgate, church, of which Kiffin was for many years the pastor, the congregation had been formed by Kiffin himself. After the Great Fire of 1666 the premises were requisitioned to provide a building for an episcopal congregation until the local parish churches were rebuilt. Then, the Baptists were permitted to re-occupy their meeting-house.[77] This form of official browbeating might well have confirmed the Baptists in their refusal to share their communion with others; the Church of England was perceived to be a persecuting church.

The true reason for demarcation lay basically, of course, in Kiffin's understanding of Scripture. He concluded his 1681 exposition by saying that 'we dare not break that Rule and Order by which we find the Primitive Saints walkt',[78] making the point that while Christians are supposed to love one another, love to the saints does not show itself 'in opposition to the Order prescribed in the Word, by which Ordinances ought to be Administred ... All true Gospel Love being Regulated by Gospel-Rule'.[79]

Kiffin's reasoning was, in effect, that love for Christians is enhanced and not prejudiced by love for Christ. If, therefore, love for Christ means doing as the Lord taught, it follows that open communion, being contrary to the law of Christ, cannot be an expression of love within and for the church. Further, a communion table to which immersed believers only are invited is nothing other than a proper exhibition of love towards those who have not been baptized.

We summarise Kiffin's additional arguments in favour of restricting the Lord's table to baptized believers. Basically, only believers should be baptized. This being so, Baptists are not guilty of schism in the matter of admission to communion.[80]

According to the New Testament,

> ... as the Grace of Regeneration gives a Right to the Enjoyment of Gospel Institutions; so *Baptism*, with respect to Priority and Order, is the first Institution, without which, none may regularly partake of other Church-Ordinances.[81]

Further,

> ... it is evident, that there is not the least Tittle either in express Terms, or Rational and plain Inference, in the whole New Testament, to Countenance the Opinion we oppose ... As for the Ages next the Apostles, for near 300 Years, we have examined the Records of those times, and find that the Ordinance of Baptism was Retained by the Churches in the same Order and Mode of Administration as is Recorded in the New Testament.[82]

In more modern times all the Reformers and the Church of England, together with

> ... all the Dissenting Congregations that own Ordinances (except a few Persons of the Baptized way and that lately too) have owned, and do own, That Baptism is an Ordinance of Christ; yea, the very first, or initiating Ordinance into Church-Fellowship, without which, no man may be regularly admitted to the Supper.[83]

This appears to be a barely-disguised reference to John Bunyan and his satellites, made out by Kiffin to be trespassers kicking against the boundaries set up by the New Testament.

Numerous objections to restricted communion were recognized and refuted by the London pastor-merchantman. The complaint that there is no express rule in the New Testament forbidding unbaptized believers from participating at the table was, according to Kiffin, tantamount to the opinion that 'whatsoever is not forbidden in Scripture, is Lawful'.[84] Such a principle could tend 'to bring all Humane Inventions into God's Worship'. In reality, 'the only Warrant we have ... must be the express Warrant, or Word of God.'[85]

In reply to the usual objection that restricted communion implies the '*Unchristianing*' of unbaptized Christians,[86] Kiffin denied the charge:

> We censure none so rigidly as to take upon us to Unchristian or Unchurch them; all that we do is ... to labour to keep the Lord's Ordinances in that Purity and Order the Sacred Records testifie they were left in.[87]

Thus did Kiffin defend the position attacked so savagely by John Bunyan.

*   *   *

Controversy among Baptists continued in the eighteenth century. Following the skirmish between John Brine and William Eltringham in the 1750s, a number of pamphlets appeared in the 1770s urging the churches to reappraise their terms of communion.[88] We should remind ourselves that, even at this somewhat later date, the overwhelming majority of Baptists, both in London and the counties, still maintained a closed-table system. Thus, Ivimey noted of the Baptist congregation which originally used Pinners' Hall, that it was 'for upwards of a century, the resort of large congregations', and that it was 'one of the very few which admitted of mixed communion'.[89]

Thomas Crosby recorded that even Paedobaptists sometimes failed to see the sense of open communion. He quoted an 'independent' whose initials were J.B. The full name was withheld, but, as the following citation shows, it does not seem to have been John Bunyan. 'J.B.', apparently, had composed an address grandiosely entitled *The sin and danger of admitting Anabaptists to continue in the congregational churches, and the inconsistency of such a practice, with the principles of both, humbly offered to the consideration of the London ministers, by their unworthy brother in the ministry.*[90]

'J.B.' was not reluctant to commit himself on the issue:

Let men pretend what they can for such a *hotch-potch* communion in churches; I stedfastly believe, the event and issue of such
practices, will sooner or later convince all gain-sayers, that it
neither pleaseth Christ, nor is any way promotive of true peace, or
gospel holiness in the churches of God's people. ... Plain it is to me,
that the *mixed communion* in churches of which many (who
consider not the thing aright, as they should) are too fond, is the very
source from which springs that visible corruption in most of the
congregational churches, now in *England*.[91]

It seems clear that this writer, together with many Baptists,
regarded 'mixed communion' as an evil; he was convinced that
Paedobaptists and Baptists, the latter rejecting infant baptism,
would never be able to enjoy happy fellowship at the Lord's table.

CHAPTER VI
THE COMMUNION CONTROVERSY
DURING THE 1700s

Arguments among Particular Baptists rumbled on. In 1727 there appeared a forty-eight-page pamphlet entitled *Some Just and Necessary Remarks upon John Gill's Defence of Plunging: Or, The Scriptural Mode of Baptizing with Water maintained*. The author was John Cogan (1698-1784), who lived at Rothwell where he both practised as a physician and was a member of the Independent church. Cogan defended Matthias Maurice's bland view of the mode of baptism, attacked young John Gill's printed thoughts on the matter, *The Antient Mode of Baptizing*, published in 1726, and Gill's defence of his own book in a further publication which appeared in 1727.[1] Relevant to the present discussion is the fact that Cogan introduced another name, that of 'Mr. Daukes'.

It is virtually certain that 'Mr. Daukes' was Clendon Dawkes. Dawkes, who died in 1758, came from near-by Wellingborough, and was both a Baptist and a high Calvinist.[2] He was, it seems, of a somewhat volatile, even unstable, character and perhaps a minor thorn in the flesh for Particular Baptists. We arrive at the identification of 'Daukes' and 'Dawkes' because, according to Walter Wilson in his *History*, John Brine preached at Dawkes's funeral while, according to the printed sermon, the occasion was, in fact, the funeral of 'Clendon Daukes'.[3]

Cogan wrote:

> I must add, that as Mr. *M*. in those few lines he writ upon free communion did not mean I verily think, communion with such as *J.G.* appears to be so, so *J.G.* in what he writ in answer thereto did not principally intend an opposition to Mr. *M*. but to his old benefactor Mr. *Daukes*, how that honest gentleman supplied him with necessaries, followed him with kindness, and what ungrateful returns he has made may another time more particularly be offered to observation.

In the mean time I must own that I am glad Mr. *Daukes* is ingaged in a good work upon good principles, which envious *Sanballats* shall not be able to overthrow. For the strengthening of his friends hands and his own in their generosity and christian principles of communion with saints as saints, I hope he will answer our expectation in reprinting Mr. *John Bunyan's* book, intituled, *Difference in Water Baptism no bar to communion.*[4]

This does not, in fact, seem to add up if we accept remarks passed about Dawkes by Wilson. According to him, Dawkes settled with a congregation at Broad Street, Wapping, and remained there as pastor until 1726. Then he transferred to a newly-founded church in Collier's-Rents, Southwark, only to depart in 1730, three to four years later, 'though', writes Wilson, 'upon what account we can find no where mentioned. The probable reason, however, was his partiality to strict communion; the Church in Collier's-Rents being formed upon the mixed plan*.'[5] The footnote indicated by the asterisk reads cryptically *'Private Information'*. Either Wilson was in error or the 'Mr. Daukes' mentioned by Cogan was not Clendon Dawkes at all. Note that, according to Cogan, 'Daukes' supported open communion in 1727, while, according to Wilson, 'Dawkes' favoured restricted communion just four years later.

Was Wilson wrong? Again, we suggest that 'Mr. Daukes' was, indeed, Dawkes. When he left the Southwark church in 1730, Dawkes went out of the ministry for about four years before accepting in 1735 the pastorate of a church assembling in Devonshire Square. Under his leadership the congregation ran down, eventually to dissolve itself.[6] Without seeking to speak ill of the dead, it might appear that the ministry proved in the event to have been an inappropriate vocation for Dawkes. We would not be greatly surprised were we to learn that about the time that Cogan referred in print to 'Mr. Daukes', 1727, Dawkes, then entering a short-lived pastorate, was in some turmoil on the matter of the terms of communion. 'Mr. Daukes' and Clendon Dawkes seem to reflect each other.

If all this is so, in Cogan's booklet Matthias Maurice is 'Mr. M.', Clendon Dawkes is 'Mr. Daukes', John Bunyan is 'Mr. John Bunyan', while John Gill is simply 'J.G.' It is not hard to estimate Cogan's opinion of John Gill, in his view a faithless friend to Daukes. The point is that Cogan seemed to have thought that the rift between Baptists as represented by Gill and Independents as represented by Maurice was such that they would never have thought about intercommunion.

Further, Cogan considered that Gill was writing against free-communion Baptists as represented, apparently, by Dawkes, and that the latter group would be well served by a reprint of Bunyan's attack upon restricted-communion Baptists.[7]

* * *

Nevertheless, in spite of men such as Dawkes (and, we might dare to say, Bunyan), in the second half of the eighteenth century restricted communion appears to have continued as the norm among the Particular Baptists. The saintly Benjamin Wallin declared in a footnote to a published funeral sermon delivered in 1769 upon the death of Mrs Rebekah Cox:

> Indeed, the party baptized, lays himself under a most sacred engagement to maintain a regular and perfect profession, and to observe all things whatsoever the Lord hath commanded, to the end of his days; which loose nominal christians do well to consider.[8]

Perhaps inevitably in the glare of the Evangelical Awakening, controversy among Particular Baptists concerning terms of admission to communion revived. As we have noted, in 1756 John Brine published his *The Baptists Vindicated*, in which he challenged open-communion Baptists to prove to the '*strict* Baptists' that baptism does not initiate into church fellowship.[9]

Brine was worried about infant baptism as well as being exasperated by Baptist opponents. According to him, restricted-communion Baptists differed from the Paedobaptists in the following important respect: the latter introduced infants into the church by baptism and then did not always permit them in later years to participate in the privileges of the church. So,

> ... the *strict* Baptists are uniform, in their Sentiments, and Practice: For, as they think, that Baptism ought to be a Term of Communion, and that it is an initiating Ordinance, into the Church, they admit all who are initiated into the Church, unto a Participation of its Privileges.[10]

John Collett Ryland, of the College Lane, Northampton, church, Daniel Turner, pastor at Abingdon from 1748 until his death half a century later, and Robert Robinson of Cambridge had written in favour of admitting non-immersed persons to the Lord's table.[11] Two of these

contributions were anonymous, appearing in 1772 under the assumed
names of 'Candidus' (Daniel Turner) and 'Pacificus' (J.C. Ryland),
urging forbearance for the sake of peace. Either the two pamphlets were
a joint effort or one of the men copied from the other.[12]

Daniel Turner, especially, would appear to have been another thorn
in the flesh for the Particular Baptists over a number of years. At any
rate, John Gill, then at the height of his influence, attacked someone
who styled himself 'Candidus' in the preface to a published sermon on
1 John 5:3, 'For this is the love of God, that we keep his commandments,' an address preached by Gill at the baptism of the Scotsman
Robert Carmichael at the Barbican, London, on October 9, 1765, seven
years earlier. Gill always had an eye for an opportunity and at this
baptism he spared no pains to unburden himself concerning the
necessity of baptism; he knew, it seems, that there was dissension
abroad. In his printed preface Gill complained about letters from
'Candidus' to a public newspaper, letters which concerned '*the controversy about baptism*', and which, allegedly, '*vilified and insulted us*'.[13]
Gill continued:

> *I shall not let myself down so low, nor do I think it fitting and decent
> to go into, and carry on a religious controversy in a news-paper, and
> especially with so worthless a writer, and without a name. This base
> and cowardly way of writing, is like the* Indians *manner of fighting;
> who set up an hideous yell, pop off their guns behind bushes and
> hedges, and then run away and hide themselves in the thickets.*[14]

It appears that an unabashed and unrepentant 'Candidus' wrote
again to the press, so further provoking the Southwark pastor. In a
postscript to another publication on baptism appearing in 1766 Gill
traded insults:

> The *first* and *second* letters of *Candidus*, in the News-paper, are
> answered in marginal notes on my sermon upon baptism, and pub-
> lished along with it. His *third* letter is a mean piece of buffoonery and
> scurrility; it begins with a trite, vulgar proverb, in low language, fit
> only for the mouth of an *hostler* or a *carman*; and his friends seem to
> have spoiled one or other of these, by making him a *parson*.[15]

We assume here without proof positive that this particular
'Candidus', a Baptist unnamed but apparently known by Gill, was
Daniel Turner. Gill, of course, died in 1771 and 'Candidus' came out

with his *Modest Plea*, in liaison with the highly respected Ryland, in the following year.

* * *

We summarise the arguments put forward by 'Candidus' in the 1772 document.

His principal thesis was that all who 'live by faith ... must have an *equal right* to All the privileges of the Gospel ... and therefore to the privileges of the *Lord's Table*'.[16] Thus, because 'all true believers hold their right to the privileges of the gospel, by the authority and grant of Christ ... *we* have no sufficient warrant to exclude them'.[17]

Exclusion from the table was a usurpation of the '*prerogative*' of Christ, and must lead to 'offending, and injuring our Christian brethren ... forcing them to live in the neglect of a known and important duty'.[18] To reject those whom Christ has accepted is a 'setting of our faces against the LORD JESUS CHRIST'. If the Lord has granted a '*dispensation*' to them, why should we have issued a '*prohibition*'?[19]

Romans 14-15 were, quite inevitably, brought to bear. According to 'Candidus', these chapters command us to receive those who are weak in faith and not to involve ourselves in questionable arguments: 'I earnestly wish our Stricter Brethren would seriously read, and without prejudice consider, the XIVth and XVth chapters of the epistle to the *Romans*.'[20]

Further, the New Testament seems to be slightly less than plain in its teaching about baptism: 'It is evident in fact, that the points in Baptism ... are not so clearly stated in the Bible ... but that even *sincere Christians* may mistake them.' Interpretations of baptism descend to the level of 'private opinion' and are '*disputable points*'. 'Besides,' asked Candidus, 'who is to be the judge of what is, or is not Baptism in this dispute?'[21]

The pragmatic argument was introduced. To paraphrase Candidus, nothing succeeded like success. In fact, the acceptance of unbaptized Christians at the Lord's table might well have led them to 'open their minds to the light and power of truth'. Conversely, a 'rigid attachment to our own peculiar opinions ... is the sure way ... to strengthen their prejudices'.[22]

Negatively, restricted communion was 'unscriptural' and involved the setting up of 'separate societies', this being the very reverse of that '*uniting spirit* which appears everywhere in the Gospel of Christ'.[23] It followed necessarily that the edification of Christians was more important than 'the order of Churches'; 'the least therefore ought to give way to the greatest.'[24]

Both Turner and Ryland described opponents of 'this free and open communion' as 'our stricter Brethren', those who indulged in '*uncommanded* strictness'.[25]

Had Daniel Turner acted in accordance with his ideas he would never have been a Baptist pastor. He might have taken the part of John Tombes (1603-76), Vicar of Leominster and, later, of Bewdley, both in the West Midlands. In his day Tombes strenuously opposed infant baptism, yet never quit the establishment. There was a reason for this. Crosby wrote that 'seeing no prospect of any reformation in the established church in this *point*, he there gathered a *separate* church of those of his persuasion, continuing at the same time minister of the parish.'[26]

In the early nineteenth century Joseph Kinghorn, minister of St Mary's Baptist Church in Norwich, argued in favour of restricted communion. He complained concerning John Tombes that he

> ... did not promote, either the cause of non-conformity in general, or of his own sentiments in particular, ... and the obvious reason is, that he was not struck with the practical importance of what he believed to be true,[27]

and that

> ... his conduct in this point excited attention among churchmen; but they approved it. For though they looked upon him as having some peculiarities, yet they applauded him for not breaking the communion of the established church. And on their own principles they were right. They knew very well, that the influence of an individual who continued among them himself, and pleaded against separating from the Establishment, would be very little, and would die with him.[28]

Thus it was in principle, though not in practice, with the Baptist ministers Daniel Turner and J.C. Ryland; they do not appear to have realized, or to have wished to realize, the implications of their joint treatises.

* * *

The assault on restricted communion was continued by a lesser-known figure, John Brown, in his *The House of God Opened and His*

Table Free for Baptists and Paedo-baptists, a twenty-three-page pamphlet which appeared in 1777. Brown became pastor of the Little Meeting at Kettering in 1752, a church which had been formed in 1730 by an amalgamation of the Baptist fellowship which in 1716 had seen John Gill baptized, and an Independent church. Brown, who died in 1800, left the church in 1771, together with some members, to form yet another congregation in the same town. His deserted people appointed as pastor George Moreton, from the Particular Baptist church at Arnesby. Following the latter's resignation in 1779 because of illness there was a vacancy for several years until 1783, when Andrew Fuller became the minister at the Little Meeting. Until 1786, when Brown left and closed his church, Kettering had two Baptist pastors who entertained opposing views about terms of admission to the Lord's table.[29]

In his preliminary remarks Brown noted that Paedobaptists admitted Baptists to their communion and that Baptists other than those who 'go by the name of strict Baptists' admitted Paedobaptists. Why, then, should 'strict Baptists ... insist on an uniformity in the outward mode of Baptism'?[30]

He maintained, too, that 'strict Baptists' failed to show the fruits of the Spirit; they 'set at nought' other Christians and 'walk uncharitably' with those with whom they disagreed on this matter.[31]

Brown conceded readily that those who would not be baptized (by whatever means) should not be admitted to communion.[32] So, for him, the question pivoted on those who believed genuinely that the sprinkling of infants was a valid baptism.[33] Brown maintained that there were good reasons for admitting such to the Lord's table. Fundamentally, because all Christians, Baptists and others, 'are in the same near relation to God, as their heavenly Father', so they all should have been admitted to the table.[34] In fact, the Lord's table was designed to exhibit the oneness of believers. Therefore, no believers should have been excluded.[35]

Baptism converts no one; therefore it should not have become a term of communion.[36] In view of the fact that water was only a 'figure or shadow, an outward sign', restricted communion tended directly to replace the substance by the sign. Realistically, the kingdom of God did not consist of, among other things, water.[37]

Further, the ordinance was a personal duty to be performed 'out of the church'. Therefore, Baptists should not have excluded others from their master's house.[38] The example of the Lord was brought to bear: because Christ allows differences in 'non-essentials', so should his followers.[39]

Brown observed that many non-Baptist churches displayed 'true Christian love', while, not infrequently, baptized churches were unspiritual. Therefore, he insisted, immersion should not have been imposed as a condition for communion.[40] It must follow that ministers who rejected the unbaptized were guilty of scattering the flock.[41] All in all, love is the royal law; admitted errors about baptism should be covered by love and acceptance.[42]

Romans 14-15, plus other New Testament passages, teach that we should receive the weak in faith;[43] strict communion showed neither love nor any capacity to convince the Paedobaptist of 'his mistakes'.[44]

Paedobaptists loved the Lord, too. Therefore, because the error of Paedobaptists regarding baptism did not necessarily debar them from serving God, they ought to have been accepted at the table.[45]

In general, the New Testament does not appear to insist that baptism by immersion is 'essentially necessary for constituting a true church of Christ, or for the admission of members into it'.[46] So, strict communion allowed our 'good be evil spoken of' and became a tool of Satan by which he broke brotherly love.[47] Spiritually-minded Paedobaptists should never have received the treatment given to the people of the world, namely, exclusion from the table.[48]

The resurrection is before us. Because all believers will eventually enter heaven we should join together now 'in the House of God and at his Table'.[49]

Brown proceeded to answer objections, noting favourably that Paedobaptists, just like Baptists, required baptism before addition to the church.[50] Further, open communion was not an alteration to the terms of communion enacted by Christ; at the Baptists' communion table the Paedobaptist gave the answer of a good conscience, so fulfilling his duty. Christ had not given Baptists the right 'to impose this or any ordinance on any, without their knowledge and choice', so preventing sincere Paedobaptists from serving their master.[51]

An answer was required to the charge that the waiving of immersion as a prerequisite for admission would lead in time to the neglect of the table. Brown considered that if 'sincere believers' only were admitted, the communion rite would never be neglected. Nor, indeed, would baptism be downgraded.[52] To the claim that Paedobaptists might well outnumber the Baptists in the latter's churches, so causing them to vanish, Brown rightly scoffed at expediency of this type as a rule for strict communion.[53] According to Brown, because Paedobaptists sometimes encountered difficulties in finding churches of their own denominations, it remained incumbent upon Baptists to welcome them to their own fellowships.[54]

He concluded with a fable about two boys who had been told by their father to wash at all times before eating at his table. One lad, Benaiah, understood this to mean the washing of the whole body, while his brother, Semei, reckoned that their father had only referred to washing the face.[55] The thrust of the story seems to be that, for some reason, the father had failed to make clear to his boys how they should wash; hence the innocent difference concerning the table. By analogy, the heavenly Father had been ambiguous about how to baptize.

No arguments could have been more moving. But, we should ask, does not the New Testament have something to say about how baptism should be administered, and to whom? Into such essential matters Brown did not go.

* * *

A response to Brown, a well-argued pamphlet of some forty-six pages prefaced with the text 'Charity — rejoiceth in THE TRUTH. I Cor. xiii.', was provided by William Buttfield shortly before the latter's death in 1778. For just three years he had been the minister at Thorn, near Dunstable.[56] Given a glancing reference only by Ivimey, he seems to have been a lesser light in the Baptist galaxy.[57] Buttfield was convinced that baptism was to be administered by immersion only. Therefore, sprinking could not be called baptism. Further, unbaptized believers, by not being baptized, had failed to give adequate evidence of their relation to Christ and should not be admitted to his table.[58]

He reckoned, furthermore, that if baptism came to be rejected as a term of communion because it could not make men Christians, then every branch of the faith may be put to one side for precisely the same reason;[59] structural Christianity would be eviscerated. On the other hand, divine institutions, such as baptism, were not to be called 'shadows', things of little importance.[60]

In his reading of the New Testament Buttfield had come to believe that baptism is the only way by which Scripture directs men into the church.[61] Therefore, immersion in water upon a profession of faith was not to be reckoned as a non-essential. It was a truly positive duty because the obligation of the Christian derived not so much from the magnitude of the effects of baptism as from the sovereign right of God to command immersion. This he has done. Non-essentials are those things alone concerning which we have received no command. It followed that baptism is by no means a non-essential. Buttfield remarked movingly:

> If, therefore, the Lord command me to pick up a pin, it is as much my duty to comply, as it is to believe that Jesus Christ is the Son of God.[62]

Going on from this, baptism, though not essential either to salvation or to the being of a true church, remained necessary for the establishment of an 'orderly' congregation. If differences on this matter were tolerated by a church there would be contention among its people,[63] while free communion would allow access even to Quakers and Roman Catholics.[64]

With regard to the view that free communion was an expression of Christian love, Buttfield remarked acutely that 'one command of God cannot require the sacrifice of another, in order to a compliance with it'. That is, the command to love one another was not advanced by putting baptism to one side.[65] He wrote that Romans 14-15 do not prove that it is lawful to dispense with a positive Christian duty; only things optional are considered by these chapters. Philippians 3:15, referring to growth in maturity, simply does not show that the Macedonian church disagreed within itself about the articles of religion.[66]

At the pastoral level, free communion in a Baptist church allowed the Paedobaptist 'to live in a sin of omission', 'doing evil that good may come'.[67] At heart, the whole issue concerned the authority of the Bible: the Baptist who asserted that baptism was a 'mere outward show' was a 'Quaker incognito', it being unlikely that he possessed an immediate revelation for his practice.[68]

Buttfield accepted the undoubted sincerity of godly Paedobaptists concerning baptism. Nevertheless, he was conscious of the distinction between a conviction about the nature of a duty and the duty itself; belief in sprinkling was not sufficient: 'we are bound ... *to keep the ordinances as they were appointed.*'[69] Inevitably, the subjective approach must be tested by objective study, all predilections falling before the clear teaching of Scripture.

Among the churches, Paedobaptists and Baptists did not in fact share the same 'spiritual view of baptism', while infants who had been sprinkled had no views at all. In a baby's sprinkling there was no representation of death and resurrection. How, then, were the advocates of two quite dissimilar rites able to allow their baptisms to admit them to a shared communion service?[70]

Furthermore, if immersion upon profession of faith was unnecessary, why should not the Baptist proceed to sprinkle infants? Why, too, did he frequently immerse those who had been sprinkled?[71]

It is true enough that the New Testament does not address 'baptized' churches. But, then, for example, no letter is addressed specifically to churches 'in which prayer is made'. In other words, the argument from silence, beloved by the open-communionists, did not stand up. Realistically, because the New Testament churches had been baptized, they were baptized churches. The sole ground upon which Paedobaptists were not invited to the table was because, 'on our principles', they were unbaptized.[72]

Coming back to the question of the sole authority for all matters of faith and practice, either the Lord, through Scripture, left on deposit sufficient directions as to how Christians should approach the table, or he did not. As it is, 'he has not left this matter undetermined.'[73]

Buttfield's closing argument was that while it was true that all believers, baptized or not, are to enjoy 'the sublime blessedness', this was no demonstration 'that they may all unite at the Lord's table'.[74]

* * *

This elegant little book did not, of course, constitute the final word. Much more was to be written on either side of the argument. John Ryland junior, who became co-pastor with his father at College Lane, Northampton, in 1781,[75] attempted to play down Particular Baptist differences on this issue: 'An artful attack has been lately made to set us on disputing among ourselves, respecting Strict and Open Communion.'[76] He declared that he had practised 'open' communion 'not from motives of policy, which I should abhor in matters of religion, but from conscience, for nearly seven and forty years'. His reason for so doing was that 'it is the Lord's Table, and not mine; therefore I dare not refuse those whom he has accepted ... unless he had commanded me', conceding that both sides 'cannot be right in their conclusion'.[77] Perhaps he was showing that he was his father's son.

The question arises, of course, as to why these men advocated open communion. Over the years Ryland senior had numerous friends among the Paedobaptists, including James Hervey at Weston Favell, a clergyman who in earlier days had been a member of the 'Holy Club' at Oxford and who remained a friend of both Whitefield and Wesley.[78] As we have noted, it was suggested by William Newman, Ryland's assistant from 1787 to 1792, that his then mentor had already turned away from the closed-communion position when he moved to Northamptonshire.[79] It is not surprising, perhaps, that his long-standing admiration for men of God beyond Baptist circles influenced his churchmanship. With regard to Daniel Turner, Ivimey was significantly reticent, recording deliberately a note from the Abingdon records to the effect that over a period of almost forty years the membership had nearly halved under Turner's leadership.[80] Ivimey was never reluctant to give praise when praise was due; in this instance he said nothing, and perhaps in so doing intended his readers to draw their own conclusions.

*   *   *

The redoubtable Abraham Booth responded to the open-communionists in 1778, the same year in which Buttfield brought out his defence of restricted communion. His vastly more detailed work, *An Apology for the Baptists*, was written on behalf of those churches which, to repeat Ivimey's observation, were then 'first designated "*Strict Baptists*"'.[81] Booth's title implied that Baptists would, if true to their principles, admit baptized believers only to the Lord's table; he wrote on behalf of 'Baptists', believing that restricted communion was an essential hall-mark of a strictly Baptist church.

As has been claimed already, Ivimey's opinion concerning the expression 'strict baptist' may be capable of challenge; it was in use some seventy years or so earlier than the publication of Booth's important book.[82]

Booth was convinced of his position. During his ordination as pastor to the church at Little Prescott Street, Goodman's Fields, London, in 1769, nine years earlier, his personal declaration of faith included the statement that 'baptism is immersion in water, *in the name of the Father, and of the Son, and of the Holy Ghost*', and that it does not 'appear from the commands of CHRIST, or the practice of his apostles, that we have any authority to administer this ordinance in any other way than immersion'.[83]

Ivimey wrote concerning Booth: 'His masterly work received no reply from his brethren (whom in return for their new coined epithet he designated *Latitudinarian* Baptists,) and at that time put an end to the controversy.'[84] Booth's *Apology* was significant because it referred back to the arguments against restricted communion offered by Bunyan at the end of the seventeenth century and because it was later attacked in detail by Robert Hall junior in the opening years of the nineteenth century. It was a central link in a one-hundred-and-forty-year debate among the English Particular Baptists.

Booth was sensitive about the fact that the champions of restricted communion were under attack:

> It is entirely on the *defensive* that the author takes up his pen; for had not the principles and practice of those professors who are invidiously called, STRICT BAPTISTS, been severely censured, ... these pages would never have been written.[85]

In his preparatory remarks Booth mentioned that 'the necessity of baptism *in order to communion*' was exactly similar to 'the sentiments and practice of our National Church'.[86] Open communion, he affirmed, was 'yet in its infancy' in Bunyan's day. He noted that Bunyan then, as 'Candidus' and 'Pacificus' in Booth's time, had charged the restricted-communion Baptists, now called 'strict Baptists', with being '*too strict and rigid*'.[87] 'Yet,' Booth confided, 'I cannot persuade myself, that either his [Bunyan's] judgment or piety appeared in this bold innovation.'[88] In the event, Booth was by no means the last 'strict' Baptist of this period who felt that his position was under siege.

Booth proposed numerous arguments on behalf of restricted communion, his fundamental thesis being that baptism and communion are positive ordinances of Christ, the former to precede the latter. This mandatory sequence can be inferred directly from the commission, Matthew 28:18-20.[89] According to the Acts of the Apostles, following the ascension of our Lord all converts were exhorted by the apostles and their colleagues to be baptized. There was no disobedience; all were baptized.[90]

The apostles were servants of the Lord Jesus and never received dispensational power; in the matter of communion they invariably applied the teaching of the Master. Booth cited 1 Corinthians 11:23, 'I have received of the Lord that which also I delivered unto you.'[91]

Furthermore, because it has a significance other than that of the Lord's table, baptism ought at all times to precede communion.[92] This was recognized by Paedobaptists who, unfortunately, baptized many who afterwards never attended communion. On the other hand, free-communion Baptists received at the Lord's table those who had never been baptized. Both groups destroyed the order prescribed by the New Testament and potentially threatened the relevance of both ordinances. 'Candidus' and 'Pacificus', as well as Bunyan, were said by Booth to have fallen into this trap. Booth suspected that a possible consequence might be that an unbaptized member who stayed away from communion would be beyond the discipline of his church, the reason being that the absentee had never committed himself in baptism either to the faith or to the congregation.[93]

For Abraham Booth, advocates of 'free-communion' were in their churches no better than the Church of England, which claimed a power to decree rites and ceremonies in the Church of God.[94] Impressive though the establishment might be, it remained that the Bible, rather than the Church, was authoritative. This being so, the clear light of the gospel increases rather than lessens the Christian's obligation to obedience.[95]

Booth felt that some people delighted in reflected glory; Daniel Turner of Abingdon was implied to have been a disciple of John Ryland rather than of Christ: he 'will hardly have courage ... openly to confront and attack his *dearest* and *most intimate* friend, Mr. Ryland'.[96] In practice, advocates of open communion allowed personal testimony, rather than the order prescribed by Scripture, to be 'the rule of admission' to the table. This meant that if a Paedobaptist who believed that he had been legitimately baptized at the font proposed to attend a Baptist communion, the Baptists would have received him. Thus, on their own principles, the free-communion Baptists downgraded the authority of the New Testament. This 'cannot be right'.[97] By embracing Paedobaptists at communion and by so doing momentarily legitimising the sprinkling of babies, Baptists 'practically approve of what, at other times, they boldly pronounce *a human invention, a tradition of men,* and *will-worship*'.[98]

Booth considered the obvious comparisons between the two

testaments: baptism was as necessary in the first and ongoing Christian centuries as circumcision used to be during the old dispensation.[99] Realistically, only if Christ had not informed us as to what baptism is, and what is requisite to communion, would his

> ... ministering servants have a discretionary power to administer them how and to whom they please. ... Then their communion would be *free indeed*; entirely free from the shackles of divine commands, and from the untoward influence of divine precedent.[100]

The reality is that Christ has informed us.

Booth concluded his *Apology* by exhorting his free-communion readers to 'be either consistent *Baptists*, or *Paedobaptists*; for, according to your present practice, all thinking and impartial men must pronounce you an *heterogenous mixture* of both'.[101]

* * *

The literary battle, it seems, rested for some years, during which time many Particular Baptist churches gently veered, or perhaps lurched, towards open communion. When Robert Hall junior took up arms in defence of the latter position he was more than a touch triumphal; he sensed that the strict communionists were suffering the trauma of losing an overwhelming majority which had formerly been taken for granted. For example, during his pastorate at Harvey Lane, Leicester, Hall established the 'Little Church', composed of Paedobaptists and separate from his own restricted-communion congregation. He administered the bread and the wine to both groups without being taken to task by the Baptists who had called him and who paid him.[102] With an overflowing congregation he no doubt basked in security of tenure.[103]

CHAPTER VII
THE COMMUNION CONTROVERSY IN
THE EARLY 1800s

Word-battles between Eltringham, Brine, Booth, Brown, Buttfield, John Ryland senior and Daniel Turner, among others, did not conclude the matter. At the end of the eighteenth century Andrew Fuller wrote to the missionaries in India that

> ... to treat a person as a member of Christ's visible kingdom, and as being in a state of salvation, who lives in the neglect of what Christ has commanded to all his followers, and this, it may be, knowingly, is to *put asunder what Christ has joined together*, see Mark xvi.16.[1]

This was strong language. Fuller was referring, of course, to the position taken by open-communion Baptists with regard to Paedobaptists. But, we ask, what about men of God such as, say, Whitefield and the American Jonathan Edwards (1703-58)? Should they not have been treated by Fuller and his like as 'being in a state of salvation'? Here we have the tragic and embarrassing anomaly presented by the exponents of infant baptism. Of course, Fuller knew that the Lord had his people both in open-communion Baptist churches as well as among the Paedobaptists; he was neither a fool nor blinkered. So it was that, in connection with the establishment of the Particular Baptist mission to India, the 1793 circular letter issued by the Baptist ministers and messengers assembled at Northampton recorded that, had no Baptist outreach been established, subscriptions would have been sent to the Presbyterians and Moravians.[2] But this was second-best; these Baptists could never get away from the New Testament. James Dore, pastor at the London Maze Pond church from 1784 until he resigned in 1815 because of a disorder which affected his voice, maintained that mixed-communion Baptist churches ought to have had written over their doors the legend 'We robbed other churches to do ourselves service'.[3] Joseph Ivimey, for his part, acknowledged quite readily that restricted communion was, in the public's perception of the Baptists, 'the most obnoxious of their principles'.[4] Nevertheless, he would not

> ... hesitate in giving it as his opinion, that the violation of this principle has been the chief cause that the Baptists have not been a more numerous, and, in the popular estimation, a more honourable body of Protestant dissenters. At every period of their history many of the principal families for wealth and respectability among them have manifested tergiversation, by occasionally uniting at the Lord's table with Paedobaptists, or have altogether left the denomination by uniting in fellowship with the Independent churches.[5]

* * *

In 1816 Robert Hall junior published his first broadside, *On Terms of Communion; with a Particular View to the Case of the Baptists and Paedobaptists*. The author was highly articulate and persuasive. Born in 1764, the youngest child of Robert Hall who had ministered at Arnesby and who had such an effect in steering many Particular Baptists away from high Calvinism,[6] Robert junior was a phenomenon. He was sent to the Bristol academy at the age of fourteen, having been taught as a lad to read from the inscriptions on the gravestones in the chapel burial yard. In later years, 'his claim to be considered the first preacher of the age has been recognised beyond the boundaries of any sect or circle,' wrote an observer in *The Athenaeum* at the time of Hall's death.[7] In 1784 he received his master's degree from the Marischal College, Aberdeen, where he had graduated. Because of Charles II's still unrepealed legislation the English universities remained closed to people such as Hall. He then assisted Caleb Evans at Bristol, both at the Broadmead church and in the academy, between 1785 and 1790. In 1791 he went to Cambridge, where he succeeded Robert Robinson. Never a well man, he resigned the Cambridge pastorate in 1806 because of severe depression probably associated with a painful illness. He convalesced, and in 1808 the Harvey Lane Baptist church, Leicester, called him to its pulpit. Here, the building was too small to accommodate Hall's swelling congregation. Although a Scots doctorate was offered him in 1817 he never adopted the title. In 1826 Hall went back to Bristol, where he died five years later.[8]

Concerning open communion, he was diametrically opposed to Ivimey:

> The Writer is persuaded that a departure from this principle in the denomination to which he belongs, has been extremely injurious, not only to the credit and prosperity of that particular body, (which is a very subordinate consideration,) but to the general interests of truth; and that but for the obstruction arising from that quarter, the views they entertain of one of the sacraments would have obtained a more extensive prevalence. By keeping themselves in a state of separation and seclusion from other Christians, they have not only evinced an inattention to some of the most important injunctions of scripture, but have raised up an invincible barrier to the propagation of their sentiments beyond the precincts of their own party.[9]

It is not easy to present Hall's exposition in propositional form because his flow of language, acute reasoning and determination to conquer tend directly to overawe the reader; frowning ramparts crumble before his verbal artillery. Any fond objection to the unrestricted system which the Strict Baptist might entertain seems to wilt before the unceasing accumulation of honeyed paragraphs.

Certain arguments stand out. His underlying assumption was that 'no man, or set of men, are entitled to prescribe as an indispensable condition for communion, what the New Testament has not enjoined as a condition of salvation'.[10]

Principally, although the Christian Church 'be branched out into many distinct societies, it is still but one'. This being so, we must not renounce the fellowship of Paedobaptists 'on account of error not allowed to be fundamental', and particularly when Baptists did or omitted nothing in their open communion which would not have been done or omitted if Paedobaptists were not present.[11] Further, Baptists admitted Paedobaptists 'to share in every other spiritual privilege', such as soliciting the prayers of the latter. So, it was surprising that the Lord's table, 'the rite which of all others is most adapted to cement mutual attachment ... should be fixed upon as the line of demarcation, the impassable barrier, to separate and disjoin the followers of Christ'.[12]

In the course of the book much was made of this point. If many Paedobaptists were perceived by Strict Baptists to be godly, why, then, were they treated as being ungodly and excluded from the table? In point of fact, restricted communion became 'the badge and criterion of a party, a mark of discrimination applied to distinguish the nicer shades of difference among Christians'.[13]

Hall conceded that the 'christian world' believed that baptism was 'an indispensable prerequisite to the Lord's table',[14] yet argued against the belief.

For him, John the Baptist's baptism occupied an intermediate station between the old and the new economies and was instituted before the appointment of the Lord's table.[15] So, Christian baptism was to be distinguished from that of the forerunner: John's baptism was not accompanied by the gift of the Holy Spirit, while Christian baptism was thus honoured, as is shown by the Acts of the Apostles. The question therefore arose as to who baptized the apostles and the disciples assembled with them on the Day of Pentecost. Hall asserted:

> My deliberate opinion is, that in the christian sense of the term, they were not baptized at all. ... it is difficult to suppose they submitted to that rite after our Saviour's resurrection; and previous to it, it has been sufficiently proved that it was not in force.[16]

From all this it followed necessarily that the apostles and many other communicants in the primitive churches had never received Christian baptism. This was suggested, said Hall, by Romans 6:3, 'Know ye not, that so many of us as were baptized into Christ, were baptized into his death.' Hall took Paul to imply that there were some at Rome who had not been immersed. It followed that such people had been 'with respect to christian baptism, precisely in the same situation' as excluded Paedobaptists, who by definition had not been baptized. Therefore, converted Paedobaptists should have been admitted to the Lord's table.[17]

The commission recorded in Matthew 28:18-20 was taken by Strict Baptists to imply that baptism should be administered invariably 'after effectual instruction is imparted, and consequently before an approach to the Lord's table'.[18] This conclusion, Hall claimed, rested entirely upon the principle that nothing which the apostles were required to teach believers should be brought to the attention of those who remained unbaptized. This, in turn, meant that Paedobaptists should not be exhorted by Strict Baptists to walk worthy of their high calling, or to 'the performance of any duty resulting from their actual relation to Christ'.[19] For Hall, such a stance, inevitable in his view, was untenable.

Hall rejected the notion that open-communionists contended for the celebration of communion prior to baptism. If Paedobaptists, who believed genuinely, though wrongly, that they had been baptized, were to be excluded from the table, it should have been proved that Matthew 28 teaches that attendance at communion depends upon prior baptism. He criticized the analogy of Jewish circumcision as a necessary condition for participation at the passover. 'But where,' Hall questioned, 'is it asserted in the New Testament that no unbaptised person shall partake of the eucharist?' He affirmed concerning baptism that 'in no part of scripture is it inculcated as a *preparative to the Lord's supper*, and that this view of it is a mere fiction of the imagination'.[20]

In short, baptism and communion were '*independently* obligatory' and lacked any essential connection.[21] Were they to have been inseparably connected, the New Testament would say so: 'The communion has no retrospective reference to baptism, nor is baptism an anticipation of communion.'[22] Strict Baptist practice amounted, then, to a punishment 'for the involuntary neglect of one ordinance'. With such 'violent remedies' which 'destroy' Hall would have nothing to do.[23]

Hall then considered the apparent fact that the Lord's teaching concerning baptism was backed up fully by apostolic practice. That is, 'the members of the primitive church were universally baptised.' It might have seemed, then, that any deviation from apostolic practice would virtually 'impeach either the wisdom of our Lord, or the fidelity of his Apostles'.[24]

He conceded readily that, with respect to baptism, in the earliest times 'converts to the christian faith submitted to that ordinance, prior to their reception into the christian church'. Further, he acknowledged that 'it is at present the duty of the sincere believer to follow their example'. Hall believed that, in spite of this, it does not appear from the New Testament that failure to be baptized disqualified from participation at communion; although 'apostolic precedent' may claim our deference, it does not decide the question.[25] This was a remarkable statement indeed. Hall admitted that in primitive times believers were necessarily baptized prior to admission to the churches and would have been rejected had they refused baptism. Unabashed, the great preacher claimed that this by no means proved such a sequence to be a permanent pattern. Then, the example of living apostles would have exposed the insincerity of all who declined immersion; now, the situation had changed. We note that at this point Hall appeared to be contradicting his comments about the baptism which the apostles, he alleged, had not received, and about Romans 6:3, and that for Hall the written word of Scripture was somehow less authoritative than the spoken apostolic word. His basic problem concerned the authority of the Bible.

According to Hall, there was a vast ideological gulf between those who opposed the apostles then and contemporary godly Paedobaptists in England 'who oppose no legitimate authority' and who, in the opinion of Baptists, mistook apostolic teaching in one particular only.[26] Restricted communion equated unbelievers in the first century with nineteenth-century pious Paedobaptists. With biting sarcasm, Hall confessed that he was 'at a loss whether most to admire the logic, the equity, or the modesty of such a conclusion'. Why should the 'great majority' of the faithful have been rejected by Strict Baptists on account of an error which was not fundamental?[27] Strict Baptist conformity to apostolic precedent was merely a 'shew'; in reality it was the open-communion Baptists who possessed a 'radical and essential' loyalty to apostolic teaching and practice.[28] If Paedobaptists had been acknowledged as Christians, they should inevitably have been judged worthy to 'enter into the full import of the rites commemorative of our Lord's death and passion'. If they enjoyed the blessings of the new covenant they should have been given access to its second ordinance, the memorial feast, and this particularly because Paedobaptists 'sincerely ... believe themselves to have complied with the first'; an 'involuntary mistake' about baptism should never have disqualified Paedobaptists from the Lord's table.[29]

In concluding this part of his attack, Hall protested that free-communion Baptists did not 'dispense' with 'divine laws'; they simply denied that the New Testament shows clearly that baptism is 'in all cases essential to communion'.[30]

The problem of universal church tradition was then faced. Why was it that free-communion Baptists seemed to depart 'from the sentiments of all parties and denominations throughout the christian world', denominations which insisted that baptism must precede communion?[31]

Robert Hall remarked that this argument presupposed 'the impossibility of the universal prevalence of error'.[32] Willing to stand alone and unintimidated by tradition, he believed that he had to show that universal Christian practice on the matter might well have been at fault. He noted aggressively that Strict Baptists ought not to have accused free-communionists of departing from universal custom; they, the Strict Baptists, had themselves effectively excommunicated the greater part of Christendom.

Hall believed that from an early post-apostolic period baptism was deemed to be vital for salvation and that primitive simplicity had soon been lost: 'There is scarcely a writer in the first three centuries ... from whom we should not be taught to infer, that baptism was absolutely necessary to salvation.'[33] So, Hall made another remarkable assertion:

> There is no doubt that the opinion of the absolute necessity of baptism, previous to communion, sprang from those lofty and superstitious ideas representing its efficacy, which our opponents would be the first to disclaim.[34]

Therefore, asserted Hall, the Strict Baptists' unwise recourse to tradition should be abandoned.

Moreover, Strict Baptists had deviated from healthy tradition as well as from Scripture: 'They are the only persons in the world of whom we have either heard or read, who contend for the exclusion of genuine Christians from the Lord's table; who ever attempted to distinguish them into two classes.'[35] The rejection of Paedobaptists by Strict Baptists amounted to the latter's verdict that the former were effectively 'men of ill lives, or ... the abettors of heresy and schism', accusations which were patently untrue.[36] In fact, 'the right of rejecting those whom Christ has received ... is not the avowed tenet of any sect or community in Christendom, with the exception of the majority of the Baptists' (note: 'majority of the Baptists'). Having rejected Scripture and sound tradition, Strict Baptists had, no doubt unwittingly, placed themselves in the dubious zone of sectarian Christianity in order to justify their conduct.[37]

In the next stage of his argument Robert Hall proceeded to provide 'positive grounds on which we justify the practice of mixed communion'.[38]

First, free communion flowed from the obligation to brotherly love among Christians. Love was the principal mark by which believers were to be distinguished in every age and was to be displayed by the preservation of union. So, when one part of the body of Christ refused to share with another part at the table, 'that very evil subsists against which we are so anxiously guarded',[39] this being contrary to the desire of our Lord as expressed in John's Gospel, chapter 17: 'We ask whether it be possible to reconcile such a conduct with the import of our Saviour's prayer.'[40] Thus, Strict Baptists misled others and themselves in that they appeared to show that 'the persons from whom they separate, are not Christians'.[41] This was not love. Why should children of the same father have refused to eat at the same table because one clause in their father's will remained in dispute? Further, the Holy Spirit revolts against restricted communion: Strict Baptists had been known to complain of 'anguish' when Christian friends were compelled to withdraw from the Lord's table after joining in other branches of worship.[42] If converted Paedobaptists were Christians, why should Baptists have placed the table, 'the symbol of christian unity', as 'the line of demarcation'? Realistically, acceptance implied neither that infant baptism is valid nor any violation of Baptist principles.[43]

Hall could not resist bringing to bear certain New Testament passages. He alleged that open communion derived from teaching about the demeanour of sincere Christians who differ doctrinally. Acts 15, Romans 14-15, the Galatian letter, 1 Corinthians 8 and Philippians 3, among other sections, were introduced. Hall made the point that in the first churches there were disagreements between Jewish and Gentile believers concerning attachment to the ancient law. Thus, in Romans 14-15 Paul commanded toleration and did not attempt to prohibit unimportant differences. 'Weakness' is presented by 1 Corinthians 8:7 as descriptive of a form of error which was not fundamental, the immature believer imagining that idols possessed a certain power. Similarly, because the error of infant baptism was not fundamental, Paedobaptists should not have been rejected from the Lord's table. Philippians 3:15, in its reference to Christians who are 'otherwise-minded', proves that non-essential differences should never lead to division.

That the New Testament never mentions baptism in these passages did not matter to Hall; the general principle of toleration concerning dietary disagreements at that period should be applied to nineteenth-century baptismal differences. If not, the principle is no principle. Although, quite clearly, Romans 14-15 do not refer to the Lord's table, Paul's insistence upon mutual reception must involve worship together at communion; failure there meant failure everywhere else in church life.

For Hall, the Strict Baptist view that Paul's command to receive the weak in faith refers only to the baptized did not count. He admitted that had the apostle specified that unbaptized converts should be tolerated, 'the inference in favor of Paedobaptists would unquestionably have been more obvious'. But it would not have been 'more certain' because, like the weak brethren at Rome, Paedobaptists retained an error which was compatible with a state of salvation and which may be held with an upright conscience.[44] To place

> ... Paedobaptists, who form the great body of the faithful, on the same level with men of impure and vicious lives, is equally repugnant to reason, and offensive to charity ... it is manifest from this mode of reasoning, that the measure contended for is considered in the light of *punishment*.[45]

But, should sincere Paedobaptists have been punished?[46] Certainly not.

Further, because Paedobaptists were a part of the true church, their exclusion from the Lord's table remained 'unlawful',[47] and for the following reason. In the New Testament the word 'church' is employed in two senses only. First, it refers to the 'universal' church and, second, to particular, 'local', Christian assemblies.[48] Baptists, Hall asserted, admitted that since faith preceded the application of water, all believers, both baptized and unbaptized, were members of the true, universal church. Because the whole church was but the sum of its parts, unbaptized Christians such as Paedobaptists must be held to be members of the local church. This meant communion.

Because infant baptism was not an error of such magnitude that it prevented the church which maintained it from being 'deemed a true church',[49] it followed that the rejection of the members of such a church from communion was schismatic. On the other hand, the admission of a Paedobaptist to a Baptist communion service in no respect upset the Baptist form of service, which remained as it was. Refusal of communion, then, was 'fraught with scandal'. More, it was 'utterly repugnant to the genius of the gospel'.[50] In earlier years secession from false churches, such as that of the Reformers from Rome and that of the Nonconformists from the Church of England, was essential; self-preservation was at stake. Restricted communion was another issue; Baptists were called neither to renounce their peculiar tenets on the subject of baptism nor to express their approbation of a contrary practice. Quite simply, they were not to sever themselves from the body of Christ.

Thus, restricted communion 'is itself a violent encroachment on the freedom of others'. 'When churches are thus constituted, instead of enlarging the sphere of christian charity, they become so many hostile confederacies.'[51] Christ became divided, particularly because Strict Baptists had remained unable to demonstrate that the New Testament forbids participation at the table by 'unbaptised Christians'.[52] If Christ has accepted all believers, so should Strict Baptists.

Hall observed with a show of reason that, if Strict Baptists disclaimed all communion with Paedobaptists and refused 'to acknowledge them as a legitimate part of the christian church',[53] which, he said, was what rejection from the table amounted to, every recognition of Paedobaptists as Christians ought to have been shunned. How could Strict Baptists have prayed for and sometimes have supported Paedobaptist churches, for example, by assisting at ordinations? Such a spectacle was as contemptible as it was amusing. In fact, the refusal of communion to a professing Christian could have been justified only upon the ground of his 'supposed criminality',[54] which meant either his retention of heretical views or an immoral life-style. If, then, Paedobaptists were to be rejected, it was because they were deemed to be delinquents. Further, Strict Baptist churches should, upon this principle, have been careful to exercise discipline of at least equal severity among their own people; there were 'doubtful' Christians retained without scruple in their communion.[55]

Love should reign. If infant baptism was practised innocently it ought not to have been punished at all, and certainly not by excommunication. On the other hand, if it was 'criminal', it could not have been as serious as various imperfections which were never perceived to lead to rejection from the table.[56] Hence, restricted communion had always been both unjust and inappropriate, inasmuch as this form of punishment could neither reform offenders nor deter others. So, this most unhappy form of discipline had become 'the scandal and reproach of our holy religion'.[57] In reality, because Paedobaptists were not reckoned by Strict Baptists as heretics, they should never have been treated as such; excommunication was an 'awful proceeding, only inferior in terror, to the sentence of the last day'.[58]

Going on from this, if it was wrong to join with Paedobaptists at communion, it followed that in their own churches Paedobaptists were 'criminal in approaching the Lord's table'.[59] Hall was perfectly well aware that Paedobaptists did believe that they had been baptized and that it was their immediate duty to commune; in neither respect had they felt themselves to be criminal. Nor did Strict Baptists, in complaining about Paedobaptists attending a Baptist communion, ever seem to have complained about communion in Paedobaptist churches, even though, on restricted-communion principles, it must have been an evil. Strict Baptists should, re-marked Hall, have had the courage to say to Paedobaptists: 'Go, sin no more,' instead of saying in effect to their brethren: 'Go, sin by yourselves, and we are satisfied.'[60]

According to Robert Hall, the practice of strict communion was incapable of accommodation to any New Testament principle. He believed that because Scripture does not debar believers from communion because of non-fundamental errors which would 'prevent their abettors from being accepted of God', Paedobaptists should not have been turned away from the table.[61] Hall could not conceive that Christ would receive believers, only to repel them from communion. For Hall, part of the problem lay in the fact that while Paedobaptists mistook the meaning of the ordinance, they simply did not reject the authority of Christ in the matter of baptism: they believed both that Christians should be baptized and that they personally had been baptized; they were serious, if mistaken, disciples. If, then, other errors entitled our indulgence, so should this. The notion that there were persons who revered neither the authority nor the laws of Christ, yet who had been received by him, was anathema to Hall.[62] Further (to repeat), because the principle of restricted communion had not been reduced by Strict Baptists to any 'general idea', the only route by which they were able to come to terms with Romans 14-15 was by stating the obvious fact that these chapters do not refer specifically to baptism. Nevertheless, re-stricted communionists were totally unable to demonstrate that the chapters in question establish a principle of toleration which does not include this case.[63]

Hall affirmed that, in his view, infant baptism did not involve any contradiction to 'the saving truth of the gospel', and did not appear to bestow any 'injurious effects' on the characters of its advocates. If damage had been done to truth or to life there would have been a case for exclusion, but this was not so: 'The hypothesis of the strict Baptists, as they style themselves, is so replete with perplexity and confusion, that for my part I absolutely despair of comprehending it.'[64] Many Paedobaptists had died in prison or in flames for their faith; Hall knew that sprinkling had not harmed them.

Under this heading, Hall allowed himself a further tilt at Abraham Booth. When Booth had insisted on baptism as a prerequisite to communion, yet denied its necessity for salvation, he appeared to Hall to have come near to disregarding Christ's authority over the Christian. How could baptism be indispensable when, in an all-important respect, it was totally unnecessary?[65]

Approaching the end of his attack, Hall considered that restricted communion was imprudent because it was contrary to the true needs of the churches. An instrument of compulsion rather than of persuasion, its proponents had allowed the issue to become a 'party distinction',[66] it being a point of honour among them to defend this peculiarity to the last. Like the Waldenses and Albigenses, who were Baptists before the time of Luther, latter-day Baptists should have allowed their view of baptism to stand upon its proper merits without having transformed it into the 'basis of a sect'.[67] When English Baptists adopted the practice of restricted communion they attracted to themselves the resentment of other denominations, who had begun to compare them to the fanatical Münsterites of Germany.[68]

According to Robert Hall, a Paedobaptist convinced of the error of his baptism would, if influenced by Strict Baptist coercion, have had to leave his own church, even a church adorned with a minister of the calibre of Jonathan Edwards. This could not be right.[69] On the other hand, free communion could and did lead Paedobaptists to think carefully about the respective merits of the two positions: 'In some societies the opposite sentiments have nearly subsided and disappeared.'[70]

The sting of Hall's onslaught against restricted communion lay at the end of its tail. Strict Baptists, just like Rome, had employed force. However, while the latter displayed the intolerance of power, the former showed that of weakness.[71] How much better, Hall maintained, had Strict Baptists felt able to trust truth to defend itself. The unchurching of every Paedobaptist community did no good at all because it rested on no clear principle, and because it inflicted a punishment both capricious and unjust, thus defeating its own purpose. He ended where he began: 'No church has a right to establish *terms of communion which are not terms of salvation*.'[72] The gospel does not consist in outward observances; if love was to prevail, Christians would soon enough come to a mind about external rites. On the other hand, coercion can only turn them from truth.

* * *

It appears that Strict Baptists writhed under the smart of Hall's book. In the same year, 1816, Joseph Kinghorn counter-attacked with his slightly smaller volume, *Baptism a term of Communion at the Lord's Supper.* According to Skeats and Miall, writing in 1891, Kinghorn 'was almost the last persistent literary opponent of open communion'.[73] In his introductory remarks Kinghorn asserted:

> *The whole controversy now before us, hinges on the question, whether we ought to obey the direct law of the Lord, and the explanation given of it in the conduct of the apostles; — or, whether we are justified in being guided by inferences, which, as I have endeavoured to shew in the following pages, are not correctly drawn from New Testament premises.*[74]

His fundamental thesis was expressed in the question '*whether persons who are acknowledged to be unbaptized ought to come to the Lord's table*'.[75] He believed not, and for the following reasons.

First, zeal for evangelical unity had led 'very excellent men' to 'neglect the positive commands of the Lord'. The view that all Christians should unite at the Lord's table, putting aside differences of opinion, was, for Kinghorn, 'this fascinating theory'.[76] Paedobaptists themselves, of course, acted upon the principle of restricted communion and were unwilling to receive unbaptized people to the table.[77]

These things being so, it remained to be proved by the advocates of open-communion that churches possessed the right to depart from apostolic tradition and practice: 'It is a serious thing to patronize *in the church* a system which directly tends to set aside any of the commands of the Lord.'[78]

It was difficult to understand how Baptists who argued for the 'perpetuity of baptism' could have believed that it was not necessary for communion.[79] Free-communionists should have proved that baptism had no connection with 'church communion' or, otherwise stated, that the Lord's supper does not depend upon baptism. Advocates of open communion who did not welcome to the table those who had not 'in some manner' recognized the law of baptism

Robert Hall, junior (1764-1831)

Joseph Kinghorn (1766-1832); an engraving reproduced by
courtesy of St Mary's Baptist Church, Norwich.

ought to have remembered that, 'on *their* principles, the strict Communion Baptists are *in the right*'.[80]

For Kinghorn, the Gospels and the Acts of the Apostles showed clearly that Christ issued a 'law' concerning baptism, and that this law was obeyed strictly.[81] Although in the first century baptism was not a term of membership with any particular church, it was nevertheless the appointed manner by which faith was professed. Only after such profession were disciples admitted to the table. The issue did not concern whether or not men should have prescribed as a term of communion that which was not essential to salvation, but what the Lord in his wisdom had prescribed: 'Christian communion must require whatever the Lord required as a mark of Christian profession.'[82] Open communion meant in practice that those who obeyed the apostolic teaching and those who opposed it 'ought to be treated *exactly alike*'. This was wrong.[83]

If, then, Christ had issued a law, that law should have been obeyed. If not, 'what is the use, either of command, or example?' The letters of the New Testament show clearly enough that 'there is a real instituted connexion between baptism and the whole of the succeeding Christian profession'. In short, 'either Christ required *too much* when he made baptism the term of Christian profession, or we require *too little* when we omit it as a term of communion.'[84]

The plea was refuted that Baptists should have admitted Paedobaptists to communion in the interests of Christian charity, yet with no sacrifice of principles. Kinghorn was happy to admit that that there were 'many excellent men in every denomination of Christians', including Roman Catholics. Nevertheless, open communion gave a constitution to the church 'which stands opposed to all the facts on record in the New Testament'; principles were at risk.[85]

Further, love towards Christians should never have been at the expense of obedience to the directions of the Lord. Indeed, separation might be more a mark of love in the event of disagreement.

With respect to Romans 14 and 15 and Philippians 3:15, which require toleration of disagreements not inconsistent with the explicit commands of Christ, Kinghorn commented at some length. All that Paul says in Romans 14-15 is that there was no law issued by Christ concerning uniformity of conduct in the matter of eating and drinking. Therefore, men may exercise their private opinions. It could not be proved that Paul advocated the reception of weak brethren when he knew that they were opposing or neglecting the revealed will of God. It followed that, because the immature emphases of some at Rome and Philippi had nothing to do with opposition to apostolic teaching, these passages should never have been used to support open communion. On the other hand, in that the kingdom of God consisted of righteousness, 'it must include obedience to practical precepts, both moral and positive,' such as baptism. The ground on which Paul requires toleration and forbearance 'is *totally inapplicable* to the case of mixed communion', infant baptism being reckoned by a Baptist as in some sense an infringement of divine law.[86] Forbearance in the matter of baptism, then, amounted to the churches' virtual repeal of the law of Christ and, as such, could well have become an ominous precedent for further serious modifications of the New Testament's rule of conduct.

In short, restricted communion must stand until it could be shown that the apostles pleaded for the reception into the churches of good men who, nevertheless, had refused obedience to a distinct command of Christ.[87]

Joseph Kinghorn then directed his attention to the view that because Paedobaptists belonged to the people of God, their exclusion from communion was a virtual punishment inflicted upon them.

In the opinion of the Norwich pastor, open communion declared in effect that the Reformation had been 'a mischievous insurrection' in which all Protestants aided and abetted a needless and schismatical project.[88] On the other hand, if it had been right to leave good men because they had left Jesus Christ, it must have been right not to admit them until they had submitted to his terms. If this was not so, why the Reformation?

So, the question returned yet again to the authority of the Bible: 'Can it be wrong, to take the New Testament as our guide; — to go where that leads us; — to go no farther than it goes with us; — and not to walk in a path opposed to its constant example?'[89]

In fact, restricted communion was no monstrous or unnatural attack upon the liberties of others. Even though mixed communion might not 'produce an immediate unpleasant effect' upon Baptist worship, it altered the constitution of every church which adopted the practice.[90] It was this which Kinghorn found unacceptable.

It followed that failure to welcome Paedobaptists to the Lord's table was no punishment. Such had never been united with a Baptist church and so could not be expelled. They were unqualified, although not unworthy, to partake. Even on Hall's principles, Kinghorn observed, in apostolic times the unbaptized would never have been admitted to the churches. Because there exists no divine law modifying this condition, it must still hold good. In practice, neither Paedobaptists nor Strict Baptists reckoned each other to be criminal; even as Dissenting Paedobaptists would have refused to unite with either Roman Catholics or the establishment because by so doing they thought that they would sanction 'corrupt appendages to the law of the Saviour',[91] so the Strict Baptist refused to welcome those whom he considered to be unbaptized. Principle, not punishment, governed such thinking.

According to Kinghorn, Strict Baptists had never blamed Paedobaptists for forming themselves into churches in which they communed together. No suspicions whatever had attached to their Christian character. Separation flowed simply from the necessary consequences of mixed communion, which, from a Strict Baptist standpoint, was a deviation from the original institution of the church. While Paedobaptists accepted the validity of immersion upon profession of faith, Strict Baptists could not reciprocate with respect to the sprinkling of infants; for them the latter procedure was no baptism. At this point Kinghorn was unduly optimistic: 'Having the honour of holding up to notice one neglected truth,' Strict Baptists believed that, with the blessing of God, they would see his cause 'gain the universal attention of all good men.' Declining to judge the hearts of Paedobaptist brethren, Strict Baptists had committed themselves quite simply to church-building with materials supplied by the 'Master Builder'.[92]

Kinghorn pointed out that, historically, separation had always been necessary for Baptists because they had found it impossible to fulfil the will of Christ when remaining in established churches. Essentially, restricted communion was capable of reduction to a clear and intelligible general principle, the obligation to fulfil the unrepealed commands of the Lord himself for the purposes which he had designed. This was far better than accommodation to systems sanctioned only by men.

Strict Baptists could not tell why God in his wisdom had allowed such vast differences of opinion in the churches; they waited for the Lord to 'elucidate his own designs'. Until then they would allow themselves to be led by 'the direct guidance of single and tangible truths'.[93]

With regard to the 'plea that Paedobaptists think themselves baptized',[94] Kinghorn asked whether they themselves would ever have received at the Lord's table someone whom they considered to be unbaptized. He believed not. It followed that Baptists and Paedobaptists could not meet on common ground. Repeating himself, Kinghorn asserted that while Paedobaptists regarded their Baptist brethren as baptized, the Baptists were in no position to reciprocate the sentiment. Moreover, true Christian liberty prohibited Baptists from receiving Paedobaptists simply because the latter considered that they had been baptized; the recipient body, in this case a Baptist fellowship, must have the final word concerning a candidate's qualifications, a principle leading to restricted communion. This was particularly the case when Baptists reckoned that, concerning baptism, Paedobaptists 'are on this point entirely wrong'.[95]

Further, because infant baptism opposed Christ's 'positive code', the New Testament must not be thought to allow forbearance in this matter. Hence, the churches were not to tolerate the neglect of a command 'so decided, useful, and universal'. The church and its ordinances were Christ's and not ours.[96]

Kinghorn shied at the responsibility which attached to the admission of unbaptized persons to the Lord's table. He believed that any deviations from the will of Christ must cause 'irremediable' mischief.[97] Thus, open communion had no capacity for doing good. The fact of the matter was that strict communion was simply an application of a general principle, which was that the church should observe all that the Lord had commanded. As it was, 'the patrons of mixed communion' had never been able to demonstrate their right to authorize men to break the law of Christ.[98] Baptists who forbore with those who abrogated Christ's institutions in Christ's church showed more love to the people in their errors than to the Lord in his wisdom. A Christian church was constituted by those who in baptism professed their faith and who joined others in obedience to Christ. Therefore, they who tolerated free communion formed a church 'visibly different from that which distinguished the church in the age of inspiration'.[99] Kinghorn barely concealed his opinion of the eloquent Robert Hall when he asked: 'Which of the corruptions that ever defiled the temple of God, did not number persons of the first talents, among its most ardent supporters?'[100]

'Expediency and policy are best tried by time.'[101] Mixed communion tended to inhibit ministers from preaching about baptism because, inevitably, they sought to avoid giving offence. Such a state of mind was always uncomfortable because the people were deprived of their food. In any event, why would Paedobaptists have wished to join as members with Baptist churches? On their own principles, they would recognize that Baptists were in the wrong, and would have avoided them to form their own fellowships. How could they who baptized babies, Kinghorn wanted to learn, commune with a church which felt that the Paedobaptists' form of baptism was invalid? Because they allowed themselves to bear the stigma of remaining unbaptized and united with Baptists on terms of inferiority, Paedobaptists, if they 'reflect on it for a moment ... will feel it *degrading*'.[102] In fact, a sincere Paedobaptist would not have wished to join with condescending free-communion Baptists.

In practice, free communion inclined to the view that religion advanced when the ritual aspects of faith lost some of their original significance. The truth was that men of differing views agreed to maintain silence, thus neutralizing each other, while the church forfeited the benediction of one of the ordinances of Christ. Kinghorn was unable to comprehend the usefulness of a Baptist congregation having a Paedobaptist minister settled over it, or vice versa. Moreover, they who held that free communion might well lead communicant worshippers to baptism tended to underestimate the strength of conviction held by many Paedobaptists. Kinghorn claimed that in his experience free communion had been known to divide the local church into two distinct parties. Conversely, 'those Baptist congregations which contained the greatest number of church members have been *strict Baptists*.'[103] This was a telling point; the Norwich pastor believed that free communion, though doubtless leading to a larger communicant congregation, tended to downgrade church membership. In sum, 'expedience and policy ought to have no weight.'[104]

Open communion demanded that Dissenters produce 'totally different' arguments to justify their separation from the establishment.[105] Earlier Nonconformists who had accepted the baptism of infants had quit the Church of England because that Church had adopted unscriptural representations of baptism and had required unscriptural ceremonies. Baptists, however, rejected infant baptism entirely and thus provided themselves with an unassailable reason for dissent. They believed that only those who had been baptized upon prior profession of their faith were to be reckoned as 'the materials of which the church should be erected'.[106] The sad reality was that the whole system of the establishment rested on a faulty approach to the baptismal issue:

For if a church is wrong in the class of members which it admits, not from occasionally mistaking their characters, but from receiving them on an erroneous principle; the evil is so deeply rooted, so extensive, and, in a national church, so irremediable, that the only thing to be done is "to come out from among them."[107]

Kinghorn was clearly out of sympathy with Anglican evangelicals and their Nonconformist sycophants. Baptist free communion invited the Churchman to exclaim that the precepts and precedents of the New Testament were not the last appeal for the Baptist. This meant that the latter's argument for separation blew itself to pieces. Although the Church of England was a 'worldly corporation',[108] annihilating the distinction between the world and the people of God, the fact remained that free-communion Baptists denied the distinction between themselves and the English Church because they, too, argued for liberty to dispense with a divine precept. Taken to its logical extreme, the Baptists' acceptance of those who clearly did not submit to Christ's institutions destroyed any ground of separation from the Church of Rome. Free-communionists had determined, as Rome did centuries ago, that apostolic foundations for the temple of the Lord were '*too small*', and that the whole structure needed to be pulled down to be replaced by 'a design, which shall comprize all the latest and best improvements of modern times!'[109]

What about Hall's assessment of John the Baptist? Contrary to Hall, Kinghorn maintained that because John's baptism was a divine institution, was administered to John's followers upon a profession of repentance and was designed to make the person of the Messiah known to Israel, it was remarkably similar to the baptism instituted by the Lord. Further, wrote Kinghorn, it was highly unlikely that the disciples would have resisted either the baptism of John or that administered by the followers of Jesus himself before the resurrection. The main difference between baptism before and after the Lord's glorification was simply that the former announced the coming of the Messiah, while the latter was the institution of Christ himself through the apostles. Essentially, both demanded assent to truth as it had been revealed at the time. John's baptism and that administered by the disciples of Jesus during his earthly ministry were, in fact, just as much Christian baptism as the Last Supper was a communion service; both anticipated and spoke about events which had not taken place. Even though some of the apostles 'had not, in the full extent of the term, *Christian* baptism, as it is *now* understood and practised, they had what the Lord esteemed requisite'.[110] Thus, the argument that the first communion service was attended by unbaptized disciples possessed no force.

Kinghorn asked how any person could profess Christ if he had not been baptized. The path of duty, in fact, had been laid down for us by the Lord himself; even Paedobaptists maintained that disciples were made such by their baptism. If the system of free communion was allowed, 'the PRINCIPLE *of obedience to the law of Christ in his church*, IS GIVEN UP'.[111]

The thesis was then defended that the idea of mixed communion had been unknown in the ancient churches and that it was not allowed by Paedobaptist writers in Kinghorn's day. While Baptists took no pleasure in contradicting the opinions of others in the matter of baptism, they felt that '*earliest antiquity* is on THEIR *side*'.[112] Over the years, the churches had never thought that 'they should partake of the *second* Christian institute, before they had obeyed the *first*'.[113] Thus, 'the Baptists do no more than was always done throughout all Christian antiquity.'[114] Kinghorn conceded that Paedobaptists acted in accordance with their own principles when attending the Lord's table in their own churches, yet the awkward question still remained: had the ancient churches ever admitted to communion those who were unbaptized? The only reply possible was negative. Hence, restricted communion as maintained by the Baptists and, in its own way, by the Paedobaptists, was entirely proper. Kinghorn quoted the Westminster Confession of Faith, chapter 27, section 1: 'Sacraments ... put a visible difference between those that belong unto the church, and the rest of the world.'[115] How, then, could Hall ever have claimed that strict communion 'destroys at once *the unity of the church*!'?[116] Baptism might not have been 'essential to the salvation of the individual Christian', but it was assuredly 'essential to the *scriptural existence of a church*'.[117]

Kinghorn's defence of restricted communion ended with miscellaneous observations. In sum, 'we are doing no more than pleading the cause of a *divine institution*.'[118] Free communion neglected baptism in the churches and represented strict communion as 'nothing better than an illiberal party zeal for a mere ceremony'.[119]

In fact, baptism was a term of Christian profession, while a Christian profession was a term of communion.

Further, if the New Testament does not explicitly prohibit unbaptized people from attending the Lord's table, it is because no such prohibition was necessary in the first century. Equally, however, the New Testament favours mixed communion no more than it does infant baptism, implying clearly that both practices would be inconsistent with the flow of its teaching. Concerning the necessity of baptism, Peter, according to Acts 10:44-8, could have omitted the command to Cornelius and his family to be baptized on the ground that they had received the Spirit. This he did not do. On the contrary, 'he considered these gifts ... as a warrant that those who enjoyed them might be baptized without scruple.'[120]

'The union of Baptist and Paedobaptist ministers in preaching for each other, and in promoting the gospel of Christ in different ways, has often been a source of great enjoyment to both,' provided that both sides avoided 'questions which related to the structure of the church, or the ordinances of the gospel'.[121] Strict Baptists rejoiced when they saw men in the establishment and elsewhere successful in turning sinners to God, yet still felt unable to commune with them, even as the latter might well have felt uncomfortable in joining at the Lord's table with Strict Baptists. Temporary practices mentioned by the New Testament, such as washing disciples' feet and the kiss of love, had been surrendered long since because they were not appointed by Christ. On the other hand, 'baptism and the Lord's supper were the general, distinguishing marks of the gospel dispensation.' Both remained 'obligatory on all Christians by the special command of their Lord'.[122]

* * *

Hall's initial attack upon restricted communion and its defence by Joseph Kinghorn were followed in 1818 by Hall's *A Reply to the Rev. Joseph Kinghorn* and by Kinghorn's further response to Robert Hall in 1820, *A Defence of "Baptism a term of Communion." In Answer to the Rev. Robert Hall's Reply.* Hall's rejoinder contained no new arguments, although it did attempt to impress upon the reader the fact that Kinghorn's treatment of his opponents 'bears no very remote resemblance to that which moderate Churchmen are accustomed to receive at the hands of their High Church brethren'.[123]

Hall deployed his considerable literary talents and powers of persuasion in an attempt to devastate Kinghorn's position.

For Hall, baptism was most certainly an obligation. But, then, if Paedobaptists were to be refused communion because they had disobeyed the law of Christ in this respect, nobody should attend the Lord's table; no one has ever fulfilled his Christian duty to perfection.[124] The flow of words lulls the reader into helpless agreement until he is startled and, hopefully, shocked by the following extraordinary statement:

> I ... assert that in the apostolic age, baptism *was* necessary to salvation. To the query which follows, how then can it be proved that it is not essential now, I reply that it is unnecessary to attempt it, because it is admitted by Mr. Kinghorn himself; and it is preposterous to attempt the proof of what is acknowledged by both parties.[125]

In his former book Hall had claimed that the sub-apostolic church was in error in holding that baptism, because allegedly a condition of salvation, should precede communion. Now, he asserted that in apostolic times the water did quite properly possess such a significance. A fundamental and quite fatal lack of consistency and control is perceptible in Hall's flow of argument.

Although he did not recognize his dilemma, Hall left himself with three self-imposed and quite impossible tasks. First, he had to show how it transpired that baptism, which he came to believe was a term of salvation in apostolic times, later lost this significance. Second, he needed to demonstrate how right-thinking Christians could depart from the apostolic standard (as he saw it) and regard immersion as unnecessary for salvation. Finally, he should have accounted for his shifting interpretations of primitive baptism. We recall that in his first book Hall had maintained that baptism was not the experience of all believers after the resurrection; in his second book he claimed that baptism was designedly indispensable. He failed on all counts to explain himself.

Hall, of course, could not understand how it was that while Strict Baptists 'are shocked at the idea of suspecting the piety of their Paedobaptist brethren, they contend it would be criminal to recognise it in the church'.[126] He failed to discern in the New Testament any necessary connection between baptism and communion; that the apostles both baptized and administered the Lord's supper was true, but this did not show that the latter depended upon the former.[127] In reality, the English Strict Baptists were half-baked (he quoted Hosea 7:8) in that they sometimes associated with Paedobaptists, yet would never commune with them. Booth, said Hall, had found this 'glaring inconsistency' an 'insupportable weight', while Strict Baptists generally 'are suspended betwixt the love of the brethren, and the remains of intolerance'.[128] For Hall, restricted communion was a system which should be discarded 'with just detestation'.[129] It was even worse than the Roman Catholic belief in baptismal regeneration because, while Rome associated the outward rite with the inward grace, the Strict Baptist, in giving baptism an undue importance regarding church membership, denied that it possessed any regenerating power. In short, Kinghorn's book might have been sweet in the mouth, yet it was bitter in the belly.[130]

Hall dealt with Kinghorn's accusation that free-communionists dispensed an ordinance of Christ unjustly, rejoining that there was a distinction between someone who 'asserts his right to deviate from the letter of legal enactments' and he who misinterpreted their meaning. The latter 'betrays his ignorance, but usurps nothing'.[131] Thus with the Paedobaptist. As far as Baptists were concerned, Christ had ordained both immersion and the table as duties of 'perpetual obligation'.[132] Nevertheless, the New Testament does not teach that they rest upon each other, a notion which 'is a mere human invention, a mere fiction of the brain'.[133] On the other hand, the free-communionist was true to the spirit of Romans 14-15 and an express law of Christ in that he received those whom Christ had received: 'It is lawful to admit a pious Paedobaptist to communion, because we are commanded to receive such as Christ has received.'[134] One of the weaknesses of the strict-communion position was that it took up a 'miserable' circular argument, assuming that which it sought to prove, namely, that baptism is a term of communion. Hall denied the assumption and therefore rejected the accusation of dispensing with the law of Christ. He suggested cleverly that, in reality, Strict Baptists confused their own interpretation of the law with the law itself.[135]

That the Church of England comprehended many abuses might be true, but Kinghorn's notion that it was 'a mere mass of corruption and error' was false;[136] Kinghorn and his brethren had no right to set Churchmen at defiance. It followed that even the godly Roman Catholic, considered simply as a member of Christ, may be admitted to a Baptist communion service; by so doing the Baptist gave away

no principles and did not acknowledge the propriety of the idola-
trous mass. In fact, Strict Baptists were not unlike the Churches of
Rome and of England in that all placed their distinctive traditions
and interpretations of Scripture on a level with the Word of God
itself.[137]

There was no need whatever, Hall maintained, for a Paedobaptist
to entertain a sense of inferiority if and when he attended a Baptist
communion service. Whatever the Baptists might have thought
about his baptism, he himself reckoned that 'infant baptism is a part
of the will of Christ',[138] and considered that the Baptists, with whom
he communed, were in error in this matter. They tolerated each
other, demonstrating 'a noble oblivion of minor partialities and
attachments', which were 'made to yield to the force of christian
charity, and disappear before the grandeur of the common salvation'.[139]

Kinghorn's opinion that free communion had undermined the
basic principles of Dissent was rejected emphatically. It was one
matter for Dissenters to leave good men in the establishment
because the latter had deviated from the will of Christ, and another
to repel them from the former's communion. The fact was that the
mystical body of Christ 'is one and one only, and that all sincere
believers are members of that body'.[140] Hence, we should not have
shrunk from those of whom we have need for fear of being
contaminated by them. Exclusion was a wrongful form of punishment because a punishment 'is exactly proportioned to the value of
the privilege it withholds',[141] in this case the illegal denial of the
fellowship of the church. Those who baptized babies 'incur the
forfeiture of all the privileges of the church, for no fault whatever',
a censure which deserved 'unmingled disgust'.[142] Although they
were in error concerning their view of baptism, their fault bore no
proportion to the punishment meted out to them by the 'insignifi-
cant' Baptist societies.[143] If Paedobaptists, as persons, were worthy
Christians, they should have been received; if they were unworthy,
they should have been rejected. Kinghorn's distinction between
unworthiness and disqualification became meaningless when seen
in the light of day.[144]

In his conclusion Hall devoted nearly thirty pages to establishing
the thesis that in primitive times open communion 'was introduced
as early as it was possible — as early as the dissimilar materials
existed, of which the combination under discussion is formed'.[145] So

it was that 'the advocates of strict communion have violated more maxims of antiquity, than any other sect upon record'. Their 'narrow, exclusive system which we are opposing' was 'repugnant'. The Lord's supper was the 'discriminating token' by which Christians were to recognize each other. Rejection from the table meant, therefore, that one class of Christians quite wrongly considered another class not to be 'parts of the church'. For this there had been no ancient precedents.[146]

Hall exhorted Christians to 'go back to the simplicity of the first ages — we must learn to quit a subtle and disputatious theology, for a religion of love'. At his most extravagent, Hall thought that Strict Baptists, who selected the ceremony of baptism 'as their distinguishing symbol', 'degrade the Christian profession ... by placing it in the due administration of the element of water'.[147] They merited the prayer of the Lord: 'Father, forgive them; for they know not what they do' (Luke 23:34).[148] Kinghorn, claimed Hall, taught that because baptism had once been necessary to salvation, it was so still, and that Paedobaptists had not been received into the Christian dispensation. In reality, had it not been for the authority of Abraham Booth and Andrew Fuller, Kinghorn's 'flimsy sophistry' in defence of strict communion would have been virtually useless.[149]

Robert Hall, in fact, impugned Fuller's sincerity concerning restricted communion. In a slim pamphlet which appeared in 1826, Hall asserted that Fuller's mind was 'all along' never completely made up on the subject. In Hall's earlier days, he alleged, Fuller had proposed 'himself to commune at Cambridge, with the full knowledge of there being paedobaptists present'. Moreover, Hall disclosed, he himself had, years before, personally asked Andrew Fuller 'whether any thing more is requisite to communion, on scriptural grounds, than a vital union with Christ'. The answer he received — and Hall, italicising, claimed to cite Fuller's exact words — was: '*When mixed communion is placed on that footing, I never yet ventured to attack it.*' Hall, in full flow, then disclosed another private conversation held with an unnamed acquaintance, one of Fuller's deacons and 'a man of primitive piety and integrity', whom he, Hall, had respected highly. When Hall asked the deacon why he objected to mixed communion, he was informed that it was for two reasons. First, the deacon's minister, Mr Fuller, did not approve of it. Second, the deacon had taken to heart Ecclesiastes 10:8, 'whoso breaketh an hedge, a serpent shall bite him.' Hall lamented that, like many others, the deacon derived his erroneous view from 'the public teachers of religion', rather than from the Bible.[150] Maybe Hall's suspicions about following men were not entirely unfounded.

To go back to Hall's *Reply* to Kinghorn in 1818, 'when the Spirit is poured down from on high, he will effectually teach us that God is *Love*, and that we never please him more than when we embrace with open arms, without distinction of sect or party, all who bear his image.'[151]

*   *   *

Kinghorn responded to this, Hall's last major book in defence of open communion, in 1820. He ventured solely to expand his previous arguments. The main thesis, again, was that the church was bound to maintain the law of Scripture:

> According to the New Testament, a profession of faith and baptism on that profession, took place *previous* to a person's being considered as a Member of the church. In following such authority we are *not* raising a wall of separation which Christ has not raised.[152]

His criticisms of Hall were more moderate than the latter's attacks upon Kinghorn. He held Hall to have failed totally to prove that

> ... we are not bound to follow the directions of the New Testament *as rules of conduct*, except in relation to duties which, in the strongest sense of the terms, *are essential to salvation*. Unless this can be demonstrated, Mr. Hall's argument is of no force.[153]

That is to say, the proposition could not be demonstrated that, because not essential to salvation, baptism should never have been made a term of communion. Robert Hall 'pleads that persons avowedly unbaptized may be received; and thus he sinks the authority of the Lord's command, and annihilates the use of apostolic precedents'.[154] With regard to the godly Paedobaptist, Hall should 'inform us whether we are *expressly commanded* to receive him as baptized or *un*baptized? If the former, then the controversy concerning *baptism* is finished'.[155]

According to Kinghorn, Hall never countered the criticism that free communion altered the constitution of the church: 'If he imagines that we esteem either his silence, or the contempt with which he treats this part of the subject a sufficient refutation, he is mistaken.'[156] Hall's allegations that strict communion is a form of punishment and that free communion was practised in ancient times were refuted.[157] Those whom Hall derided as 'little Baptist teachers' had an advocate on high who would plead their cause. Realistically, Kinghorn remarked that it signified nothing whence these men originated; the business of such ministers was 'to keep in the path trodden by primitive Saints, holy Apostles, and the Son of God'.[158]

* * *

To conclude, free communionists, it appears, seem never to have taken the view that while restricted communion ought to have been the order for the churches, the needs of the day demanded a more relaxed approach; like their strict-communion brethren they sought the authority of the Bible. The present writer believes, nevertheless, that their arguments were specious, that is to say, plausible but not right. He would go further, and suggest that the pragmatic arguments offered were an example before their time of what is now occasionally referred to as 'Situation Ethics'.[159] According to this, the individual works out for himself what he ought to do in the light of the overall command to Christians to love one another. The exponent of situationalism takes this route in preference to applying the specific laws of Christ with total inflexibility. In thus doing he depreciates the wisdom of the Word of God, fails to act in love, and so prejudices the cause of Christ.

The writer would add a final comment. Sadly, restricted communion is contrary to the spirit of the times and is unacceptable in most evangelical communities. It follows that the very best advertisement which 'Strict Baptists' can give for their practice is holiness of life accompanied by love for those of the Lord's people who do not agree with them. Further, a proper exclusiveness at the Lord's table should never cancel appreciation of the Lord's people in general.

CHAPTER VIII
HIGH CALVINISM AND THE PARTICULAR BAPTISTS

During the eighteenth century English Particular Baptists were influenced enormously by what Andrew Fuller termed 'high Calvinism'. He considered this to be a species of Calvinism essentially unlike the 'moderate' and 'strict' varieties. For Fuller, 'high' Calvinists were 'more Calvinistic than Calvin himself', while a 'moderate Calvinist' was 'half Arminian'. Fuller claimed 'strict Calvinism to be my own system'.[1] It is to the phenomenon of 'high Calvinism', or 'hyper-Calvinism', as it has often been called, that we now turn.

'High Calvinism' was a theological system which would appear to have co-ordinated two denials. First, there was the denial that God calls all who hear about Christ to believe in him; no man is obliged as a matter of duty to trust in Christ as a condition of salvation. This denial applied to both the reprobate and to the elect. The 'reprobate' are all those who were not originally chosen in Christ before the world began, for whom Christ did not die, who will be left in their sinful state by God, and who therefore will never repent and believe. The 'elect' are all those who were originally chosen by the Father to form the church of God, for whom Christ did die, and who will certainly come to a living faith in the Saviour. The reasoning was that if God alone can, and sometimes does, give repentance and faith, such should be demanded of no man, whoever he might be; sovereign grace is irresistible. Second, high Calvinism denied that it is the responsibility of the churches to call upon all men indiscriminately to repent and to believe in Christ for the salvation of their souls.

Positively, high Calvinism tended to address the claims and the consolations of the gospel only to those who apparently displayed genuine signs of rebirth and, therefore, of their original election to salvation. Faith tended to be redefined as an inner awareness that one had been born again and was therefore among the number for whom Jesus died.

Furthermore, high Calvinism might be considered to have been a benign form of 'Antinomianism', which means 'against the law'. In its most virulent form, this fundamental error has taught that the benefits of the death of our Lord can be enjoyed without the Spirit of God leading the sinner to repentance and to holiness of life. Thus defined, the emphasis is contrary to the nature and design of redemption. The Anglican Augustus Toplady, Vicar of Broadhembury, Devon, and no Antinomian, has bequeathed the following interpretation:

> By Antinomianism, I mean, That doctrine, which teaches, "That believers are released from all obligation to observe the moral law as a rule of external obedience: That, in consequence of Christ's having wrought out a justifying righteousness for us, we have nothing to do, but to sit down, eat, drink, and be merry; that the Messiah's merits supercede the necessity of personal inherent sanctification."[2]

The charge of Antinomianism was often hurled against the high Calvinists. This was because they appeared now and then to incline to the view that repentance is not necessary for salvation; sin does not have to be given up. This notion, if indeed it was held, was an application of the belief that the elect, converted sinner is always without spot before God. So, his obedience to the moral law does not bear upon his final salvation, a salvation which, because decreed, remains certain. Looked at in another way, high Calvinism was maligned by its critics as a protest against holiness, a protest which maintained that trying to be pure was like the religion of the Pharisees; salvation was by the law.

At the time, accusations of immorality were never, it seems, brought by their opponents against those Particular Baptists who were known high Calvinists; their lives were perceived to have been incapable of public reproach. Nevertheless, it was all very suspicious. Young Isaac Watts wrote to his brother, Enoch, at about the time of the 1689 Particular Baptist assembly:

> Those called Antinomians now-a-days ... vent dangerous errors under such dangerous expressions as these: 1st, That God sees no

sin in his people, and therefore Saints need not ask pardon. 2d, Christ was a murderer, a blasphemer &c. because he had those sins imputed to him. Christ believed and repented for us as well as died for us. ... faith is not so properly an acceptance of Christ as an assurance that he is ours.[3]

Watts might have misunderstood, of course, but that was how he perceived, or chose to perceive, Antinomianism.

Among the Baptists of the period, John Gill was without doubt the most prominent exponent of high Calvinism. Towards the end of the eighteenth century most Particular Baptists had come to accept Gill's works as the final word on orthodox interpretations of Scripture. He produced an entire theological library which became standard reading material for the constituency.[4]

With regard to the notion that the law of God is not the rule of conduct for believers, 'Dr. *Gill*, Mr. *Brine*, Mr. *Toplady*, &c. utterly condemned so vile a sentiment,' wrote John Ryland junior.[5] Nevertheless, as the eighteenth century passed by, men were not slow to realise the practical implications of high Calvinism. Thus it was that Ivimey wrote:

> There can be no doubt, (at least, so the writer thinks,) but what those who sow the seed of the actual justification of the elect before faith, or from eternity, will have to reap a crop of Antinomian practices in the lives of their hearers. Even the correct statements of Dr. Gill upon this subject, it should seem, did not prevent some of his members from "denying the necessity of the internal work of the Spirit as a sanctifying principle of grace and holiness."[6]

To repeat, high Calvinism denied that a person insensitive to his sinfulness should ever be summoned to conversion. This approach rested firmly upon the dogma that fallen humanity is beset by an inability to turn from sin and turn to God. So, what men cannot do in their own strength, they need not do.

*   *   *

The question arises as to what was meant by 'inability'? Here was, and is, the crux of the issue. For the high Calvinist, man's incapacity to repent was seen sometimes as a natural limitation rather than as a culpable evil arising from a perverted and sinful heart. The high

Calvinism of the period tended to assert that men do not turn to Christ because, quite simply, they are naturally and constitutionally unable to do so; their inability is inborn rather than wicked. Further, their incapacity to depend upon the Saviour derived not from the fall of Adam and the corporate guilt of the race but, rather, from the manner in which innocent Adam was originally created. Lewis Wayman, who pastored an Independent church at Kimbolton in the East Midlands until his death in 1764, held that 'Adam had not the faith of God's elect before the fall, and did not lose it for his posterity; therefore, they [the elect] are not debtors to God for it while in unregeneracy.'[7] So, faith is by no means a duty. This accounts for Wayman's remarkably inaccurate comment about 1 Peter 1:23; he confused the written word of Scripture and the eternal word, Christ: 'They [the elect] are not said to be begotten by that word which was not so soon as time began, and when time shall be no more shall cease to be, but by that word which *liveth and abideth for ever*.'[8] It followed for Wayman that the sinner's response to the gospel is neither a necessity laid upon him by Scripture nor an experience triggered by Bible preaching; Christ in the Spirit is the unique and sovereign medium of renewal. Faith is neither a demand imposed upon those who will never believe nor a demand laid upon those to whom by grace it will be given.

The approach was developed by the Baptist John Brine. He taught that Adam, prior to the fall and in his innocency, was not required and therefore not equipped to repent and trust in God. It followed that his fallen children had never, as sinners, acquired a capacity with which their first father, in his integrity, was not endowed. If innocent Adam was not constitutionally capable of exercising faith, much less will his sinful seed be able. In consequence, their present incapacity to repent and believe the gospel presupposes that, like Adam, they have never been required to do so. Nevertheless, Brine taught that Adam's sinful children, like their originally innocent father, were still obliged to heed every revelation from God. When preaching at the ordination of John Collett Ryland in 1750, Brine based his remarks upon 2 Timothy 4:1-2. Ryland was told to 'comfort *the Mourners in Zion*, by proposing to their Consideration the sweet Promises and precious Truths of the Gospel'. Brine also told Ryland what to say to those who did not mourn:

> You must *exhort* Men in general to shun the Practice of Sin, and to avoid all Occasions of it: And put them on the Practice of Duty. Exhort them to read the Scripture; and exhort them to Prayer, which

is a Part of natural Religion, and a Duty incumbent on all Men. Exhort them to hear the Word of God preach'd; this is also their Duty: For the Gospel justly demands the Attention of every Man.[9]

Here, the high-Calvinist distinction between so-called 'legal' and 'evangelical' repentance comes over the horizon, a distinction which might appear to have been its fundamental self-contradiction. The fact remains that because Adam's fallen children, according to Brine, are obliged to believe the truth and every revelation from God,[10] we might reasonably conclude that they ought to love both God and their neighbours (Deuteronomy 6:5; Leviticus 19:18). These are duties which would embrace repentance and faith in Christ, should some of Adam's children be privileged to hear the revelation of the gospel.

According to Ivimey, high Calvinism dominated the Particular Baptist scene by the mid-1700s. Writing concerning the reign of George II and, specifically, about the period immediately following the 1745 invasion of England by the Young Pretender, Charles Stuart, he asserted:

> The manner of preaching the gospel, by some of the Baptist ministers, to unconverted sinners, had been greatly altered during this reign. From the zeal which they displayed for the peculiar doctrines of Calvinism, and their tenaciousness for the sentiment that *salvation is of the Lord,* and by grace alone, without human endeavours, they were led into an extreme, so as to deny that all who hear the gospel are called to that exercise of repentance and faith which is connected with salvation; thus taking the negative side of what was then called the modern question, "Whether it be the duty of all men to whom the gospel is published, to repent and believe in Christ?" So far as I have been able to discover, this subject had never been made a question by our ministers, previously to the end of the last reign.[11]

We shall examine the 'modern question' and the controversies associated with it later in this chapter.

* * *

Quite when high Calvinism appeared in the churches is uncertain, although it must have been at an early time. Relevant to the matter is an excerpt from a letter written in 1675 to Andrew Gifford, pastor of the Pithay Baptist church, Bristol, by, among others, the eminent William Kiffin. The letter declared:

'Tis certain no man can, without the assistance of the Holy Spirit, either repent or believe; yet it will not therefore follow, that impenitency and unbelief are no sins; if these be sins, then the contrary must be their duty.[12]

To repeat, we have here the whole issue addressed negatively by high Calvinism. Does God require those who were not foreknown by him to yield to him a humble trust which they will never want to give, and that which he, because he had not decreed their renewal, will never enable them to provide? Further, does God require the elect to offer that which will inevitably be generated by the Holy Spirit, that is, repentance and faith? We would say 'yes' on both counts.

We can trace high Calvinism back to the earlier part of the sevententh century. Dr Tobias Crisp, Rector of Brinkworth in Wiltshire from 1627 until his death in 1642, held, as did John Gill after him, the doctrine of eternal justification. By 'eternal justification' was meant the view that the elect were justified in Christ before the beginning of the world. This implies that the elect person, prior to active faith, was never a child of wrath 'even as others' (Ephesians 2:3). Although Crisp was never foolish enough to disapprove of good deeds, he did write: 'There is not one act of righteousness that a person doth, but when that is finished, there is more transgression belonging to him, than before he had performed it.'[13]

Whatever Crisp intended by such a remark, the Antinomian implication for the unwary was clear: it was better to avoid righteous acts than to perform them. John Gill saw problems in this area, and wrote in response to Crisp's observation that believers need not be afraid of their sins: 'I must confess, I do not like the expressions, but am of opinion they ought to be disused.'[14]

Gill was not the last to express reservations. In 1887 a note in *The Sword and the Trowel* remarked concerning the publication of short-hand records of Crisp's works by his son forty-five years after the former's death: 'This will account for the crudeness of some of his expressions. ... Many of his statements, however, while they readily admit of an orthodox sense, lie open to the charge of being beyond the truth.'[15]

No doubt this was so, yet John Gill republished Crisp's works in 1755. Ivimey's view seventy years later was that he personally had come to regret 'that Dr. Gill should have sweetened a poisonous drug, or put his indorsement to a bad bill, by explaining and recommending the works of Dr. Crisp'.[16]

At this point Richard Davis enters the scene again. As we have observed, in 1689 he became minister of the Rothwell, Northamptonshire, Independent church. Some, perhaps many, of the people there were inclined towards high Calvinism. The 1700 account of Davis's beliefs and practices bears this out.[17] It claimed concerning the Rothwell Independents that, in their view, 'it is to no purpose to pray for, or endeavour after Repentance; because the Sins of the Elect, past, present, and to come, are already forgiven; and therefore they ought to pray only for the Manifestation of their Pardon'.[18] Unquestionably, this was high Calvinism. Davis himself interpreted Galatians 2:16, 'we have believed in Jesus Christ, that we might be justified by the faith of Christ,' in the following way:

> Not only justified by God, to our Surety in Heaven, for that was done ever since he rose from the Dead, *Rom.* 4.25. *Ch.* 8.33, 34. And consider'd as such, 'tis in him one continued Act: But the meaning there is, that God may justifie us, or apply Justification to our Persons, and so to our Consciences, that we may come to the knowledge of it ourselves. Now in God's Act, upon our receiving Christ, there is a continuation of his former judicial Act to our Surety, and there arises nothing in it new, but as it respects us, and that determination of it on our Persons and Consciences, that we may come to know God's Heart therein concerning us.[19]

In mentioning the divine application of justification to the believing sinner's conscience Davis might have meant that the believer realises that he is justified rather than enters into a state of justification.

Furthermore, it appears that, at that time, there was no surprise felt when some high-Calvinist Independent churches reacted against infant baptism. Edmund Jones of Pontypool commented acidly in 1741: 'When they become Antinomians, they will readily turn Anabaptists.'[20] High Calvinism and the Baptists' restricted communion were perceived in some quarters to be coming together. It would have been, for example, the baptismal issue alone which separated men such as Richard Davis and John Gill, his earlier near neighbour at Kettering.

Joseph Hussey, pastor of a Congregational church in Cambridge, emphasized early in his ministry the divine invitation to sinners to accept Christ. Later on, he moved his position. In his 1707 publication, *God's Operations of Grace, but No Offers of His Grace*, Hussey developed the view that because saving grace is irresistible and available for the elect alone, to preach Christ is scriptural.

However, to offer grace and salvation indiscriminately to sinners will not help them to believe since faith is the sovereign gift of God. Because eternal life is granted to the elect alone it is wrong to offer this blessing promiscuously to all men. Hussey's views were widespread and moulded many people, including the Baptist John Skepp.

Skepp had become pastor of the Particular Baptist church at Curriers' Hall, Cripplegate, London, about 1710. According to Hussey, from whose Cambridge congregation Skepp came, he had pressed himself into the ministry in opposition to the opinions of both pastor and church.[21] A subscriber at the Salters' Hall synod in 1719, Skepp died in 1721, just after Gill had moved to London. After an intervening pastorate at Curriers' Hall, Brine became the pastor there. As far as Ivimey was aware a century later, Skepp was the first Baptist minister to imbibe the new method of gospel preaching: 'Mr. Skepp, it should seem, would not persuade sinners to listen to the calls of the gospel, lest he should despoil God of the honour of their conversion.'[22]

Skepp, long suspicious of the Calvinism of his time, wrote in later years:

> I well remember, that when I was young, having learned the Assembly's Catechism, and read some Confessions of Faith, and the doctrinal Articles of the reformed Churches, with their arguments against Papists and Arminians, I used to be stumbled at Arminian discourses, from such who were accounted Strict Calvinists. I call them Arminian Discourses; for it is not the throwing in a few words, by way of a parenthesis, that will mend the matter, nor sufficiently atone for an hour's practical discourse in the Arminian dialect, where the Spirit's work, both as to previous renovation, or continued influences and assistance, is not so much as mentioned, till just at last; and then only with this Arminian or Semi-pelagian close — 'I know you cannot do these things of yourselves, unless God enable you; and therefore you must rely upon him, and earnestly beg the Divine assistance.'[23]

'Semi-Pelagianism', a fifth-century error, claimed that the beginning of salvation lies with men; God assists them when they seek him.

Skepp emphasized, too, that an elect person is passive during the process of regeneration, the Spirit leading him to see himself as he really is:

> This passive, yet efficacious work of God upon the hearts of his people in effectual calling and conversion is what our Lord taught Nicodemus under the Similitude, of a new birth.[24]

It is easy to see that this approach redefined and reduced conversion to an act of God in which the elect sinner did nothing. Certainly, he was not to be urged to undertake a positive and radical action like actually repenting of sin. Ivimey asked with regard to Skepp's depreciation of the Westminster Confession:

> But was it modest in Mr. Skepp to be so certain that the Assembly of Divines, and the compilers of all the Reformed Creeds, and most other ministers, were all Arminians and Semi-pelagians, while they had always considered themselves to be Calvinists?[25]

Ivimey claimed about 'Mr. Skepp's *non-invitation, non-application* scheme' that it 'was by him introduced among the Baptists ... a river that has plentifully watered our churches'.[26]

Back at Rothwell, Richard Davis was followed in 1714 by another Welshman, Matthias Maurice. We have already come across Maurice in his controversy with John Gill about the mode of baptism. The degree of personal misunderstanding in the air might be illustrated by a remark of Philip Doddridge in 1726 to the effect that, in his view, Maurice was 'the Antinomian preacher at Rothwell'.[27] In fact, Maurice was no high Calvinist, at least not in later years and probably never before. Interestingly, he inclined to the view that the coming of the Lord might occur in 1941.[28] No man's man, he worked out his own position with regard to high Calvinism, and in 1737 published a thirty-two-page pamphlet entitled *A Modern Question Modestly Answer'd*. In this he sought to maintain the thesis that

> ... any Person surely, who lays aside all Affectation of Singularity, and sincerely and unfeignedly makes the Bible the Rule of his Faith, must say, that God does by his *Word* plainly and plentifully make it the duty of unconverted Sinners, who hear the Gospel, to believe *in Christ*.[29]

Maurice died in 1738, but a reply to him, *A Further Inquiry after Truth* by Lewis Wayman, who, according to Ivimey, was almost idolized by the Baptists,[30] appeared soon after. Dr Abraham Taylor, theological tutor at the Independent academy, Union Street, London, warned that such writing could lead to 'Doctrinal Antinomianism'.[31] A further contribution, *The Modern Question Affirm'd and Prov'd*, by Maurice, came out posthumously in 1739. This contained a commendation by the provocative London Congregationalist Thomas

Bradbury. He wrote concerning Maurice: '*The Church, to whom he was an affectionate Pastor, has lain under a Reproach, which this Book, and their Desires to have it publish'd, will effectually roll away.*' The book included '*The* TESTIMONY *of the Church of* CHRIST *at Rowel, against the pernicious* NEW OPINION', in which testimony it was declared by the male members 'that God does in his Word make it the *Duty* of poor unconverted Sinners, who hear the Gospel preach'd, to be truly concern'd for their Souls, and believe in *Jesus Christ* for Salvation.'[32]

So, controversy had now spread to London, where Abraham Taylor was a more dangerous opponent than Maurice of the high Calvinists. Gill took up arms against Taylor, as did Wayman at Kimbolton.[33] Maurice's pamphlet, meanwhile, was answered not by Gill, who perhaps had had quite enough to do with him, but by John Brine. Brine, we recall, was a confessed 'Strict Baptist', and, like Gill, now a London pastor. He was also somewhat of a disciple of John Skepp.

In 1752 Alvery Jackson, a Baptist minister in Yorkshire, went into print on the affirmative side of the 'Modern Question'. This was given a response by John Brine in his *Motives to Love and Unity among Calvinists differing in opinion* and also in his *A Dialogue between Christophilus, Philalethes, and Philagathus.* In the latter, he wrote against Jackson that

> ... to declare to unregenerate Persons the Necessity of Faith in order to Salvation ... falls very far short of asserting it to be their present Duty. *According to the Commandment of the everlasting God, the Gospel is made known to all Nations*: That Commandment refers to the Publication of the Gospel among all Nations, and not unto *the Obedience of Faith.*[34]

A Mr Johnson of Liverpool was also attacked by Brine for confounding what Brine called 'actuating' and 'acting' faith: 'The former is the Work of the Blessed Spirit upon us. ... The latter, viz. the Acting, or Exercise of the Grace of Faith, is proper to us. For, the Holy Spirit does not believe, but we ourselves.'[35] Brine, like Skepp, accepted that the believer is required to do nothing because he can do nothing.In 1760 Brine wrote daringly:

> I hope you will hear it with Reverence; *Omnipotence itself cannot cause Enmity to Love.* For, that implies a contradiction. ... In our depraved Nature, there is nothing but a mere passive

Capacity to receive a holy, spiritual Principle from God, in a way
of Creation, or Infusion.[36]

* * *

Of the three Baptist high Calvinists, Brine, Skepp and Gill, Gill was
held as the greatest. This eminent man had been born in Kettering
in 1697, and was taken by his family to a Dissenting congregation
in that town.[37] When Gill was about eleven years of age the local
schoolmaster decided to make daily attendance at the parish church
compulsory for the boys. As the Gill family would not, for reasons
of conscience, agree with this imposition, young John had to quit
school. In 1716 he was immersed in a river upon profession of faith.
He soon began to preach. The capacity of the nineteen-year-old
might be measured by the hymn which he wrote on the day of his
baptism, a hymn which the people sang. The fourth verse seems to
dismiss any possibility that Gill would grow up to be a practising
Antinomian:

> That we should follow Christ the Lamb
>   In owning his commands;
> For what we do, he did the same,
>   Though done with purer hands.[38]

When in his early twenties, and by that time a married man, he
accepted an invitation to his London pastorate. A considerable
scholar, his prowess in rabbinic studies has seldom been equalled;
in 1748 an honorary doctoral degree was conferred upon him by a
Scottish university in recognition of his work in that field. The
Doctor remained as pastor to his church until his death in 1771 and
was constantly in demand as a preacher at funerals and ordinations.
His voluminous writings show clearly that over the years he immersed himself in those doctrines which, as a boy, he had begun to
learn in Northamptonshire.

The authority of John Gill among Particular Baptists was, said
Ivimey, virtually 'oracular'.[39] Moreover, he was a formidable controversialist. Augustus Toplady wrote about Gill that

> ... what was said of Edward the Black Prince, That he never
> fought a battle, which he did not win; what has been remarked of the
> great Duke of Marlborough, That he never undertook a siege, which

he did not carry; may be justly accommodated to our great philoso-
pher and divine: who, so far as the distinguishing doctrines of the
gospel are concerned, never besieged an error, which he did not
force from its strong holds; nor ever encountered an adversary,
whom he did not baffle and subdue.[40]

But Robert Hall junior complained to the Welshman Christmas
Evans (1766-1838) about Gill's works that, if they were written in
Evans's mother tongue he would have been spared from reading
what he considered to be 'a continent of mud'.[41]

It is arguable that Gill did, in fact, write too much; originality seems
at times to be half-buried by repetition. In defence of Gill, it might be
said that, although his sentences are frequently long, his style is clear
and concise. His writings show that he always took pains to understand
and assess his opponents' positions as fairly as possible.[42]

A good example of Gill's preaching is contained in a funeral
address for one of his deacons and a messenger from his church to
the Baptist Fund, John Davenport, when Gill was fifty-seven years
of age. In addressing the bereaved family and others, Gill exhorted:
'Attend the means of grace, and may the Lord call you by it, in due
time, that you may fear and serve your father's God, and fill up his
place in the world and the church.'[43] It might be that Gill was
inhibited by emotion and so did not express himself freely. On the
other hand, Ivimey asked: 'Is this preaching Christ *the hope of glory*,
as Paul did?'[44] We might contrast Gill unfavourably with our earlier
citation from a funeral sermon by John Piggott, as also with George
Whitefield when pleading on one occasion with young people:

> But I must not forget the lambs of the flock. — To feed them was
> one of my Lord's last commands. — I know he will be angry with me,
> if I do not tell them, that the Lord may be their righteousness; and that
> of such is the kingdom of heaven. — Come then, ye little children,
> come to Christ; the Lord Christ shall be your righteousness. — Do not
> think, that you are too young to be converted. — Perhaps many of you
> may be nine or ten years old, and yet cannot say the Lord is our
> righteousness; which many have said, though younger than you. —
> Come, then, while you are young. — Perhaps you may not live to be
> old — Do not stay for other people. — If your fathers and mothers will
> not come to Christ, do you come without them.[45]

In fairness, it might be added that Whitefield did not find favour
with everybody. The somewhat erratic John Martin (1741-1820)

John Gill (1697-1771); a portrait reproduced by courtesy of the
Metropolitan Tabernacle, London

Dear Brother

I need not tell you that I have been some years past engaged in writing on exposition of ye new Testament which is now just finishing, & thro' ye sollicitations of my friends, I have printed proposals for ye publication of it, some of which I here send you by which you will see yt ye work is large & heavy, & will require all ye assistance my friend, can give me & the whole strength of our interest to get it out into ye world; but inasmuch as nothing of this kind has been done by any of our denomination, & such a work seems necessary both for minist-ers & private christians, that they may have something to have recourse to in their own way; it may be hoped that our friends will exert themselves in giving cheerfull assistance & encouragement to it; I send these proposals to you because I dont know ye brother, nor his name who ministers to our friends at northampton & I doubt not but you will get me all ye service you can, if you think fit you may send one of ye specimens to Dr Doddridge, & spread some of ye proposals among the pupils. what subscriptions may be obtained, in either way of subscribing, proposed, be pleased to send to me with ye names of ye subscribers, in convenient time afforn as you can. I hope you are in health both in soul & body I wish you much of ye divine presence & ye discoveries of ye love of God to you: you will excuse brevity in writing, having much of this work upon my hands, who am your

affectionate friend &
Brother in X
John Gill

London Jan. 28th 1744-5.

Facsimile of a letter from Dr Gill to Mr Yeomans of
Northampton, 1744

travelled to London from Spalding in Lincolnshire to learn, as he wrote in his autobiography, published more than twenty years before he died, 'that part of the watch business which is called finishing'.[46] In the event, he was more eager to sit under the feet of Gill than attend other preachers. He wrote concerning the Kettering man:

> Having found out his meeting, I kept closely by him while I staid in Town. Occasionally, indeed, I heard Mr. Whitfield, and some other popular preachers, but none of them pleased me so well as the Doctor. His discourses were more evangelical, better studied, and argued, and, as I thought, much more consistent, than those which I heard at the Tabernacle.[47]

It should be said that Martin was always something of an odd man out and could be calculated to have made an observation like this. He was, for example, a person who 'rendered himself obnoxious to his brethren in the ministry by his unkind misrepresentations of their political sentiments', according to Ivimey.[48]

Somewhat of a recluse, Gill never met his people overmuch. Always punctilious in the performance of his pastoral duties, men were converted through a ministry which extended over half a century. He held firmly to the reins of office until the end. Ivimey recalled an incident which was said to have happened during the last two years of Gill's life. It seems that when the suggestion of a co-pastor was raised because some younger folk were leaving for other churches, Gill retorted that, according to Ephesians, chapter four, some are appointed as pastors, but not, apparently, as co-pastors.[49] His tenacious retention of office was due, commented Ivimey tartly, either to the fact that the Doctor was in his dotage or that he allowed himself to be influenced by an improper selfishness.[50] What, then, could have been said about other Baptist ministers of the time in the light of the remark of Gill's successor, John Rippon, to the pastorate in 1773. He reported that Gill, when he learned of the death of his mother, gave up pipe-smoking. Commented Rippon darkly, in defence of Gill, that prior to his bereavement, '*he*' (note Rippon's italics) 'never disgraced himself as a great smoker.'[51] When his wife passed away in 1764 at the age of sixty-eight, Dr Gill in his funeral address for her referred once only to his loss, and this in the most indirect way. It had been so, too, when he lost his twelve-year-old daughter some twenty-six years before. It seems that just before her death she asked her father about baptism and communion. The girl was told that her salvation did not 'depend upon' the ordinances. So, 'persons may be saved without them, through the grace of Christ, who have not an opportunity of submitting to them.'[52] While not desiring to appear indelicate, we should like to know why it was that Ivimey did not record that the father actually encouraged his daughter to believe in the Saviour. No doubt he did so.

It is possible that Gill might have had some indirect influence upon the division between John Wesley and Whitefield. In 1740 came Wesley's notorious sermon 'Free Grace'. At the time, Wesley seems to have read some of John Gill's writings. It was certainly the high-Calvinist view which Wesley attacked in the printed sermon. With ruthless logic he tore into what might appear to have been Gill's brand of Calvinism. According to Toplady, Wesley had once remarked to him concerning Gill: 'He is a positive man, and fights for his own opinions through thick and thin.'[53] At any rate, Whitefield soon wrote to Wesley, begging him 'for CHRIST's sake, if possible, dear Sir, never speak against election in your sermons'.[54]

In 1752 Gill published *The Doctrine of the Saints' Final Perseverance* in answer to Wesley's *Serious Thoughts on the perseverance of the saints*. Gill noted about the Methodist that 'sometimes he is for free-will, sometimes for free-grace; sometimes for resistible, and sometimes for irresistible grace',[55] and that, with respect to Wesley's repudiation of predestination,

> This is an article agreeable to the Scripture; an article of his own church; an article which he as a true son of the church, has treacherously departed from; an article which Mr. *Wesley* must have *subscribed* and *sworn* to; an article which will stare him in the face for as long as *subscriptions* and *oaths* stand for any thing with him.[56]

It might be that John Gill, great scholar and divine that he was, has been the target of more harsh and even malicious criticism than any other English Baptist of similar attainments.[57] Joseph Ivimey, indeed, seems to have taken every possible opportunity to attack the Southwark pastor.[58] So, for example, the nineteenth-century historian came to the conclusion that 'it appears, that neither the Doctor, nor his brethren, Messrs. Skepp or Brine, had so learned Christ as Paul and Peter had understood him'.[59]

Andrew Fuller, in his definitive work *The Gospel Worthy of All Acceptation*, first published in 1785, smote high Calvinism hip and thigh, yet treated Gill far more leniently than he did John Brine and

Lewis Wayman, both classic high Calvinists of the earlier part of the eighteenth century. Perhaps Fuller, who lived nearer to Gill's time, was a touch more perceptive than later writers, permitting us a degree of reserve when we come to Ivimey's castigations. It is not to be denied that there are some remarks of Gill which, when taken in isolation, appear to reject the truth that saving faith is the duty of all who hear the gospel.[60] On the other hand, Gill sometimes implies that trust in Christ for salvation is indeed the responsibility of such people, whether or not they are spiritually renewed. This point will be considered below.[61]

* * *

We should return to John Brine, born into a poor family in Kettering in 1703, six years after Gill's birth. This outstanding man never went to school. Converted under the ministry of Gill, Brine became in 1730 the pastor at Curriers' Hall, Cripplegate, where Ann Dutton was a member and where, we have noted, Skepp had formerly laboured. Brine, not unexpectedly, cultivated a particular friendship with Gill, and accepted Hussey's view that it was wrong to offer the grace of God to all. He contented himself with what he considered clear statements of doctrinal truth without making any application to his subjects.[62] Ivimey observed that John Brine was 'a very pious and useful minister' and 'a very considerable writer, whether the number of his publications or the ability displayed in them are considered'.[63] John Martin, however, thought that 'his delivery was not at all engaging'.[64] Ivimey cited with approval Robert Robinson of Cambridge, describing the latter as 'no mean critic, who, at the time he wrote ... was an orthodox minister'. Robinson claimed that

> ... those doctrinal Divines, who affect to discharge their office fully, by narrating and reasoning, and who reject persuasions, should not forget that reasoning is *persuasion*; and that they themselves slide almost as often as any men, into personal application, especially in discussing certain favourite points of divinity.[65]

In London John Brine took an active part in the affairs of the Particular Baptists until his death, defending, as we have observed, the 'strict Baptists'. John Ryland junior, ever ready to smooth over differences, said in later years about Bunhill Fields, where Brine was buried: 'There lie the ashes of the three great Johns; — John Bunyan, John Gill, and John Brine.'[66]

We quote from Brine's *The certain Efficacy of the Death of Christ asserted*, which appeared in 1743 in response to a publication by Isaac Watts. In commenting upon John 3:18, 'He that believeth on him is not condemned: but he that believeth not is condemned already, because he hath not believed in the name of the only begotten Son of God,' Brine observed:

> It is one Thing, to say that Punishment will certainly be inflicted on such as believe not, and another, that it is the Want of Faith, which demerits that Punishment ... it follows, that the Want of Faith, is the Cause of Men's lying under the *sentential* Curse and Condemnation of the Law; this is expressed by the Particle ALREADY, in which lies the Emphasis of the Words; But from this, it is not to be apprehended, that the *Want* of Faith *demerits* the Punishment threatned.[67]

The word 'demerit' meant 'deserve'. Brine did not, in context, seem to have given due weight to the latter part of John 3:18 and verses 19 to 21. He appeared to assume that lack of faith is the instrumental cause rather than the basis of condemnation, just as, conversely, faith is the instrument, but never the ground, of salvation. He took no account of verse 19, which asserts that the condemnation of men is based upon their deliberate rejection of 'the light', Christ, and this because their deeds are evil. This affirmation is surely only another way of saying that unbelief, while admittedly symptomatic, is in itself positively sinful and blameworthy. The impression given is that John Brine was more the besieged servant of an enclosed and slightly synthetic theological system than a candid expositor of Scripture. He wrote: 'As no Man can receive evangelical Consolations, until he sees his Need of Christ, and Salvation by him; So *none* have a right to those Consolations, before they are the Subjects of such Convictions.'[68]

*   *   *

Later in the eighteenth century high Calvinism was to be criticized by some in the Particular Baptist constituency. The renowned Abraham Booth, pastor for thirty-seven years at Little Prescott Street, Goodman's Fields, wrote on the subject. Concerning Booth, William Newman said that 'such a degree of majesty attended him ... you could not help feeling that you had a prince or a great man in the house'.[69] Booth was a soul-winner; he was heard on one occasion to affirm of ministers that 'our great business is ... to preach the gospel of God, and to watch for the souls of men. ... To entertain and to please, are the design of an actor on the stage, not of a minister in his pulpit.'[70]

In his *Glad Tidings to Perishing Sinners* Booth asserted:

> To contend, indeed, that regeneration must be prior to faith, and to justification, is like maintaining, That the elect son of a nobleman must partake of the human nature, before he can have that filial relation with his father ... human nature, derived from his parents, and the relation of a son, being completely of the same date; there is no such thing as priority, or posteriority, respecting them ... Thus it is, I conceive, with regard to regeneration, faith in Christ, and justification before God.[71]

This meant that, as Booth saw it, the sinner may believe even when he possessed no awareness whatever that the Spirit was leading him to faith.

At this point there was some disagreement between Booth and Andrew Fuller. Fuller, pastor from 1783 until 1815 of a Particular Baptist church in Kettering, John Gill's home town, and of a mind other than Gill on many matters, wrote that 'a sinner ... *cannot actually* come to Christ for life, while he is unwilling'. According to Fuller, it was here that Abraham Booth was somewhat confusing. The latter wrote, for example, that 'no holiness is necessary to *coming* to Christ, any more than to *warrant* our coming'. 'If so,' commented Fuller dryly, 'faith must be an act of an ungodly mind.'[72] In other words, Fuller considered that regeneration makes faith possible, although 'a *consciousness* of holiness is not necessary to coming to Christ.'[73] As we might imagine, he was not really so very far from Booth at this point; both men held that a realisation of having been born again is not necessary for a sinner when he turns to the Lord.

Abraham Booth emphasized admirably the truth that regeneration is inextricably associated with preaching: the elect are born again by means of incorruptible seed, the Word of God (1 Peter 1:23). Then, the reality of rebirth, even though the sinner might not be aware that he has been born a second time, inevitably leads to faith in the proclaimed Christ. Booth cited, for example, the Puritan Stephen Charnock (1628-80): 'The gospel is the instrument whereby God brings the soul forth in a new birth.'[74]

With regard to the classic high Calvinists of a somewhat earlier time, such as Hussey, neither Gill nor Brine produced a treatise specifically to defend the 'no-offers-of-grace' theology,[75] although it was a belief which all three held. Gill wrote in opposition to Wesley:

> And that there are universal offers of grace and salvation made to all men I utterly deny; nay, I deny that they are made to any; no, not to God's elect; grace and salvation are provided for them in the everlasting covenant ... published and revealed in the gospel, and applied by the Spirit.[76]

He then remarked caustically:

> Till it is proved that there are such universal offers, then Dr. *Watts's* reasoning on that head, will require some attention, but not till then.[77]

Surely, Dr Gill was absolutely right at this point. He believed that the initial act of election, from which the final salvation of the church must issue, was, as he expressed it elsewhere, an 'act of grace'.[78] That is, the grace of God infallibly conveys salvation; it should not be interpreted as the possible experience of being redeemed. So, even if something is to be 'offered', let it never be the grace of God. Nevertheless, without denying the churches' duty to carry the gospel to all men so that they will be saved, we ask if Gill was not, perhaps, somewhat misleading when he taught that salvation (as distinct from 'grace') should never be offered. Rather, when a preacher properly urges all his hearers, some of whom may not be among the elect, to trust in Christ, he will do so with the promise that forgiveness of sins is given to all who do repent and believe.

The incisive remark of Andrew Fuller concerning Gill's refutation of the belief that repentance and faith are duties for the non-elect is interesting. Gill, he thought, 'in general, opposed those principles; yet frequently, when his system was out of sight, he established them'.[79]

* * *

Among the Particular Baptists the high Calvinism of Hussey and Brine took deep hold for many years. Clendon Dawkes might be taken as one example of the way in which the tendency worked itself out in the churches.

Dawkes, who has appeared already in the strict-communion controversy,[80] became in 1735 pastor of a church which twenty-seven years earlier had moved to Pinners' Hall, filling the vacancy created by the departure of Isaac Watts's Independent congregation. They assembled on Sunday afternoons only until 1723-4, when they moved yet again, this time to Devonshire Square. As mentioned in an earlier chapter, they met here on Sunday mornings and after-noons alternately.[81] These people are not to be confused with the Devonshire Square church established by William Kiffin on the same site as early as 1640. The latter congregation continued until 1727. Then, to benefit from a substantial legacy to be received by another Particular Baptist church, that at Turners' Hall, the one hundred and fifty-eight members at Devonshire Square dissolved their church state to amalgamate with the former congregation. This act of dissolution was described scathingly by Ivimey as an act of suicide initiated by timid and worldly-minded deacons unwilling to guarantee a salary for a minister of their own. The new, united, church continued to use the Devonshire Square premises for many years.[82] So it transpired that for some while the building was host to two quite separate Particular Baptist congregations meeting at different times on the Lord's day. By 1751 Dawkes's ministry was perceived to have been without notable success; either then or, perhaps, ten years later, the church dissolved itself.[83]

Dawkes moved to Hemel Hempstead, where he died. John Brine, who preached his funeral sermon, referred to Dawkes's 'enlarged Acquaintance, with the evangelical Scheme, and a spiritual Savour, of the Truths of the Gospel', which probably meant an affinity with his own views.[84] Ivimey remarked about the sermon that it would have been pleasant had Brine been able to say something of the effect of Dawkes's 'enlarged' understanding in the 'enlarging' of his congregation in London. This, according to Ivimey, 'under his hands ... soon became extinct'.[85] Ivimey laid some stress upon 'soon'. He proceeded to observe that John Brine's own church 'gradually degenerated in purity of sentiment, and declined in numbers, till it too ranked with the dissolved churches'.[86]

Happily, decline was not the experience of all high Calvinists; some did preach the truth to perishing sinners and were blessed for their labours. For example, John Noble (1659-1730) was followed by Samuel Dew, who died in the 1760s, in the pastorate of the then-prosperous congregation meeting at Tallow Chandlers' Hall. Noble

knew how to preach, whereas Dew did not. In consequence, the
latter was destined to preside over the falling away of his people.
Discouraged by losses and unable to renew the lease on their
premises in 1760, they dissolved their church-state. Most of the
people, Samuel Dew included, joined John Gill's congregation. A
generation earlier, John Noble had been, wrote Ivimey, 'precisely of
the sentiments of those worthy men, Skepp, and Brine, and Gill, and
of many in our own time; who ... are opposed to the general
invitations of the gospel'.[87] In Noble's time the church grew. Edward
Wallin, by no means a high Calvinist, yet invited by Noble's church
to preach the funeral sermon for their late pastor, said:

> He well knew how to lay open the miserable case of sinners by
> nature, and preach full and free salvation to such by Christ alone, in
> a very plain and affecting manner.[88]

Clearly, there were considerable differences of approach among
the high Calvinists. Dew's only published sermon was that preached
at the funeral of Mrs Mary Bevois. Practically the only encouragement in it to the bereaved was a bare repetition of the text, John 6:27-
9, which exhorts men not to labour for the food which perishes, but
to believe in Christ. Ivimey's assessment of Dew's ministry was that
he urged men to

> ... use the means which God has appointed; hear the gospel
> preached, in which Christ is revealed as the object of faith, and by
> which men are instructed in the way of salvation.[89]

He remarked that Mr Noble 'preached the doctrines of sovereign
and distinguishing grace, spiritually, experimentally, and practically; and the other [Samuel Dew], systematically, speculatively,
and controversially'.[90] This seems to be why the sheep drifted away.

CHAPTER IX
JOHN GILL AND FAITH

No study of the eighteenth-century English Particular Baptists would be complete without a review of elements of the high Calvinism of John Gill. Basically, Dr Gill was a 'systematic theologian'. That is to say, as a Bible teacher, the Southwark pastor spent much of his time in arranging or systematizing the central truths of Scripture as he saw them. John Calvin (1509-64), as also the Particular Baptists who published their confession in 1689, had done this, and there have been many others. Because Gill wrestled with the connection between divine sovereignty in saving sinners and men's responsibility in responding to the gospel, the meaning of faith, in particular, occupied his attention.

* * *

Gill insisted that faith, understood as assent to the facts of the gospel, is an exercise demanded by God from all who hear; we ought to believe what we are told. In discussing John 6:37, 'All that the Father giveth me shall come to me; and him that cometh to me I will in no wise cast out,' Gill commented that the Jews could be 'reasonably accused' for not believing in Jesus as the Messiah, even though none but those among them whom the Father had given to the Son would ever trust the Lord 'to the saving of their souls'. And, added Gill,

> ... even not coming to Christ, and believing in him, in this spiritual manner, when he is revealed in the external ministry of the word ... is criminal and blameworthy, notwithstanding men's want of both will and power; since this does not arise from any decree of God, but from the corruption of nature through sin.[1]

This may seem surprising in the light of what has been said already about Gill and high Calvinism. In point of fact, such is the vastness of Gill's writings that it is not always easy to pinpoint what Gill thought exactly about some matters, this included.

For Gill, the sinner's inability to believe, a central dogma of main-line Calvinism, appears in the passage quoted as wicked rather than natural and innocent. Let's look at this distinction from the point of view of traditional (not 'high') Calvinism. The difference between things which are 'wicked' and things which are 'natural' might be illustrated in the following way. Because men were not created with wings so that they could fly, their inability to imitate the birds (apart from building aeroplanes) remains a blameless rather than a self-imposed and unlawful limitation; it is not their fault. But it is quite another matter with unbelief. Whereas the total inability of men to fly is perfectly natural, their age-old inability to believe, apart from God's grace, has always been unnatural and evil, a direct consequence of Satan's successful temptation of Adam and Eve. Men never trust the revealed truths of God because, a long time ago, in Adam, they rebelled and damaged themselves. So, their inability remains solely their fault. This self-inflicted wound to the heart was an iniquity: 'all have sinned' (Romans 5:12). Paul was referring to that which all mankind did in the person of Adam. It followed that even non-elect Jews who heard Christ were in the wrong when they did not trust him for their salvation. Gill, as quoted above, was absolutely right.

Further, that which is blameworthy must be a neglect of duty (1 John 3:4, 'for sin is the transgression of the law'). Correctly enough, Gill implied that saving faith is a responsibility incumbent upon all who hear the gospel. In fact, his writings seldom focussed upon this truth, usually drawing a distinction between 'evangelical' and 'legal' repentance. So:

> Evangelical repentance is not in the power of a natural man, but is the gift of God's free grace. Legal repentance may be performed by particular persons, who are destitute of the grace of God, and by all the inhabitants of a place, as the *Ninevites*, who repented externally at the preaching of *Jonah*; though it does not appear that they had received the grace of God, since destruction afterwards came upon that city for its iniquities.[2]

Gill properly emphasized that when the gospel is preached it should never include the assertion that Christ died for all men, that is, for the reprobate together with the elect.[3] But his application of this truth was less satisfactory. The 'external' revelation of the gospel tells out the glorious truth that they who believe in Christ must be saved. Nevertheless, only when the Spirit convinces a gospel-hearer of his lost state should he be encouraged to believe savingly in Christ.[4] This the renewed sinner may and will do on the ground that he now has an interest in Christ; it has been revealed to him by the Spirit that Christ died for him personally.[5]

It is just at this point that we arrive at one of the most puzzling features of Gill's idea of faith. In discussing John 5:34, 'but these things I say, that ye might be saved,' Gill denied emphatically that Christ intended seriously to save some who, in the event, were not saved.[6] We would suggest that the Doctor's exegesis ignored the element of mystery in John 5 (and elsewhere). He proceeded upon the view that the text and context of John 5:34 may very well refer to the temporal preservation of the nation rather than to the eternal salvation of individuals within it. Gill cut through the problem rather than endeavouring to unravel it.

Such an interpretation is dubious, given the thrust of the chapter. Take, for example, John 5:24, according to which he who hears the word of Christ 'shall not come into condemnation; but is passed from death unto life', while John 5:39 is concerned with the quest for 'eternal life' rather than national security. The fact would appear to be that Gill was at odds with himself. He was utterly dominated by the view that because saving faith is an imposed gift from the triune God it cannot be a demand. It is true, of course, that he did in a way maintain that inability to believe does not cancel responsibility to do so, and at times taught almost explicitly that trust in Christ for salvation is nothing less than a duty incumbent upon all who hear about salvation. To repeat, he usually distinguished between 'legal' and 'evangelical' repentance and faith to prove that men are not required to believe in order to be saved.

* * *

The fundamental differentiation between 'evangelical' and 'legal' repentance often comes to the surface in Gill's treatment of those passages in the Bible which urge men to turn to God. For example, with respect to Ezekiel 18:30-1, which urges Israel to 'repent ... cast away from you all your transgressions ... and make you a new heart and a new spirit', Gill insisted that Israel in exile was exhorted by the prophet to a 'national' repentance, 'for national iniquities, and to prevent national judgments'.[7] Concerning the apparent demand by Ezekiel that they should renew their hearts, Gill, characteristically, considered that these words 'may be designed to convince men of their want of one [a new heart] ... and so be the means ... of his elect enjoying this blessing'.[8] On balance, Gill preferred to believe that many of the initial addressees of the house of Israel were regenerate, the exhortation not referring to 'the first work of renovation'.[9] His argument was weak. While it is true that God alone can create a new heart and a new spirit (so, Ezekiel 11:19), the exhortation was surely designed to convince the unregenerate person of his need to turn to God for help. John 3:3,5 are similar in meaning. It does appear that the idea of 'national judgments' was superimposed by Gill upon the text in the interests of his general scheme. The Israel addressed by Ezekiel was already suffering a catastrophic judgement, that of exile. The prophet's cry was for something more radical than social reformation. We might compare Ezekiel with Jeremiah's earlier ministry in the Jerusalem of King Josiah. Jeremiah did, in fact, witness an external reformation, yet this did not suffice him. Judah had returned to the Lord, though not 'with her whole heart, but feignedly' (Jeremiah 3:10). Ezekiel, too, was concerned with more than orthodoxy.

Gill's treatment of Acts 3:19, 'Repent ye, therefore, and be converted,' was equally tortuous. Insisting again that repentance is either 'legal' or 'evangelical', Gill asserted, rightly, that this passage does not suppose repentance and conversion to lie in the power of men.[10] Less surely, he went on to claim that 'the conversion here pressed unto us, is not an internal conversion of the soul to God, which is the work of almighty power; but an outward reformation of life'.[11] Again, Gill does not convince us. So,

> ... if therefore evangelical repentance and internal conversion were here intended, it would only prove that the persons spoken to were without them, stood in need of them ... and therefore ought to apply to God for them.[12]

This seems right. But why did Gill refer to 'evangelical repentance' as no more than a possible interpretation? Does the apostle Peter summon his conscience-smitten audience to true conversion in Acts 2, only to call his hearers in Acts 3 to a mere outward reformation, a reformation which would have involved the dangerous recognition that Jesus is the Messiah, yet falling short of a baptismal confession of Christ as Lord? Acts 4:4 shows that the address recorded in Acts 3 led to the addition of some two thousand souls to the newly-born church. Supposing Gill's approach to have been correct, namely, that Peter was only aiming at an outward reformation, the apostle's ministry achieved more than he thought possible or even desirable.

According to Dr Gill, Paul's exhortation to the Athenians to repentance (Acts 17) means at most that

> ... it is both the duty and interest of men to repent, and turn to God, that they may have a discovery of the remission of their sins through the blood of Christ, and not that they shall hereby procure and obtain the thing itself.[13]

Gill meant that the sinner who turns to God will discover wonderfully that he has been forgiven.[14] Nevertheless, no man is required to turn to God in order to be forgiven, and this because 'forgiveness of sin is indeed only manifested to converted penitent sinners'.[15] The argument lacks strength. What is the difference between calling upon men indiscriminately to turn to God so that they might discover that their sins have been forgiven and urging them to repent in order to 'procure the thing itself'? Gill denied the equation, of course, because he did not believe that God issues a serious call to the non-elect.[16] To do so would be 'unsuitable to his wisdom and sincerity'.[17] Gill denied rightly enough that prayer should be made by Christian people for the salvation of all men 'collectively'.[18] Further, and more controversially, 'for those who shall not be saved, salvation was not purchased, nor should it be offered to them, nor indeed to any.'[19] We ask: does the premiss about the limited atonement demand this negative conclusion about evangelism? Further, with regard to reprobates, was Gill right concerning 'evangelical' repentance and faith in declaring that 'it will be difficult to prove, that God requires these things of them'?[20]

To some extent Gill deserves his readers' sympathy, bearing in mind that he lived through the Methodist revival, the theology of which was scarcely reformed. So, concerning the Jews who did not believe in Jesus,

... nor were they, nor are any, condemned for not believing that Christ died for them, but for the transgressions of the law of God, and the disbelief or contempt of his gospel.[21]

True. But was not Gill off the track in appearing to make a general call to saving faith depend upon the erroneous belief that Christ died for all who hear the gospel? He assumed that only if Christ died for all men must all be required to believe savingly in him. Conversely, Gill believed that if Christ had not died for all Adam's children there should be no promiscuous call to saving faith: why should men be told to believe in a Saviour who possibly did not love them and had not suffered for them specifically? Instead, there should be a simple call to outward reformation ('legal repentance'). Only thus did Gill cope with the general exhortations to repentance found in Scripture.

*   *   *

It needs to be emphasized again that the heart of the issue for Gill was not that of any incompatibility between a man's unwillingness to believe God's revelation in Christ and his responsibility to do so; it is probable that Gill found little difficulty in this area. Rather, he considered pardon as an unconditional gift of God, bestowed infallibly upon the elect. This is why salvation was not even to be proffered to those perceived to be elect, let alone to others:

> God never calls persons to evangelical repentance, or requires them to believe in Christ to the saving of their souls, but he gives them that special grace, and puts forth that divine energy which enables them to believe and repent.[22]

To repeat, Gill was right to teach that it is no sin for unbelievers if they do not accept that Christ died for them personally. Rather, they will be judged for 'the contempt of his gospel'.[23] But, what is 'contempt'? We ask: how can Christ be treated with contempt by evil men if they are not required first to believe certain truths about the Saviour, principally that he died as the great sin-bearer, and then, on the basis of what they now accept, to come to him personally for salvation? Martha, sister of Mary and Lazarus, knew the reality of this (John 11:25-7), as did those Christians in Rome who had 'obeyed from the heart' the pattern of teaching to which they had been delivered (Romans 6:17).

Perhaps Gill worked backwards, as it were. Because effectual calling generates faith, the gospel becomes 'the power of God unto salvation' (Romans 1:16).[24] Because God's call is decreed, it is inevitable and irresistible. Gill perceived no necessity for any man to believe in Christ. Dominated completely by his own interpretation of the application of sovereign grace, Gill rejected the view that mortal man can be required to appropriate salvation. Again, we ask: was Gill right in holding that the Bible does not require all who hear the gospel to turn to Christ? He theorized rather than expounded. The fact is that Gill did believe in a universal responsibility to obey at the very least 'the law and light of nature'.[25] This implied a universal duty to obey the fuller revelation of Jesus Christ by yielding the obedience of faith (Romans 1:5, 16:26). In reality, his writings tended to redefine faith, and it is here that they seem to have departed from Scripture. For Gill, people convicted of their sinfulness were not to be summoned to trust in Christ. The reason for this was that their eternal destiny did not rest upon faith. Quite simply, as born-again Christians, they became aware of their blessed state; they did not enter into it for the first time. This perception was at the heart of Gill's theology and ministry.

CHAPTER X
JOHN GILL AND ETERNAL JUSTIFICATION

Another main feature of John Gill's interpretation of Calvinism was the doctrine of 'eternal justification', a doctrine which dovetailed into his idea of faith. A sermon issued in 1762 entitled 'The Doctrine of Justification by the Righteousness of Christ, Stated and Maintained',[1] from which most of the following quotations are taken, dealt with the subject in detail.

Gill defined 'eternal justification' as

> ... an act in God, all whose acts in him are eternal; that this is the grand original sentence of justification; of which that pronounced on Christ, as our representative, when he rose from the dead, and that which is pronounced by the Spirit of God in the consciences of believers, as well as that which will be pronounced before men and angels, at the general judgment, are no other than so many repetitions, or renewed declarations; that this includes the whole complete *esse* of justification.[2]

Further, to quote Gill, 'justification is a pronouncing a person righteous according to law, as though he had never sinned.'[3] This was quite correct, yet Gill did not stop there. For him there was a distinction between what he termed 'active' and 'passive' justification:

> Active justification is God's act, it is God that justifies; passive justification is the same act, terminating on the conscience of the believer; active justification is strictly and properly justification, passive justification is improperly so; active justification precedes faith, passive justification is by faith.[4]

This view of the relation between justification, both 'active' and 'passive', and conversion was exhibited consistently in Gill's works over a period of some forty years. If we might repeat from the previous chapter, the idea, stripped to its skeleton, was that at their conversions the elect do not enter into a state of justification. Rather, they come to a new perception: they are given a blessed awareness that they had always been and always will be justified in the sight of God, and this because of their eternal union with Christ their Surety.

> We see the sun shining in its brightness, but did it not exist before, it could not be visible to us; the same observation we hold good in ten thousand other instances. Faith is the hand which receives the blessing of justification from the Lord, and righteousness ... but then this blessing must exist before faith can receive it.[5]

The justification of the believer was declared by God to himself before the world began: 'It is an eternal, immanent act in God.'[6] This conviction led to what must be to the uninitiated a quite astounding declaration:

> God does not justify any because they believe in Christ ... A man is not more justified after faith, than he is before faith, in God's account.[7]

And, with regard to faith:

> Nor is it *causa sine qua non*, or that without which a man cannot be justified in the sight of God ... all God's elect are justified in his sight, and in his account, before faith; and if before faith, then without it.[8]

It goes without saying, of course, that Gill was absolutely right in holding that the New Testament does not teach that a Christian is justified 'because' he believes. However, does not the Bible teach that the child of God is justified before God and by God only when he believes (so, Galatians 2:16)? Is it not true that even if, as Gill said, faith is not the 'cause' of our justification, it is nevertheless the necessary means by which the sinner is actually justified? The Christian is saved because of Christ, yet, equally, he is saved through faith (Ephesians 2:8). Gill denied the latter assertion; for him, faith was not even the 'efficient cause', that is, the instrument or means of justification.[9] This is doubtful. Would Paul, for instance, have told the Galatians that God's elect are justified 'without' faith? John Gill was, of course, far from being a heretic. Nor was he strictly unorthodox. Nevertheless, the fact that he was a truly great man and a defender of the faith does not prevent the suggestion that there were serious defects in this area of Gill's teaching.

With respect to Galatians 2:16, 'Even we have believed in Jesus Christ that we might be justified by the faith of Christ.' Gill claimed:

> Here the apostle is speaking of justification, as it terminates upon the conscience of a believer; and this is readily granted to follow faith, and to be a consequent of it.[10]

Apparently, Gill assumed that the apostle Paul, too, believed in a distinction between 'active' and 'passive' justification. Let us accept this supposition for the sake of the argument. So, on such a construction, Paul writes that elect sinners, when led to renounce the 'works of the law', turn to Christ to experience for themselves the joy of a justification which had always been theirs; it was theirs even when they had been cursed by God for their sins. The unsophisticated student of John Gill might, perhaps, be forgiven if he asks how it is that any of the elect could be convinced that when unbelievers they had been cursed by the law yet were in a state of actual justification. The student might be forgiven, too, should he conclude that here Gill is difficult and, arguably, quite impossible.

We doubt, too, that Paul differentiated between 'active' and 'passive' justification.

* * *

Gill's explanations of specific texts in defence of eternal justification were sometimes weak. Concerning Romans 8:1, 'There is therefore now no condemnation to them which are in Christ Jesus, who walk not after the flesh, but after the Spirit,' he wrote:

> Justification is not only before faith, but it is from eternity, being an immanent act in the divine mind and so an internal and eternal one: as may be concluded ... if they bore this character of elect from eternity, or were chosen in Christ before the world began; then they must be acquitted, discharged, and justified so early ... for *there is no condemnation to them which are in Christ*, Rom. viii.1; and therefore must be considered as righteous, and so justified.[11]

The point here is that it is just possible that Gill, an acute scholar who seldom missed much, misquoted Paul to suit his own exposition. To repeat, the apostle actually wrote: 'There is therefore now no condemnation to them which are in Christ Jesus.' Notwithstanding the eternal union between Christ and the elect, Paul apparently makes the assertion that 'now', that is, since faith was born, they who were elect are not condemned. Before they came to faith the elect had, in fact, been condemned and were far from being in a state of justification; 'now' it is not so. Gill dropped 'now', a most important little word which implies quite clearly the believer's transfer from condemnation to justification. A keen controversialist, Gill could hardly have let 'now' slip accidentally; his omission would seem to have served an interest.

An even more glaring weakness in his defence of eternal justification is to be discerned in Gill's references to the saints of the previous dispensation:

> It deserves regard and attention, that the saints under the Old Testament, were justified by the same righteousness of Christ, as those under the New, and that before the sacrifice was offered up, the satisfaction given, and the everlasting righteousness brought in; for Christ's blood was shed for the remission of sins that were past, and his death was for the redemption of transgressions under the first Testament, Rom. iii.25; Heb. ix.15, Now if God could, and actually did, justify some, three or four thousand years before the righteousness of Christ was actually wrought out, taking his Son's word and bond as their Surety, and in a view of his future righteousness; why could he not, and why may it not be thought he did, justify all his elect from eternity, upon the word and bond of their Surety, and on the foot of his future righteousness; which he had engaged to work out, and which he full well knew he would most certainly work out? and if there is no difficulty in conceiving of the one, there can be none in conceiving of the other.[12]

We might ask, what of the eleventh chapter of the Epistle to the Hebrews? This chapter teaches in the clearest possible fashion that the saints who lived before the first advent of Christ were justified by or through faith; for the 'fathers' and the 'elders' (Hebrews 1:1, 11:2) faith was indispensable to salvation. So, for example, by means of faith Abel obtained witness that he was righteous (Hebrews 11:4). In Gill's terminology, of course, Abel would have experienced 'passive justification' and did so through the medium of 'faith'. In reality, the chapter tells us that the justification of those of the elect who lived before the turn of the ages was not owing to a notional doctrine of eternal justification, but was 'by faith'. In failing to introduce the eleventh of Hebrews, Dr Gill's argument would appear to collapse.

A further weakness in Gill's defence of eternal justification surfaced in his misinterpretation of 2 Timothy 2:13, 'If we believe not, yet he abideth faithful: he cannot deny himself.' In writing that 'a man is as much justified before as after it [faith], in the account of God', Gill added: 'After he does believe, his justification does not depend on his acts of faith; for though *we believe not, yet he abides faithful*; that is, God is faithful to his covenant engagements with his Son, as their Surety.'[13] We disagree. In the words of William Hendriksen, 'if Christ failed to remain faithful to his threat as well as to his promise, he would be denying *himself*.'[14] In short, Paul's words have nothing whatever to do with 'covenant engagements'; they concern that which will happen to spurious believers who deny the faith they once professed. Gill's argument only served to weaken his position.

* * *

In his presentation of eternal justification Gill employed the illustration of a royal pardon being issued to a condemned criminal. Receiving by faith the righteousness of the Saviour, the soul

> ... is set at liberty, and filled *with a joy unspeakable and full of glory*. So that faith is just of the same usefulness in this respect, as a condemned malefactor's actually receiving the king's pardon into his own hand is to him; when, in consequence of this, he is not only delivered from prison and confinement, and all the miseries which attended such a state; but also freed from all those fears ... which arose from his daily expectation of just punishment.

So,

> ... though faith does not justify us, it being neither the whole, nor a part of our justifying righteousness, nor the cause or condition of our justification; yet, as it apprehends and receives Christ's righteousness for our justification, it brings much peace, joy, and comfort into our hearts.[15]

The point of the illustration seems to be that the condemned malefactor was in principle pardoned before he was made aware of the matter; the royal decree came into being before it was received by the criminal. Similarly, the elect sinner, pardoned and justified previously by virtue of his eternal union with Christ, only comes into an awareness of his state when, by the grace of God, he leans and relies on the Saviour. Real before, justification becomes real to him then.

Does such a construction correspond to the New Testament? Here we read that unbelievers, including those who are elect, are condemned 'already' (John 3:18). Their condemnation is objective, rather than (for the elect) an unenlightened fiction of the imagination. Does God ever justify a sinner before Christ is accepted by that person? Gill's metaphor is questionable.

Second, the illustration does not appear to parallel the New Testament's understanding of conversion. For example, on the Day of Pentecost all who had been convicted of their sins were told by Peter to repent and be baptized for the remission of their faults (Acts 2:38). The sorrow which they displayed on that occasion was a godly sorrow; they repented of the fact that they had been involved in the death of Jesus. It does not appear that they were sorrowful simply because of a promised judgement from God. In Gill's illustration, however, the malefactor neither exhibits nor needs to exhibit sorrow for offending the monarch. Before receiving the pardon, his sorrow would apparently not have been for sin but for the melancholy consequence of sin, a gnashing of teeth rather than tears of contrition.

The two types of sorrow are very different. The malefactor's sorrow, if any, would have been what Gill understood as 'legal' rather than 'evangelical',[16] the criminal of the illustration appearing to know nothing of the truth of 2 Corinthians 7:10, 'For godly sorrow worketh repentance to salvation ... but the sorrow of the world worketh death.' On this further count, Gill's parable seems inadequate.

*   *   *

Another problem concerning eternal justification arose from Gill's understanding of Ephesians 2:3, in which Paul asserts that believers once 'were by nature the children of wrath, even as others'. The Doctor wrote:

> God's elect may be considered under two different *Heads*; and as related to two different covenants at one and the same time. As they are the descendants of *Adam*, they are related to him, as a covenant-

head, and, and, as such, sinned in him; and, ... are all, by nature, children of wrath, even as others. But then, as considered in Christ, they were loved with an everlasting love: God chose them ... and always viewed and accounted them righteous in Christ, ... So that it is no contradiction to say, that the elect of God, as they are in *Adam*, and according to the covenant of works, are under the sentence of condemnation; and that as they are in Christ, and according to the covenant of grace, and the secret transactions thereof, they are justified and freed from all condemnation.[17]

Gill seems to have been confused at this point. He taught that before conversion elect believers were simultaneously in both a state of condemnation and a state of justification. This scenario is even more complicated than the situation of the criminal who genuinely believed that he was condemned, not knowing that he had been justified. According to Gill's treatment of Ephesians 2:3, Christians enjoy a justification which existed alongside their now cancelled condemnation, and this because they were considered 'under two different heads, Adam and Christ'. This does not seem to fit Paul's thought. Ephesians 2:3 asserts that 'we ... were by nature the children of wrath', and that condemnation has given place to justification. What others are, believers were. Their situation has changed dramatically; no longer do the wrath and curse of God hang over them.

This criticism of Gill might be directed, too, to John Brine, with whom Gill always stood. Brine had written in 1732 concerning Ephesians 2:3:

As God put the elect into Christ, or united them to him in eternal election, he views and considers them in him, and so justifies them, and takes infinite pleasure in their persons as members of the Mediator, in whom he always had the fullest satisfaction and delight; tho' they are under a sentence of condemnation by the law, as violaters of it, while in unbelief.[18]

If we try to relate such teaching to Romans 5:12-19, in which Adam and Christ are both compared and contrasted, is it possible to believe that the elect, in Gill's words, are 'related to two covenants at one and the same time'? Strictly speaking, as Andrew Fuller pointed out,[19] the unbeliever is not required to maintain the original covenant of works in order to satisfy God. As a sinner he has fallen already under the penalty of that long-since shattered command; he is cursed by that law which, in Adam, he had broken. To know peace with God he needs

another wáy, a way which, graciously, has been revealed, a 'righteousness of God without the law' (Romans 3:21). All this is in spite of the
fact that, because he remains wilfully an unbeliever, the unrepentant
sinner is still bound 'to do the whole law' (Galatians 5:3).

It follows that if, by God's grace, the curse has vanished in place of
justification, the convert will have been transferred from one situation,
that of condemnation, to another, that of imputed righteousness. It
might seem that Gill did not focus sufficiently upon the New Testament's teaching concerning the fundamental and dramatic alteration of
status brought about through faith.

The problem was intensified by Dr Gill in that he paralleled a
notional simultaneous justification and condemnation of the elect
sinner by God with a simultaneous divine justification and condemnation of Jesus at Calvary:

> Jesus Christ was the object of his Father's love and wrath at the
> same time, he sustaining two different capacities, and standing in two
> different relations, when he suffered in the room and stead of his
> people; as the Son of God he was always the object of his love; as the
> Surety of his people, bearing their sins, and suffering for them, he was
> the object of his wrath, Psalm lxxxix.38.[20]

Was this so? Does Scripture indicate that Jesus was at the time of
his sufferings the object both of divine favour and anger? At Calvary
was Jesus both beloved and cursed? Unquestionably, there is mystery
here, yet Gill's employment of the complex relationship between the
Father and the Son when our Lord was crucified, taken to buttress the
doctrine of the eternal justification of the elect, was unsubtle; the
unique experience of the God-man should not, perhaps, have been
adopted as a parallel for our own previous situation. The evidence of
the inspired record would appear to be that the Saviour who was for a
while forsaken by his Father was not at that time aware that he remained
in his Father's favour. Rather, he was absolutely certain that he had
been abandoned, even though remaining obedient to his Father's will
(Philippians 2:8). Hence the agonized question, 'Why hast thou
forsaken me?' (Matthew 27:46). God neither condemns when he
justifies nor justifies those whom he condemns.

* * *

In discoursing upon the everlasting love of God to the elect the

Doctor declared that the 'law-enmity' of God to his people was slain at Calvary. There never was 'enmity in the heart of God to his elect; that would be inconsistent with his everlasting and unchangeable love'.[21] Here is a problem, in that Gill might have differentiated unhelpfully between God and the law of God. He seems to have held that, in a legal sense, God had been hostile to us because we were law-breakers. Nevertheless, in himself he never was our enemy. This appears to mean that even though the elect had been willing transgressors they were always accounted righteous; they were justified. If this is what Gill meant, it might be that he misinterpreted the New Testament's doctrine of reconciliation.

While Scripture does teach the everlasting love of God to his people, a love that sent Jesus to die, is it correct to say, as did Gill, 'agreeably, the scriptures never speak of God's being reconciled to his elect either in eternity or in time, but of their being reconciled to him'? Was he wise to have asked the question: 'Where does the scripture ever represent the end of Christ's sufferings and death to be, to reconcile God to his elect; that is, to remove any enmity in his heart against them, or to procure for them his love and favour?'[22]

In reality, when Romans 5:11 asserts that believers have 'now received the atonement', Paul surely means, in the words of John Murray, that 'what we have received is reinstatement in the favour of God'.[23] The New Testament would seem to show clearly that one of the glorious paradoxes of the gospel consists in the fact that God regarded himself as the holy enemy of the elect, yet loved them so much that he sent his Son to die for them (Romans 5:8-10). That is, he loved those with whom he would not nor could be reconciled unless Christ died as a propitiation. It appears that Gill, rather like some more modern theologians of a liberal tendency,[24] attempted to short-circuit this complex matter by denying that the holy God was ever hostile towards his sinful though chosen people. The Doctor attempted to crash his way through a mystery, namely that those whom God always had loved were at one time the objects of a holy, personal and divine enmity.

* * *

In order to highlight the radicalism of Gill's theology we quote Benjamin Keach and Thomas Crosby, both of whom had been in the Southwark church to which Gill was called originally, and also the

Dutchman Herman Witsius (1636-1708), whose work *The Oeconomy of the Covenants between God and Man* appeared in English translation in its second edition in 1775 with a commendatory foreword by, among several others, John Gill and John Brine. Andrew Fuller and Joseph Ivimey will then have the last word.

In his delightful little volume *The Child's Delight: Or Instructions for Children and Youth*, Benjamin Keach wrote:

> Justification is an act of God's rich Grace, through the Redemption which is in Christ, wherein he freely pardoneth and acquitteth us of all our Sins, and accepteth us as Righteous, only for the sake of Christ and his Righteousness, which is imputed to us.[25]

It seems that Keach was deliberately probing a sensitive issue in his church; he sensed that not all would necessarily agree with him, such as, for example, a 'gracious' lady in his congregation who could not accept his view that the elect were under wrath 'before calling, or before they are united to Christ by the Holy Spirit'.[26] Keach, in a detailed sermon entitled 'A Medium between two Extremes', declared that others in London held to this 'mistake'. He wrote that such people '*do not carefully distinguish as they ought between our Fundamental and Virtual Justification in Christ, as our Head and Representative, and our actual and Personal Justification when we are united to him*'.[27] 'Virtual', of course, does not mean 'actual'. All this is significant in that Keach rejected the view that faith in Christ is a 'condition of our Justification': 'But how that which God himself gives to us by his free and absolute promises, can be a condition of the Covenant, or of our Justification, I see not.' Nevertheless, he was prepared to 'offer' Christ to 'all' men.[28]

He appears to have been quite clear about when it is that a sinner is actually justified. We might be allowed to wonder if Keach, although backing away from eternal justification, was not entirely uninfluenced, even confused, by the high Calvinism of the London Particular Baptists of that early period.

In a barely-concealed criticism of young Mr John Gill ('Mr', because Gill did not receive his Scots doctorate until eight years later), Thomas Crosby wrote approvingly about another Calvinist, Edward Wallin, that he

> ... did not run into those flights of *justification* before *faith* ... but with the *English Baptists* in general held, That none can be said to

be *actually* reconciled, justified, or adopted, until they are *really* implanted into Jesus Christ by faith.[29]

Herman Witsius taught that 'the satisfaction of Christ being supposed, and apprehended by faith, by which the whole righteousness of the law is fulfilled, the man is then justified', and wrote with reference to Galatians 2:16, 'the MEAN by which we receive the righteousness of Christ, and justification depending thereon, is FAITH, and that ONLY.'[30]

We believe that, in employing the words 'then' and 'depending', Witsius was nearer the mark than was Gill.

With regard to Andrew Fuller, when inducted to the Kettering pastorate in 1783, his personal confession of faith acknowledged:

> Before our believing in Christ, we are considered and treated by God, as a lawgiver, as under condemnation; but, having fled to him for refuge, the law, as to its condemning power, hath no more dominion over us, but we are treated, even by God the judge, as in a state of justification.[31]

It might be borne in mind that Fuller spent his earliest years in a high-Calvinist church, that at Soham in Cambridgeshire. When he moved to Kettering he had already changed his position.

Joseph Ivimey remarked that Dr Gill, when on his death-bed, repeated the following lines from Isaac Watts:

> He raised me from the deeps of sin,
> The gates of gaping hell,
> And fix'd my standing more secure
> Than 'twas before I fell.

Ivimey went on to recall a personal experience:

> The writer once by accident went into a meeting-house in London, where the minister is a *very high* Calvinist. The clerk, too, on that occasion, proved himself to be as sound as his minister! Being quite sure Dr. Watts had mistaken the subject, he ventured to alter the last two lines of the verse above mentioned, thus,

> "And fix'd my standing *most* secure
> *In Christ* before I fell."

It was easy to perceive that this sound clerk was *very high*; but then
it was quite easy to discover that this scheme was not *scriptural*; as
that standing could not be *most secure*, which did not prevent the
elect from *falling*.[32]

In other words, if the elect were actually justified in Christ before
they fell, when they were, allegedly, 'most secure', how was it that
they fell at all? Does the Bible ever teach that there can be
justification without sanctification?

*   *   *

It is said in the Bible about Absalom that, when standing in the city
gate, he declared: 'Oh that I were made judge in the land, that every
man which hath any suit or cause might come unto me, and I would
do him justice' (2 Samuel 15:4).

In context, 'to do justice' means to pronounce someone righteous, and to do so in public rather than privately. This is totally in
keeping with the Bible's idea of justification. Deuteronomy 25:1
shows this clearly. In Absalom's situation the rebel prince wished
and, indeed, fully intended to say that others were righteous,
although he realised that this was impossible until all concerned
acknowledged him 'in the city gate'. There, both they and he could
be heard. For him, then, the issue revolved around just when
righteousness was to be declared and actualised. The reality was that
Absalom's revealed plan to justify the people was by no means their
actual justification; notwithstanding his intentions, the time for him
and for them had not yet arrived.

All this shows exactly how the Bible leads us to consider the
point in time when God justifies the elect sinner and before which
point the latter is not reckoned by God as righteous. It is true, of
course, that the imputation of the righteousness of Christ to the
believer was decreed before the beginning of the world. It follows
that this imputation remains absolutely inevitable: the perfect righteousness of the Lord Jesus shall most certainly be reckoned to the
account of him who, because he has been graciously chosen, must
and therefore will come to trust in the Saviour. But when is he
reckoned as righteous? Before creation? When Christ died? When
our Lord rose from the dead? Or when the believer is converted?

The Word of God indicates that mutual reconciliation between an offended God and an offending sinner never becomes real, either in the mind of God or in the experience of the sinner, until faith is born. The sinner must cleanse his evil heart and, so to speak, bow the knee in obedience. Set apart by the Holy Spirit so that he will turn to the Saviour (1 Peter 1:2), the elect believer is clothed with the righteousness of Christ for the first time ever. On the other hand, before repentance and faith are born in his heart, he is still a rebel and no more than a child of wrath. That is why he must believe in Christ.

Gill and others like him travelled beyond these limits. We suppose that in so doing they did not help the cause of the Particular Baptists.

CHAPTER XI
JOHN GILL AND THE MESSAGE OF THE GOSPEL

In our review of John Gill's Calvinism we turn finally to his ideas about how the gospel should be proclaimed. That there is good news to be announced to all men was a matter about which Gill entertained absolutely no doubts whatever.

> It is a part of the ministry of the word to lay before men their fallen, miserable, lost, and undone state by nature; to open to them the nature of sin, its pollution and guilt, and the sad consequences of it; to inform them of their incapacity to make atonement for it; and of their impotence and inability to do what is spiritually good; and of the insufficiency of their own righteousness to justify them in the sight of God: and they are to be made acquainted, that salvation is alone by Christ, and not otherways; and the fulness, freeness, and suitableness of this salvation, are to be preached before them; and the whole to be left to the Spirit of God, to make application of it as he shall see fit.[1]

Would that all ministers of the gospel were similarly inflamed. John Gill preached truth; we thank God for such candour.

The point to be made is that while Gill did not concede that the gospel should urge men personally to saving faith in Christ, his interpretation of the ministerial commission was virtually such a call. This is because the obligation Gill placed upon the hearer, even though the latter might be reprobate, amounted to the requirement that he should exercise saving faith. Gill, of course, was usually reluctant to say this explicitly; he hedged himself:

> The ministers of the gospel, though they ought not to offer and tender salvation to any, for which they have no commission, yet they may preach the gospel of salvation to all men, and declare that *whosoever believes shall be saved*; for this they are commissioned to do.[2]

In practice, this meant that the Christian minister is to endeavour to preach to all men because preaching is the servant of election:

> As it is the will of God that his chosen people and others should promiscuously dwell together, so he sends his gospel to them in general, and by it takes out a people for his name ... the condemnation of men is aggravated by it [the gospel], inasmuch as, though they are surrounded with light, they love darkness rather than light.[3]

Sinners generally ought to turn to Christ, and failure to do so is an aggravation of their sin. Nevertheless, Gill, quite typically, declined to say that unbelievers should be pressed personally to turn to the Saviour. This was consistent with the high-Calvinist principle that faith, because a gift, is not an exercise to which men should be summoned. So, in a 1762 sermon Gill exclaimed to those alone 'who are seeking to flee from the wrath to come' that 'there is no other way of escaping' save by 'fleeing to Christ, turning to him'.[4]

Gill tended to lean heavily upon the proclamation of the truths of the gospel without sensing any need to press them upon his hearers. The truth will speak for itself, if blessed by the Spirit, without the personal intervention of the preacher. This is because Gill knew

> ... what encouragement is there for poor sensible sinners, to commit their souls into the hands of Christ, who is able to save to the uttermost; and who hath assured us, that whosoever believeth in him shall not perish, but have eternal life.[5]

Furthermore, the simple statement of the truths of the gospel is sufficient because, basically, the good news is in no sense a demand which lays any obligation upon its hearers:

> Nor is the gospel a law, it is a pure declaration of grace and salvation by Christ; it has no commands but all promises; there is nothing in it that looks like a law.[6]

By 'promises' Gill meant those things which God will do, and not those blessings which he would give in the event of certain conditions being fulfilled by men. Here, Gill was not entirely consistent. In commenting upon 'obedience to the faith', Romans 1:5, Gill noted that Paul and his colleagues had received their office 'that men might be brought by the ministry of the word to obey the faith, Christ the object of faith ... or to obey the doctrine of faith, which is ... to embrace it heartily by faith'.[7] But, surely, a requirement to obey presupposes the existence of some sort of demand, or even a 'law'?

Nevertheless, it is because saving faith is essentially a gift from God that Gill, when he focussed upon the matter, could not consider obedience as a needful step to salvation. 'Obedience is not the condition of pardon, though a declaration of pardon is an excellent motive to induce to obedience.'[8]

Gill believed firmly that

> ... Christ died for all the elect of God, and them only; that by his death he has procured for them actual pardon, reconciliation, and salvation; and that in consequence of the absolute and uncondi-tional covenant of grace being ratified and confirmed by his blood, faith and repentance are bestowed upon, and wrought in these persons, not as conditions, but as blessings of that covenant.[9]

The question could be raised: why cannot certain blessings also be conditions? May we not suppose that Gill allowed logic to lead him to conclusions which were perhaps beyond Scripture? In some confusion, he fell back upon his distinction between 'legal' and 'evangelical' repentance:

> And as for commands and exhortations to regeneration, or promises of pardon to such who regenerate themselves, or threats of death to those who neglect it, or complaints against those who would not do it, I know of none in the whole word of God; what is referred to, only regards an external reformation of life and man-ners, and not regeneration, or the first work of conversion.[10]

But, if this should be so, how could Gill have written elsewhere concerning all men that God 'ought to be the sole object of their worship; it is their duty to worship him, and that in a spiritual manner, suitable to his nature as a Spirit'?[11]

As noted, Gill did from time to time proclaim strongly that saving faith is a virtual duty incumbent upon all who hear the gospel. So, for example, with respect to John 6:44, 'No man can come to me except the Father ... draw him,' Gill claimed that failure to come to Christ in a 'spiritual manner' is due to men's 'corruption and vitiosity of nature', which renders men 'blame-worthy'.[12] It does appear that here and there throughout his long ministerial career Gill expressed the view that the gospel is, in some sense, an ultimate demand upon all its hearers and that the fact that saving faith is the gift of God does not necessarily cancel men's responsibility to

190   *Picking up a Pin for the Lord*

believe; God commands a reluctant world both to repent and to trust in the Saviour proclaimed to it.

If we do accept that they who are privileged to hear about Christ ought to trust him for their salvation, and even if Gill did sometimes express himself in such terms, it does not follow that, as he said in commenting upon Romans 11:32, 'that he might have mercy upon all', universal offers are to be made to all men.[13] Perhaps it would be better if the word 'offer' was put diplomatically to one side. While Gill claimed that 'the ministry of reconciliation ... does not propose to men to make their peace with God',[14] a truly chilling statement, he declared concerning the ministerial commission that 'all that a true and faithful preacher of the gospel can do, is to ... declare, that whoever repent of their sins, and believe in Christ, shall receive the forgiveness of them; and which declaration of theirs God abides by and confirms'.[15]

Nevertheless, is not such encouragement to all who hear the gospel tantamount to a command? At the very least it is an encouragement backed up by a magnificent promise, perhaps, even, an 'offer'. Remarkably, this provocative word had been deployed by Herman Witsius, so much admired by John Gill. In discoursing upon the covenant of grace between God and the elect sinner, the Dutch divine asserted that faith is the 'instrument' proposed to the sinner by God rather than the 'condition' by which the sinner lays hold on the Lord Jesus.[16] Doubtless, the first proposition is true, yet is not man's employment of such an essential instrument a necessary condition for his salvation? With regard to divine offers, Witsius wrote that faith comprises

> ... the acceptance of the benefit offered by the covenant, and makes the promise firm and irrevocable. "Here is my Son," says God, "and salvation in him. I offer him to whoever desires him, and believes, that he shall find his salvation in him. Who desires him? who believes this?" "I do," says the believer, "I greatly long for him. I believe my salvation to be laid up in him. I take him as thus offered to me." "Be it so," saith the Lord.[17]

Gill declined the word 'offer', yet scarcely, if at all, differed with Witsius concerning the manner of appropriation of salvation. We ask: is a sinner's refusal to trust in the Saviour about whom he has heard really a matter of indifference to heaven? Is not rejection of the truth as it is in Jesus a dishonour to God and a sin and, because a sin, a punishable transgression of a righteous demand? Is not the man who preaches good news in fact projecting faith as the condition of salvation because, quite simply, he tells out that saving faith, or trust in Christ, leads to salvation, while the absence of it leads to damnation? Listen to Gill as he expounded Acts 2:39, 'the promise is unto you and to your children':

> The promise is no other than the promise of life and salvation by Christ, and of remission of sins by his blood ... the persons addressed ... are told, for their relief, that the same promise would be made good to their posterity also, provided they did as they were directed to do.[18]

Note the words 'provided they did as they were directed to do'. Gill evidently considered the gospel to have been a command both to those present in Jerusalem on the day of Pentecost and to their quite possibly reprobate children. We might remember at this point that, unlike the Presbyterians and the Independents of his time, as well as evangelical Anglicans, Gill was not a Calvinist who sprinkled babies in the name of the Trinity. This was because he did not believe that the covenant of grace embraces both believers and their children. The quotation shows that he reckoned the salvation of all concerned at Pentecost, parents and offspring, as conditional upon their individual faith; the promise of God would be 'made good' 'provided', or if, they did as they were commanded. Not only does saving faith become a condition of salvation, it is also an act, something which sinners 'do' (Gill's word). Would Gill have been able to disagree with Andrew Fuller's sentiments to the effect that although the gospel, in the strict sense of the term, might not be a law but, rather, a declaration of God's grace, it requires in practice faith as an expression of obedience?[19]

In short, with regard to Gill's understanding of the message of the gospel, we would suggest that he frequently allowed himself to be controlled by a quasi-theological system which led him beyond New Testament boundaries. On the other hand, in his extensive writings he did from time to time shed elements of the system to exhibit an evangelical Calvinism not much different from that, say, of Whitefield.

CHAPTER XII
ANDREW FULLER, CALVINISM AND HIGH CALVINISM

We come now to consider Andrew Fuller, a man who perhaps more than anyone else led the Particular Baptist reaction against high Calvinism. Fuller, the son of a Cambridgeshire farmer, and in his younger days an effective wrestler, was one of the leading original thinkers among late eighteenth-century Particular Baptists. Fuller exercised considerable influence upon denominational affairs and through his writings moulded the minds of many, including William Carey, the pioneer missionary. A thirty-two-year pastorate at Kettering saw the membership of his church increase gradually from less than 90 to over 170. Many travelled in from the villages to hear him. Fuller's biographer, John Ryland junior, saw it as no discredit to him that, in a town which had a population of not much more than 3,000 in 1815, his own congregation had never exceeded 1,000. The paucity of numbers was attributed to evangelical preaching in the parish church and to the fact that Thomas Toller, the Independent minister, was deservedly popular.[1] Toller's son, Thomas junior, when preaching his valedictory sermon in 1875, mentioned that around the year 1800 'Kettering in the neighbouring towns was called, perhaps derisively, the Holy Land ... because of the almost universal practice of all classes of the inhabitants attending some place of worship'.[2] By 1828, when a religious census was taken, there were in Kettering nearly 1,200 Episcopalians, a similar number of Independents, over 600 'Baptists', 200 or so 'Calvinistic Baptists' (a distinction was noted), 500 or more Wesleyans, nearly 30 Quakers and just 40 of no sect.[3]

Andrew Fuller was secretary to the Particular Baptist Mission from 1792 until the year of his death, 1815. According to Ivimey, 'he considered that neither himself nor his friends would have so deeply compassionated the condition of the heathen world had they re-

tained the hyper-calvinistic scheme of doctrine, as to have undertaken such self-denying efforts to establish a Society to promote
their conversion.'[4]

* * *

Fuller's most important work, *The Gospel Worthy of All
Acceptation*, was written as a response and objection to that form of
Calvinism in which he had been reared and which had influenced
many English Particular Baptists during the greater part of the
eighteenth century. The book appeared first in 1785 but was
modified as years went by. We outline some central points, citing
mainly from the second edition of 1801.

Fuller reacted strongly against Gill's concept of 'evangelical' as
opposed to 'legal' repentance, projecting the distinction between
the two as a fiction.[5] Here we are at the core of the Kettering pastor's
rejection of high Calvinism. He was quite unable to agree with Gill
that there were duties required by God which were not spiritual;
rather, all duties were to be performed in 'a spiritual state of mind'.[6]
He confessed that, in his earlier study of the preaching of John the
Baptist and that of Christ and the apostles, he had come to the
conclusion that the repentance and faith for which they called were
'such as are connected with salvation'.[7]

Through his reading of Jonathan Edwards as well as the Bible
Fuller became convinced that because men would not come to
Christ they therefore did not come to him, and that this refusal to turn
to the Saviour was evil. It followed that even when no grace (that is,
a God-granted ability to believe in Christ) was given, sinful men
who heard the gospel were obliged to believe and must render
themselves guilty when failing to do so.[8]

In this connection, Fuller focussed attention on what he believed
to be the fallacy of 'legal' repentance:

> God requires the heart, the whole heart, and nothing but the
> heart; that all the precepts of the Bible are only the different modes
> in which we are required to express our love to him ... and that, so
> far from their [that is, unregenerate sinners] being exhorted to
> everything excepting what is spiritually good, they are exhorted to
> nothing else.[9]

With regard to the typically high-Calvinist view that faith

'consists in a persuasion of our interest in Christ',[10] Lewis Wayman of Kimbolton being cited, Fuller made the telling point that if a persuasion of salvation was saving faith, then faith could not be a duty incumbent upon the unsaved. This was because, quite clearly, the unsaved were not interested in Christ and entertained no persuasion about him as their Saviour. Therefore, it could not possibly be their duty to believe a lie.[11] True, yet what was saving faith? For Fuller, a personal interest in salvation was not so much faith as a consequence of faith.[12] To prove this, he returned to the scriptural data: 'By saving faith, we undoubtedly embrace Christ *for ourselves* ... But this is very different from a persuasion of our being in a state of salvation.'[13]

Fuller commented upon Abraham Booth and some unnamed writers who considered faith in Christ as a 'dependence' on him, 'receiving' him, 'coming' to him and 'trusting' in him for salvation.[14] The Kettering pastor held that 'trust' is the most appropriate term: 'We may credit a report of evil tidings as well as one of good, but we cannot be said to trust it.'[15] That is, saving faith consisted in believing the good news to be both accurate and relevant and then personal dependence upon the Christ proclaimed in the gospel.

Abraham Booth was taken to task by Fuller. The former maintained in his *Glad Tidings to perishing Sinners* that the sinner will receive mercy should he apply for it. In Fuller's opinion, he avoided the question 'whether faith in Christ be the *duty* of the ungodly':

> If the ungodly be not *obliged*, as well as warranted, to do this [that is, to believe in Christ], they are at liberty to do as the Jewish nation did, to *receive him not*, and to go on depending upon the works of the law for acceptance with God.

Would they have been 'guiltless in so doing', Fuller asked. He commented that 'whatever was Mr. Booth's reason for being silent on this subject, he will not say they are'.[16]

* * *

Fuller's next task was to demonstrate that 'faith in Christ is the duty of all men who hear, or have opportunity to hear, the gospel'.[17] We summarize his arguments.

In the Bible, 'unconverted sinners are commanded, exhorted, and invited to believe in Christ for salvation'. Fuller assumed that

Andrew Fuller (1754-1815)

Abraham Booth (1734-1806)

'whatever God commands, exhorts, or invites us to comply with, is the duty of those to whom such language is addressed'.[18] Numerous references were brought to bear to prove the point. Contrary to John Gill,[19] Fuller maintained that the thirsty mentioned by Isaiah 55:1-7 are not those who desire spiritual blessings but all who have a 'natural desire of happiness'.[20] It is to such men of the world that the invitation of the gospel is addressed.

This approach came out well in a letter to a friend on the subject of 'Sandemanianism', an error which took its name from Robert Sandeman (1718-71), who held that bare assent to the work of Christ is alone necessary for salvation.[21] Fuller complained thus about high-Calvinist preaching:

> For a minister to withold the invitations of the gospel till he perceives the sinner sufficiently, as he thinks, convinced of sin, and then to bring them forward as something to which he is entitled, holding up his convictions and distress of mind as signs of grace, and persuading him, on this ground, to think of himself one of God's elect and warranted to believe in Christ, is doing worse than nothing.[22]

John Brine, Fuller noted, believed that John 6:29, 'This is the work of God, that ye believe on him whom he hath sent,' concerned the necessity but not the duty of an exercise of faith by unregenerate Jews in order to be saved. In response, Fuller wished to know, 'how can our Lord be supposed in answer to their question to tell them of an act which was necessary, acceptable, and pleasing to God, but which was not their present duty?'[23]

Because 'every man is bound cordially to receive and approve whatever God reveals',[24] Fuller wrote:

> The same law that obliged Adam in innocence to love God in all his perfections, as displayed in the works of creation, obliged Moses and Israel to love him in all the glorious displays of himself in his wonderful works of providence, of which they were witnesses. And the same law that obliged them to love him in those discoveries of himself obliges us to love him in other discoveries, by which he has since more gloriously appeared, as *saving sinners through the death of his Son*. To suppose that we are obliged to love God as manifesting himself in the works of creation and providence, but not in the work of redemption, is to suppose that in the highest and most glorious display of himself he deserves no regard.[25]

The point was then made that 'though the Gospel, strictly speaking, is not a law, but a message of pure grace; yet it virtually requires obedience, and such an obedience as includes saving faith'.[26]

Not unnaturally, Romans 1:5 was brought to bear: 'We have received grace and apostleship, for obedience to the faith among all nations.' Fuller observed that although repentance towards God and faith in the Saviour are blessings bestowed by God, they are, nevertheless, 'exercises of *obedience*', obedience presupposing prior obligation, or duty.[27]

Want of saving faith in Christ is shown by Scripture, claimed Fuller, to be due to the depravity of human nature and a 'heinous sin'.[28] The fact that certain sinners were never elected to salvation is not represented by Scripture as their fault; Fuller knew that God passed them by to glorify his just anger. On the other hand, persistent failure to believe in Christ, arising from voluntary ignorance, pride, dishonesty and aversion of heart, is portrayed as evil.[29] Fuller mentioned that John Gill sometimes inadvertently established this and other principles when not focussing upon his own system.[30]

In this connection, Fuller observed: '*Unbelief is expressly declared to be a sin of which the Spirit of truth has to convince the world*, John xvi. 8,9. But unbelief cannot be a sin if faith were not a duty.'[31]

Further, 'God has threatened and inflicted the most awful punishments on sinners for their not believing on the Lord Jesus Christ'.[32] Because sin, as a breach of duty, occasions God's punishment and because a want of saving faith is punishable, saving faith must be a duty. While faith is not the 'procuring cause', that is, the meritorious ground of salvation, culpable unbelief is the procuring cause, or ground, of damnation. Men ought to 'receive the love of the truth' (2 Thessalonians 2:10-12).[33]

Fuller developed the view that 'other spiritual exercises, which sustain an inseparable connexion with faith in Christ, are represented as the duty of men in general', among which were love for God, the fear of God, sorrow for sin and humility.[34] This meant, quite simply, that if the laws of God were both 'spiritual, and remain in full force as a standard of obligation', it followed that 'God's gift' remained as 'man's duty'. Fuller cited the Independent divine John Owen (1616-83) to the effect that he who was ignorant of this 'has yet to learn one of the first principles of religion'.[35]

The case of the people of Nineveh was raised, Fuller being aware that John Gill had stressed that the repentance demanded from that city was 'legal', not involving repentance with a view to salvation.[36] Fuller remarked tellingly: 'I do not know that the repentance of the Ninevites was genuine, or connected with spiritual blessings; neither do my opponents know that it was not.'[37] Fuller was attacking Gill for tying Nineveh into his own somewhat synthetic system.

With regard to 'the inability of sinners to believe in Christ, and do things spiritually good',[38] Fuller remarked convincingly concerning the inability which stems from total disinclination: 'It is just as impossible ... for any person to do that which he has no mind to do, as to perform that which surpasses his natural powers.'[39]

However, natural inability and total disinclination may not be placed in parallel. If a man, 'from the constitution of his nature', is unable to believe a certain kind of truth, he would equally be quite unable to reject it. Fuller meant that constitutional inability to believe in Jesus would be no more than one effect of a total inertness to the gospel. Such a person would no more be able to decline the good news than to approve it. Fuller's reasoning was acute and admirable at this point. He realised that because 'all men' rejected the truth of God in preference to embracing it, it followed that their inability was not due to the way in which God made them but was, rather, the product of their evil hearts.[40]

It was precisely for this reason, wrote Fuller, that the 'godly in all ages have considered themselves insufficient to perform those things to which nevertheless they acknowledge themselves to be obliged'.[41] So, for Fuller, the necessity of a work of the Spirit in the heart 'prior to believing, is perfectly consistent with its being the immediate duty of the unregenerate'.[42] That is, sinful men who will never renew their hearts are duty-bound to do so. 'If an upright heart toward God and man be not *itself* required of us, nothing is or can be required; for all duty is comprehended in the acting out of the heart.'[43]

* * *

Objections to these observations were then countered by Fuller. He noted that, whereas his views had been criticized as tending towards Arminianism, the fact was that the high-Calvinist criticisms themselves 'are of *Arminian* original'. Nothing if not daring, he cited John Brine in support of this thesis.[44]

High Calvinism occasionally approached the vexed question of duty-faith by contemplating the holiness of Adam and Eve before they fell into sin. With this procedure Andrew Fuller would have nothing to do:

> Our disordered souls are incapable of forming just ideas of so glorious a state. To attempt, therefore, to settle the boundaries of even *their* duty [Adam and Eve prior to the fall], by an abstract inquiry into the nature of their powers and principles, would be improper; and still more so to make it the medium by which to judge of *our own*.[45]

Further, he stressed that his views were no different from those held by earlier men who believed in the divine decrees. He claimed the support of Augustine (A.D. 354-430), Calvin and other Reformers, the sixteenth-century Puritans, the Synod of Dort (1618-19) and various seventeenth-century Nonconformists.[46] In this fashion Fuller attempted, with some success, to show that the high Calvinists were in error if they claimed to be the only ones in step.

Concerning the principle of holiness possessed by Adam, Fuller observed that it had never been proved that Adam, as a righteous and innocent man, was not able to live by faith. This point was developed to counter the view that if sinless Adam had not lived by faith, and, indeed, was not obliged to do so, it followed that his sinful offspring did not labour under such a necessity.[47]

Fuller then came to the objection that a general invitation to sinners to be saved by Christ is inconsistent with the election of some rather than all. Leaning upon John Owen for support, Fuller observed sensibly that 'God's word, and not his secret purpose, is the rule of our conduct'. The duty of the minister is clear: he is to exhort, invite and warn sinners to believe in Christ. In Owen's words, cited by Fuller, the minister is not to 'trouble himself about, those secrets of the eternal mind of God, viz. whom he purposeth to save, and whom he hath sent Christ to die for in particular'.[48]

* * *

Fuller was at his weakest when trying to reconcile the doctrine of particular redemption with his conviction that all who hear the gospel should believe in Christ for their salvation. Apparently, he rejected as an hypothesis 'manifestly inconsistent with the Scriptures' the view that the sufferings of Christ are 'the literal payment

of a debt ... according to the number of those for whom he died, and
to the degree of their guilt'. He asserted that this 'commercial'
interpretation, if true, might well be 'inconsistent with the free *forgiveness* of sin, and with sinners being directed to apply for mercy as
supplicants, rather than as claimants'.[49] In all this he was correct to the
extent that the Bible never teaches that the satisfaction rendered by our
Lord was a *quid pro quo*, a measured price paid for the sins of the elect,
sins which, on this construction, would have been counted and then
estimated according to the punishment due for each and every one.
Nevertheless, Scripture is clear that the death of Jesus was a real,
adequate and precise sacrifice for God's people; the redemption
rendered by the Saviour was exact.

According to Andrew Fuller, the particularity of redemption is to be
seen in the sovereignty of its application. Although, as he saw it, the
sacrifice of Christ was sufficient for all men's sins, God reckons it to
the account of the elect only. It was for these that Christ died,
notwithstanding the infinite dignity of his sufferings. Indeed, Christ did
not introduce a merely conditional provision of redemption for all
mankind.[50] Yet consider these words:

> If satisfaction was made on the principle of debtor and creditor,
> and that which was paid was just of sufficient value to liquidate a given
> number of sins, and to redeem a given number of sinners, and no more;
> it should seem that it could not be the duty of any but the elect, nor
> theirs till it was revealed to them that they were of the elect, to rely
> upon it: for *wherefore should we set our eyes on that which is not*? But
> if there be such a fulness in the satisfaction of Christ as is sufficient for
> the salvation of the whole world, were the whole world to believe in
> him; and if the particularity of redemption lie only in the purpose or
> sovereign pleasure of God to render it effectual to some rather than to
> others, no such consequence will follow.[51]

These beliefs were brought out clearly in Fuller's *Reply to
Philanthropos*, 'Philanthropos' being the General Baptist Dan Taylor
of Yorkshire (1738-1816), the founder in 1770 of the 'New
Connexion' of General Baptist churches. According to Fuller, Taylor
assumed the name 'Philanthropos' in order to remind Fuller of the
superiority of his, Taylor's, Arminian system 'in point of *philan-
thropy*'.[52] Fuller wrote that, notwithstanding the fact that Christ, in
laying down his life, intended to save the elect alone,[53]

... Calvinists in *general* have considered the particularity of redemption as consisting not in the *degree* of Christ's sufferings, (as though he must have suffered more if more had been finally saved,) or in any *insufficiency* that attended them.

Rather,

The sufferings of Christ, in themselves considered, are of *infinite* value, sufficient to have saved all the world, and a thousand worlds, if it had pleased God to have constituted them the price of their redemption.[54]

Andrew Fuller's claim that he did no more than reflect historic Calvinism was not entirely untrue. Witsius, whose *The Oeconomy of the Covenants between God and Man* was commended by John Gill, had penned:

The obedience and sufferings of Christ, considered in themselves, are, on account of the infinite dignity of the person, of that value, as to have been sufficient for redeeming not only all and every man in particular, but many myriads besides, if it had so pleased God and Christ, to have undertaken and satisfied for them.[55]

It looks as if Fuller had copied from Witsius, who wrote further that the infinite value of Christ's sufferings is a truth which 'should, without distinction, be proposed both to them that are to be saved, and to them that are to perish; with a *charge* not to neglect so great salvation'.[56]

At any rate, it was thus that Fuller explained the churches' obligation to preach the gospel indiscriminately and the duty of all who hear it to turn to the Saviour. While unregenerate sinners should never be urged to believe that Christ died deliberately for them, they should be informed that the sufferings of Christ suffice for their salvation. In this lies their great encouragement to believe.[57] It seems that Fuller was struggling in order to provide unnecessary justification for the practice of preaching the gospel to the unconverted. Ivimey, who knew Fuller, wrote:

Mr. Fuller, too, by some of his explanations respecting the sufficiency of the atonement as a sacrifice equal in value to have effected the salvation of all mankind, was supposed to have pleaded for universal redemption; nothing, I am persuaded, was farther from his intention, as he considered the Holy Spirit's application of the atonement confined to the objects of the Father's election, and of the Son's redemption. ... The writer has long been of opinion that, if instead of proving by the above representations the general invitations of the gospel to the unconverted to be scriptural, it would be much more easily supported, and be better understood, by a reference to the manner in which the Lord Jesus and his inspired apostles preached the gospel. Who can deny but that those infallible specimens support the practice of calling on the unconverted to "repent and believe the gospel."[58]

Fuller's partial misinterpretation of the connection between Calvary and evangelism did not, of course, remain unnoticed; he stirred up a hornet's nest. For example, in 1831 William Rushton of Liverpool insisted that even the word 'redemption' provides a strong argument against the indefinite scheme. Thus: 'The very nature of redemption, therefore, comprehends something vicarious, something definite.'[59] Unfortunately, limitations of space prevent a detailed study of later reactions to Fuller's rationale for evangelism; if we investigated the matter we would travel into the bosom of the 1800s and well beyond the designed *terminus ad quem* of this book.[60]

In closing, we ask: does the New Testament ever proclaim the universal 'sufficiency' of the cross? It says clearly, and requires the Lord's people to say with equal clarity, that all who believe in the Saviour shall be saved (so, for example, Acts 2:38-9, 3:19, 10:43, 13:38-9, 16:31; Romans 10:9-10); the death of Christ is either implied or said to be efficient in the event rather than sufficient in its promise. There is, we believe, a great deal of difference between the two approaches. It is at this point that we disagree with Andrew Fuller.

CHAPTER XIII
THE LATE 1700s

As the eighteenth century wore on the churchmanship of the leaders of the Evangelical Awakening, plus the Arminianism of the Wesleys and their followers, effectively inhibited any serious co-operation between them and the vast majority of the Particular Baptists; they passed each other by. In 1778 the Carlton, Bedfordshire, church, desirous of a pastor, was told by John Ryland of Northampton about Mr Mark Wilks, who was seeking a settlement. Wilks came to Carlton for two Sundays in early 1779. The church book states that he was

> ... a rank Methodist Indeed who refused all rule, Order or Dicipline in the Church of God. In this Person We Was all Unanimous in refusing and rejecting him for the above reason. And he Left us to our great joy the 21st of Feby. 1779.[1]

Such perceptions were typical and had carried over from the earlier years of the century. Indeed, throughout the whole period there seem to have been at the most only limited contacts with evangelical Anglicans. George Whitefield excelled as an evangelist but did so as a minister of the Church of England, a Church with which the overwhelming majority of Particular Baptists would, on their principles, have nothing to do. John Gill, in his *Body of Divinity, Cause of God and Truth*, his principal published sermons and other works, never mentioned George Whitefield; as far as the patriarchal Baptist was concerned the two men might have lived on different planets rather than in the England of the eighteenth century. Why was this? Was the Doctor resentful of the Anglican's evangelistic success? One is reluctant to criticize thus a man as truly great as Gill. Was he suspicious of the lasting worth of Whitefield's work? We cannot tell, but would not discount the possibility. Consider Wesley's comments concerning his fellow clergyman. He claimed that on Whitefield's own admission,

> ... in a few years, the far greater part of those who had once "received the word with joy," yea, had "escaped the corruption that is in the world," were "entangled again and overcome."[2]

Wesley then gave his own appreciation:

> But those who were more or less affected by Mr. Whitefield's preaching had no discipline at all. ... They were formed into no societies: They had no Christian connexion with each other, nor were ever taught to watch over each other's souls. So that if any fell into lukewarmness, or even into sin, he had none to lift him up.[3]

Might this, if correct, not teach us what the eighteenth-century Particular Baptists knew well: that evangelism and churchmanship are, or ought to be, intimately related? Converts need a home, and the local church is the situation provided by the New Testament. Given that Gill could have been distrustful of Whitefield's Calvinism, although he did not say so, did he, perhaps, also perceive that para-church evangelism might not be the answer? Gill was no mean preacher, and if Whitefield slew his ten thousands, Gill boasted not a few conquests. It might not just have been Calvinism reinterpreted which led Dr Gill to keep himself to himself; a low view of the Church of England led him, perhaps, to remain silent when, seemingly, many thousands in both Old and New England were being brought to faith through the ministry of an establishment clergyman. This could explain Gill's eloquent silence, a silence which he might have felt to be wise when God seemed to be blessing Whitefield's labours so abundantly.

In this connection, what can be said about the highly respected William Grimshaw, evangelical Rector of Haworth from 1742 until his death in 1763? A reliable tradition recounts that on one occasion Grimshaw left his congregation to sing Psalm 119 (all of it) while he took his horsewhip to scour a nearby tavern for absentees from his service. Scared delinquents cascaded from windows and doors to flee before him into church to hear the sermon, while others escaped through the back door.[4] Servants of God though they most certainly were, they of Grimshaw's kind were reckoned to be establishment men maintained by a commonwealth sprinkled with

Christianity. Whether evangelicalism or Anglicanism came first for them would have been, as far as the Baptists were concerned, by no means an open-and-shut issue. Or perhaps it was; such people were perceived to be Anglicans from first to last.

Thus it is possible to understand the complaint levelled against Howell Harris by William Herbert, a Baptist minister in Trosgoed, Breconshire. Herbert bemoaned the fact that Harris, always an Anglican, was like a farmer who cured many scabby sheep of the rot, and, when he had nearly healed them, turned them out into a field, the Church of England, which was filled with sick sheep. The newcomers became as rotten and scabby as ever. His annoyance might have been exacerbated if, as has been claimed, Herbert was influential in making Harris a Calvinist.[5]

Again, it is not difficult to see why it was that although the renowned John Newton wished to attend the Northamptonshire and Leicestershire Particular Baptist Association annual meeting at Olney in 1774, he decided to stay away. His diary recorded: 'I should have liked to have gone myself, but thought my presence would not be agreeable to some. Ere long the effects of bigotry and a party spirit will cease.' In his entry for August 7, 1776, having heard Robert Hall senior preach with 'narrowness of spirit' on the subject of 'love, the bond of perfection', Colossians 3:14, Newton affirmed with apparent condescension that the Particular Baptists were the objects of his Christian love, 'notwithstanding they cannot break through the prejudices of education which fence them to keep them aloof from those who wish them well.'[6]

Doubtless, Hall and his people would have said that the Church of England needed no instruction about prejudice, bigotry and party spirit.

On one occasion an open letter was sent by Robert Hall junior, in his Cambridge days, to the Revd Charles Simeon (1759-1836), Vicar of Holy Trinity, Cambridge from 1782 until his death. The latter's evangelical beliefs were fostered by Henry Venn (1724-97), Vicar of Huddersfield, who had given funeral orations for both Grimshaw and George Whitefield, and who had been such an encouragement to the Baptist Abraham Booth in the latter's earlier days.[7] In 1795 Simeon preached in his own church in favour of Roman Catholic priests who had escaped from France, and had said, according to Hall, that 'you complained ... that the BAPTISTS in particular, would never be satisfied till they got your people under the water'. Hall criticized Simeon on the ground that, for Baptists, water was simply 'the *symbol* of a Christian profession, while you profess to believe it *regenerates* the partaker, and makes him a child of God'. He also took the evangelical Anglican to task because the latter had acknowledged the French priests to be his 'Christian brethren'.[8] Such skirmishing reveals all too clearly the deep distrust in the establishment felt by Baptists in those days, even when the former donned low-church canonicals. It might follow that, if we are to call for revival in our time, we need to be better informed about what did happen in the eighteenth century, a century which experienced true revival, and about why the Particular Baptists usually stood back.

Intolerance towards the Baptists was still prevalent. In 1769 a young couple in Durham were refused marriage by their local clergyman because their parents were Baptists and because they had not been christened. This meant that they could not be married in England. Determined to become man and wife, they went to Scotland where they were duly joined in matrimony. When they returned home, the clergyman demanded to be paid fees for a ceremony which he had not performed. Not unnaturally, the couple refused to pay, whereupon the priest began proceedings against them in the ecclesiastical court. When Dissenters in London took up the case the priest dropped the matter.[9]

In 1772, encouraged by the bold example of some clergymen who petitioned Parliament to be relieved from subscription to the articles of the Church of England because they did not believe them, a meeting of Dissenting ministers, including Dr Samuel Stennett, the Particular Baptist, gathered to discuss the issue. In due course, a bill was passed by the Commons, only to be rejected by the upper house. In 1774 Robert Robinson of Cambridge took up his pen on the matter under the title of 'Arcana' ('mystery' or 'secret'), and in 1779 a bill was passed by both houses whereby Dissenting ministers were relieved of the duty of subscription to the Thirty-Nine Articles; they were required to state only that, as Protestants, they accepted the Old and New Testaments as the revealed will of God. In addition, Dissenting schoolteachers were at last relieved of the penalties to which they had been exposed for teaching without being licensed by their local bishops or without taking the Anglican sacrament.[10] Nevertheless, the Corporation and Test Acts remained on the statute books. In 1787 a deputation of Dissenters waited upon several leading members of both houses to seek their repeal. The Commons, however, voted against such a motion by a narrow majority. Then came the French Revolution; on this side of the Channel people generally were nervous concerning any changes in favour of personal liberties. So, the year 1790 saw the defeat of another bill for the repeal of these acts. A standing committee of Dissenters was formed in 1792 dedicated to the overthrow of Charles's legislation, although this did not come to pass for many years.[11]

We can, perhaps, understand the public attitude towards Nonconformists if the latter were perceived to hold the view expressed in 1798 by John Martin in a lecture at the Broad Street Chapel, London. He was reported to have said about the Dissenters: 'Should the French land, some, yea many of these different and differing people would unite to encourage the French, and to distress this country, provided they had a fair opportunity.'[12] After being written to by Abraham Booth, and being interviewed by some of the managers of the lecture, Martin was dismissed from the lecturership, as also from the society of Baptist ministers meeting at the Jamaica Coffee House.[13]

* * *

Ivimey noted that in 1775 Robert Robinson had in his possession a list of English Dissenting churches. The figures, which the historian reckoned to have been 'tolerably correct', totalled 1,118 churches, of which 390, that is, 35 per cent, were Baptist. Not stating whether the latter figure included both General and Particular Baptist churches, Ivimey implied that the average membership of a Baptist church might have been somewhat in excess of 50.[14] At the time, most Baptist churches met in county or district associations, the practice of the associated churches being to address an annual letter to the assembled body.[15]

In 1790 John Rippon initiated *The Baptist Annual Register*, the edition for that year indicating that there were then 310 churches in England and 48 in Wales, with the Welsh churches having several branches each.[16] According to Ivimey, there were by 1798 326 churches in England, and 84 in Wales, 'consisting in the whole of about nine thousand members.' Rippon, however, gave the number of the English churches as 361.[17] If the figures for Wales are correct, the number of Welsh churches had increased by exactly 75 per cent during the years 1790-8, while the English situation had remained far more static. The minutes for 1790 of the Northamptonshire and Leicestershire Particular Baptist Association claimed that the Welsh Association contained 46 churches which 'had large additions to several of them, both *this* year, and *last*; in some Churches more than 60 Members were added in a year'.[18] The same minutes record that in 1789 the Western Association included 39 churches, the Bourton Association, 16, the Kent and Sussex Association, 11, while the Yorkshire and Lancashire Association 'gave no account of their members'. Increases in membership were commonplace.[19]

The records of the Northamptonshire and Leicestershire Association from 1766 to 1794 inclusive, a period of twenty-nine years, indicate that in that time 2,134 new members came into the churches, giving a net increase of 952. It appears that the vast majority of new additions were by conversion or, as the records have it, by testimony of 'faith and experience'. For example, in 1777 there were 69 additions, of which no less than 56 were by profession. It is interesting to note that the churches were by no means reluctant to 'exclude' members. So, again in 1777, there were 52 losses, including 14 by exclusion. That is, in that year one quarter of the number received by profession was excluded, although, of course, those who were removed would not necessarily all have been included among those initially accepted. We cannot tell because the names of those concerned have not been recorded. During those twenty-nine years there were increases for every year except in the period 1782-5, in which there was a net reduction in membership of 37; admissions tailed off, while deaths, dismissals and exclusions increased. The record gives no reason for this.[20]

* * *

New times were bringing in men who were not blind to the fact that there had been an awakening in which, for a variety of reasons, Particular Baptists had neither sought nor achieved prominence. Ivimey recorded his emphatic view that a meeting of the Northamptonshire and Leicestershire Association held at the College Lane, Northampton, church in 1779 'was ... the commencement of a new era in the history of our denomination'.[21] Robert Hall senior, pastor, we recall, at Arnesby and the father of the similarly-named champion of free communion, preached on Isaiah 57:14, 'Take up the stumbling block out of the way of my people,' and later expanded his address into a pamphlet, *Help to Zion's Travellers*, which appeared in 1781. Wrote Ivimey:

> The principles of this admirable little work were those of modern Calvinism in opposition to the system of high or hyper-calvinism, which had so generally prevailed in our churches, chiefly in consequence of the preaching and writings of Messrs. Brine and Gill.[22]

Hall's address was magnificent:

> If any one should ask, have I a right to apply to Jesus the Saviour, simply as a poor, undone, perishing sinner, in whom there appears no good thing? I answer, Yes; the gospel proclamation is, whosoever will, let him come. ... The way to Jesus is graciously laid open for every one who chooses to come to him. His arms of mercy are expanded to receive the coming soul. Fear not, poor sinner, to approach him. He will not, on any account, cast thee out. John vi. 37.

Further,

> There is no preventive bar in the sinner's way to the Saviour, but what ariseth from a carnal heart; such as impenitency for sin, an attachment to self-righteousness, and an avowed aversion to the holy perfection of God and his sovereign methods of grace.[23]

Observe the provocative words 'every one who chooses to come to him'. We ask: do sinners 'choose' to come to Jesus? Not, of course, without the grace of God. But Gill would never have taken the qualification into account: regenerate sinners accept that which is given them; they never choose. Hall, frequently moderator of his association, was yet more vile; he struck at the roots of high Calvinism in holding that in some respects there is not much difference between that system and Arminianism:

> To doubt of personal safety is accounted by such the damning sin of unbelief. ... It is somewhat singular that this notion of faith, as consisting in an assurance of a personal interest in Christ, which was in the last age reckoned a distinguished tenet of those that were then called *Antinomians*, should be principally maintained by the most zealous *Arminians* of the present day.[24]

Robert Hall, always fiercely independent in his thinking, had been influenced already by the younger John Ryland, pastor at College Lane, Northampton, who, in turn, had read *An Inquiry into the Freedom of the Will* by Jonathan Edwards, and two sermons on the same subject by another American, John Smalley. Smalley's sermons, copies of which had been obtained from John Newton at Olney, were transcribed and lent to Robert Hall by Ryland, who noted that they

> ... contributed much to strengthen his conviction, that the *moral Impotence* of sinners is no more than an excuse for their slighting the *Call of the Gospel*, than it is for their violating the *Commands of the Law* ... so the utter aversion of a sinner, to regard the *Kindness* of God our Saviour, cannot release him from an obligation thankfully to comply with his *Invitation.*[25]

It is fascinating, and by no means unmoving, to see how the Northamptons of Old and New England united, albeit unwittingly as far as Edwards was concerned, to unfasten the cold hand of an ultra-high Calvinism, a hand which had tended to throttle the life out of the English Particular Baptists. Nevertheless, it is to be regretted that Jonathan Edwards did not think his way through to a more biblical form of churchmanship when he began his ministry. It was because he changed his mind on the question of attendance at the communion table that he stirred up an unexpected opposition in his congregation, an opposition which led ultimately to his dismissal from the Northampton, New England, pastorate.[26] In time this issue was perceived to be relevant to the baptism-communion question among the English Particular Baptists. Joseph Kinghorn remarked thus about Edwards's practice of admitting unconverted people to communion on the ground that it was occasionally the means of their conversion:

> This sentiment had been introduced by Mr. Stoddard, the President's grandfather; and was generally received in and about Northampton. Mr. Edwards hesitated concerning it when he first settled in that town, but on the whole, thinking it right, he had complied with it for twenty years. ... his opinion altered, and a controversy was one of the results.[27]

Edwards spent no less than twenty years in the ministry before changing his mind so courageously on the terms of admission to the

Lord's table. If the matter caused a man of his calibre such problems over so many years, it is no wonder that there have always been confusion and evasion in the churches about the issue of restricted communion.

Hall's attack on high Calvinism did not happen by chance. We have noted already Matthias Maurice's response to high Calvinism, *A Modern Question Modestly Answer'd*, which had appeared in the 1730s. In 1770 the Northamptonshire and Leicestershire Particular Baptist Association issued a circular letter which asserted that 'every soul that comes to Christ to be saved from hell and sin by him, is to be encouraged ... The coming soul need not fear that he is not elected, for none but such would be willing to come and submit to Christ'.[28]

The letter has sometimes been taken to indicate a swing from high Calvinism by many of the Particular Baptists of the time. Strangely, perhaps, John Martin, the immediate author of the letter, a disciple of Gill, and the man who distressed the London ministers over the issue of a possible French invasion, was subsequently an opponent of Andrew Fuller.[29] In his autobiography Martin wrote rather pompously:

> I must now turn from imposters to men of moral worth; for with such was I next engaged, in a controversy of an unpleasant kind. In the year 1787, I was informed, that several ministers of my acquaintance, were determined to propagate more Arminian tenets than they were once inclined to preach. Among these respectable ministers, the Rev. Mr. Andrew Fuller, of Kettering, was much applauded for a Treatise which he published with this Title: The Gospel of Christ worthy of all Acceptation; or the obligations of Men, fully to Credit, and cordially to approve, whatever God makes known.[30]

Martin added that Fuller's 'leading propositions' were 'obscure, inconsistent, and erroneous'.[31] The impression which Martin leaves behind him was that of a self-appointed and somewhat unwelcome trouble-shooter (or trouble-seeker) and controversialist among the Particular Baptists, many of whom, as we have noted, eventually turned away from him. Martin held tenaciously to the view that if faith is a gift it cannot be a duty.[32] But, why not? Fuller said about Martin that when he lifted up his feet he was always careful to put them down in the same place.[33] This might have meant that, in Fuller's view, Martin had not thought his way through to Jonathan

The original meeting-house at Arnesby, Leicestershire. Part of the building was used as a stable; photographed by courtesy of

William Carey (1761-1834)

Edwards's position, eventually that of Fuller, who wrote: 'To be dead *in sin* is to be *sinfully* dead.'[34]

Hall's preaching and writing were decisive. It was Hall who introduced Andrew Fuller to the works of Jonathan Edwards.[35] Further, in Hall's congregation at Arnesby there was occasionally seen a young man, one William Carey, who had to walk more than twenty miles to hear Hall preach.[36] The good which came from that country church in Leicestershire is incalculable. When just twenty-one years of age Fuller became pastor of a Particular Baptist church at Kettering, having developed the conviction that Calvinism and evangelism not only could but should be reconciled. The major theses of his *The Gospel worthy of All Acceptation*, which we have considered, came to be accepted generally as the new orthodoxy.

Nevertheless, old emphases perpetuated. Ivimey wrote:

> The Antinomian error, in regard to the moral law not being obligatory on a believer as the rule of a Christian's moral conduct, greatly prevailed at the close of this century.[37]

Not only high Calvinism was under siege. In 1789 Robert Robinson suggested that as the Particular Baptist Fund, instituted for assisting Calvinistic Baptist ministers, was augmented year by year by voluntary subscriptions, its generosity might well be extended to those who were not Calvinists in any sense of the term. He asked 'why the *Christian* should be overlooked and the *Calvinists* only regarded?', adding that 'to be in want and to be a Christian, were sufficient qualifications to receive charity'. Robinson was, doubtless, speaking from the fulness of his heart because he had both surrendered his earlier Calvinism and, remarked Ivimey, spoke concerning the Trinity 'with a degree of sceptical embarrassment' as well as 'levity'.[38] This is why Robert Hall junior, in his attack on strict communion, did not employ Robinson's work on the same subject. Referring to himself in the third person, he wrote about the treatise in question that 'it rests on principles more lax and latitudinarian, than it is in his power conscientiously to adopt'.[39]

At the Northamptonshire and Leicestershire Association meeting held at Clipstone in 1791, William Carey, pastor at Harvey Lane, Leicester since 1789, asked 'if it were not practicable, and our bounden duty to attempt somewhat toward preaching the gospel in the heathen world?'[40]

The awareness that the world was larger than England, impressed upon him by the weekly editions of the *Northampton Mercury* delivered to his village when he was a lad,[41] had done its work. In 1785 William, who then belonged to a group which met at Hackleton, near Northampton, had requested the Baptist church at Olney, of which John Sutcliff was pastor, to consider sending him out into the work of the ministry. Following his admission to membership in July of that year, he preached once on the following Lord's day. His address, it seems, was something of a disappointment both to his hearers and to himself. However, less than a year later the church book stated that he was 'sent out by the Church to preach the Gospel, wherever God in his providence might call him'.[42] In the event, providence led him to his life's work in India. His book, *An Enquiry into the obligations of Christians to use means for the Conversion of the Heathen*, elaborated his burden. At the association meeting in 1792 Carey was the preacher, his text being Isaiah 54:2-3, 'Enlarge the place of thy tent.' He expanded on the oft-quoted dictum 'Expect great things from God, and attempt great things for God'. Later, in the parlour of Mrs Martha Wallis's home at Kettering, there was formed 'The Particular Baptist Society for propagating the gospel among the Heathen'.[43] Some thirteen pounds were collected in Andrew Fuller's snuff-box. In 1793, in his address to the missionaries during their parting meeting at Leicester, Fuller commissioned them:

> Go then after your Saviour's example, go in pursuit of the lost sheep; follow after them, search and find them out, that they may be brought home to his fold, from the dark mountains whither they have wandered ... that they be delivered from the errors and abominations of the Heathen, and be brought to the knowledge and enjoyment of God.[44]

When, in 1793, William Carey set sail for India in the Danish East-Indiaman *Krön Princessa Maria*, together with John Thomas, a member of the Little Wild Street, London, church, he had been influenced profoundly by Edwards. The telling remark of Andrew Fuller in the year of the Kettering man's death, 1815, is worth citing:

> We have some, who have been giving out, of late, that "If Sutcliff, and some others, had preached more of Christ, and less of

Jonathan Edwards, they would have been more useful." If those who talk thus, preached Christ half as much as Jonathan Edwards did, and were half as useful as he was, their usefulness would be double what it is. It is very singular, that the Mission to the East should have originated with men of these principles; and, without pretending to be a prophet, I may say, If it ever falls into the hands of men who talk in this strain, it will soon come to nothing.[45]

The impact on the home churches must have been considerable, as witness the note dated March 24, 1793 in the records at Harvey Lane, Leicester, the pastorate of which Carey had surrendered to go to the Far East:

> Revd. Mr. Carey our Minister left Lester to go on a mishan to the East Indies in order to take the Gospell amongst the poor Heathen. This is inserted to show the love he had to the souls of his Fellow Creaturs.[46]

Such activity, said Ivimey, 'enkindled a spirit of zeal which had not been before manifested, or felt on behalf of heathens at home.'[47] Fuller at Kettering and Sutcliff at Olney both testified to the fact that when their people became interested in the mission parochial bickerings ceased; they acknowledged the folly of squabbling over minor differences at home when whole continents were without the Word of God.[48] Children at home were in dire need, too. In 1786, six years before the establishment of the mission, John Sutcliff had written in the Northamptonshire and Leicestershire Association's letter for that year:

> It may be hoped, that the prevailing practice of establishing schools upon the Lord's-day, may be attended with the most beneficial effects. ... The proper education of youth, is a matter of the highest importance. ... According to the present laudable plan, many are in a great measure preserved from what would be hurtful; and, by being taught to read, and regularly brought to the public worship of God, are in the way to learn that, which ... may be profitable to themselves, and render them more useful members of society at large.[49]

In 1797 there was formed 'The Baptist Society in London, for the encouragement and support of Itinerant and Village preaching'. The preachers had to be both Baptists and Calvinists. Abraham Booth, in his address circulated on behalf of the society, wrote that

... *reading* the inspired volume, and the *preaching* of divine truth, are the grand means appointed of God, to excite serious reflection and earnest prayer; to produce conviction of sin and interest the conscience in what the Scriptures reveal; to renew the heart, and give a holy bias to the whole soul.[50]

Although 'as a divine' Abraham Booth was reckoned in his time to have been 'a star of the first magnitude', according to his friend, Dr Newman,[51] Fuller, we recall, claimed that Booth did not say that faith is a duty because he would not. Allegedly, he evaded the question.[52] All this illustrates the perennial truth that a mature expression of Christian doctrine has never been attained either quickly or easily, not even by great men such as he. The Lord is patient when we are slow to understand, and we should be patient with each other; we remain disciples. The fact was that Booth's view of such matters was a touchy issue in his constituency, as is shown by a comment passed by John Rippon shortly after Booth's death in 1806. He concerned himself with the latter's conviction that the gospel provided a complete warrant for the ungodly to come to Jesus and with his view, as expressed by Rippon, that 'what men have a *right* to do in the Church they have a *command* to do'. He concluded that Booth would have maintained that 'every one knows that what men have a *right* to do, and are *commanded* to do, must certainly be their duty to do'.[53] The diplomatic Rippon was trying to cover up for Booth.

* * *

As the eighteenth century drew to its close many among the English Particular Baptists reverted gradually to the original Calvinism of their seventeenth-century forefathers. Reformed scholasticism retreated before leaders whose alert minds as well as warm hearts had been inflamed both by Scripture and by revival. In time, the pendulum swung the other way; sadly, the nineteenth century gave abundant testimony to a widespread surrender of the doctrines of grace among the Baptists. In 1855, Spurgeon, lonely in his popularity, wrote to another minister that the Tabernacle pulpit made it possible for him 'to revive the *old* doctrines of Gill, Owen, Calvin, Augustine, and *Christ*'.[54] Even John Gill was embraced by the young pastor at the New Park Street Chapel, Southwark.

CONCLUSION

We have arrived at the end of our study of the English Particular Baptists of the eighteenth century. Would you, the reader, allow some final remarks?

First, who were those among the Particular Baptists who came to be denominated as 'Strict Baptists'? William Jeyes Styles, in his 1887 attempt 'to state and advocate the tenets of the Strict and Particular Section of the Baptist Denomination',[1] put forward doctrines which, earlier, had been held by John Brine, John Skepp and John Gill. Styles wrote that because 'spiritual repentance' is an 'effect of a supernatural birth of the Spirit', it is not 'the duty of natural men'.[2] The impression given by Styles is that if one does not agree with him in this and in other related matters one is not a Strict Baptist.

The eighteenth century shows otherwise. The people who came to be called 'Strict Baptists' were then considered such simply because they insisted that their churches and the Lord's table should be opened to baptized believers only. It is perfectly true that a high Calvinist, John Brine, appears to have been the first to have acknowledged the epithet 'Strict Baptist'. Nevertheless, it does not appear that even he perceived any connection between his interpretation of the doctrines of grace and specified terms of communion as if the two stood or fell together. The question of whether or not saving faith is a duty, together with other controverted matters, does not seem to have impinged on this definition; evidence fails to show that either high Calvinism or any form of Calvinism had anything to do with being a Strict Baptist. We recall that Joseph Burroughs was characterized by Ivimey both as a Strict Baptist and an Arminian.

To this extent, Styles seems to have misappropriated the title. To quote Abraham Booth again, 'it appears that the epithet *strict* ... is no dishonour to us ... every Baptist ought to be a *Strict* one, or else renounce the name.'³ We recall that he concluded his *Apology* with the following exhortation to the increasing number of Baptists who advocated free communion:

> Be either consistent *Baptists*, or *Paedobaptists*; for, according to your present practice, all thinking and impartial men must pronounce you an *heterogenous mixture* of both.⁴

This complaint had nothing to do with high Calvinism.

We recall, too, Bunyan's sarcastic references to 'the brethren of the baptized way'.⁵ It seems that he distanced himself from many, even most, of the Baptists of his time, some of whom in neighbouring Northamptonshire were stigmatized as Strict Baptists shortly after his death in 1688. Our point is that the eighteenth-century Baptists provide a clear case for a new look at the adjective 'strict'. If the arguments presented by the advocates of restricted communion are accepted it might even be claimed that Baptist churches which operate 'mixed' communion, even on an occasional basis for the benefit of visitors, at one stroke forfeit their Baptist identity. 'Baptists' become such when, after their immersions, believers commit themselves to the joy and the challenge of a local baptized church, surrendering themselves to the Lord and to each other. The logic seems as right as it is unassailable.

In short, we assert on the basis of this period of Baptist history that a Strict Baptist congregation should not be considered as a church which by definition embraces high Calvinism. This may surprise some. Between the eighteenth century and our own time there have been many changes in every area of English society; in certain fundamental respects our situation is not that which must have both depressed and stimulated our forefathers. But some things do not alter. It could be that the definitions forged in the heat of controversy at that period still retain their value. We might draw an analogy from more recent history and from a quite different situation. When, in the 1940s, the men of the British 7th Armoured Division were ridiculed as 'Desert Rats' by their enemy, they adopted the desert jerboa as their shoulder flash. The name remains as an unofficial title. Similarly, the epithet 'Strict Baptist' might not be without some usefulness, indeed honour, nowadays. At least, it offers an instant definition of one aspect of applied New Testament churchmanship. Nevertheless, 'Strict Baptist' should not be adopted as a denominational title. For theological reasons Gill would not have done this, and Gill would have been right. If, in our time, we have to have some label, that of 'Baptist' will suffice.

Second, controversy about 'strict' and 'open' communion leads us to suppose that this will always be a divisive issue among Particular Baptists (let alone between them and others). That is, even orthodox Calvinism as such is not enough to bind churches together at a voluntary associational level. If they cannot agree upon terms for local-church communion they will tend to splinter and go their own way. Ivimey, we noted, observed that some churches, particularly those in Bedfordshire, kept away from the 1692 assembly because the former did not practise restricted communion.[6] John Bunyan was a great and a good man, yet he could and did lose his temper with the advocates of the restricted system. What likelihood, then, is there that Baptists who disagree now on this issue will be able to liaise fully either on an inter-church basis or even in a gathered church? One side would have to yield.

For example, the Independent church at Over, Cambridgeshire, originated in the 1730s with Mr Fisher as their first pastor. After his death in 1760 or 1761 the church was attracted by the preaching of Thomas Ladson, who remained with this 'destitute' people for a year or so. When they differed among themselves because most were traditionally Independents and he a Baptist, the Baptist faction departed, together with Mr Ladson, and founded their own church at Needingworth, thereby weakening considerably the Over group.[7] Baptists who take the New Testament seriously (and not all do, as some who have had dealings with the Baptist Union, for example, have found) will inevitably have problems about free communion, which says in effect that baptism is optional. It follows that one of several inescapable conclusions in the debate about terms of communion is that Paedobaptists who insist upon baptism as they understand it are more consistent than their Baptist brethren who open the Lord's table to unbaptized believers.

Furthermore, the tensions of the past might give guidance for present-day ministers. The fact of the matter is that there are always men in the ministry who believe sincerely enough that restricted communion reflects New Testament practice. C.B. Jewson, a member of St Mary's Baptist Church, Norwich, where Kinghorn had ministered continuously for fifty-two years, observed that in the communion controversy between Robert Hall and Kinghorn,

... while Kinghorn's logic was correct, the peculiar circumstances of the Baptist denomination in its relationship to other
evangelical bodies in England made his position impracticable, as
his own Church later proved.[8]

This was an admission that open-communionists sometimes
know better than they practise and that they permit pragmatism to
control churchmanship. We might be forgiven for making the
following suggestion about young ministers who allow themselves
in their earlier years to remain in open-communion churches.
Although such brethren could be reluctant to admit it, it might be
that they are not entirely happy about their situation; the New
Testament worries them. Further, they realise that, unless they make
their own arrangements at an early date, their fleeting years in the
Lord's work might well be controlled by a system of churchmanship
which, at heart, they perceive to be pastorally unsatisfying because
in this respect beyond the Word of God. They have a problem, a
problem exacerbated by an insistent awareness that transfer to a
restricted-communion situation would probably be fraught with all
manner of difficulty.

There is little doubt that this type of situation is the unhappy lot
of some. Facing what is something of a self-inflicted defeat, some
ministers so afflicted wish that they could alter the system which
pays them. Nevertheless, unwilling to face resignation and possible
redundancy, which might well be financially disastrous, they remain as they are. Later on, because they know that years have bound
them inextricably to a free-communion situation, they make the best
of it and choose to convince themselves that open communion is a
secondary matter of no primary importance; conversion, after all, is
the great thing. They ache with the awareness that what Christ has
commanded, though not necessary for salvation, is never to be
reckoned as non-essential in church building, and that what is not of
faith is sin. Perhaps the eighteenth century might teach would-be
pastors that they do need to apply their beliefs as soon as possible in
this area if they wish to avoid permanent regrets and vocational
defects. They who apply themselves to teaching future ministers
might take note, too.

Third, evidence from the eighteenth century shows clearly
enough that during this period there were in England two Baptist
groups, 'General' and 'Particular', and that they usually went their

own ways. Immersed Calvinists and Arminians did not, it seems, enjoy intimate fellowship together. Because, historically, men have always been dominated by the theological systems in which they have placed themselves, we ask if it could be otherwise now.

Fourth, with regard to the 1689 confession of faith, the period under review might serve to show that, unlike the Bible, Baptist confessions, however venerable, valuable and instructive, always reflect a sort of built-in obsolescence, and this because they were the products of their age.

The 1689 endorsement of the 1677 confession was to a considerable extent a needful political ploy. The confession was reintroduced after William of Orange became king to demonstrate that the Particular Baptists, after all, did agree in most matters with other Dissenters and, indeed, to a considerable extent with the Thirty-Nine Articles of the Established Church. This was, no doubt, largely why the distinctive terms of communion held by the majority of churches at the assembly were not mentioned explicitly; differences had to be played down.

Communion controversies before, during and after the eighteenth century surely indicate that that august confession might not be sufficient for our own time; no longer do Particular Baptists need to underemphasize their views about baptism and communion. To elevate the 1689 declaration to the status of an all-time standard might, then, be a positive mistake: different times and different situations demand new groupings and new formulations. We look back to our fathers, thank the Lord for them and, if we are wise, learn a great deal from them. Nevertheless, we do not suppose that their definitions are necessarily adequate for time and eternity.

Fifth, the eighteenth century shows the vulnerability of high Calvinism, at least as represented by the exegetical idiosyncracies of great John Gill and other men. Fuller, though not without some theological weaknesses, exploded the high-Calvinist distinction between 'legal' and 'evangelical' repentance. We should remember that preaching the command to all men everywhere to repent and to believe in the Lord Jesus Christ is nothing less than the ordained servant of election as well as an instrument of reprobation. Such preaching should attach to itself the loving promise that Christ will, indeed, receive and never cast out those who come to him, this being the unchanging warrant for any sinner to turn to the Lord. It is through exhorting men personally and indiscriminately to trust in Christ that the Lord both brings to himself all for whom he died, and becomes the great stumbling block of those who will not believe.

Finally, the eighteenth century has something to teach us concerning the preparation of men for the ministry. Although such giants as Brine and Gill were entirely orthodox with respect to their churchmanship, judged by numbers they appear to have failed almost disastrously where Whitefield and other establishment men succeeded so brilliantly. But, should we be too dismissive? What would Gill, Booth, Carey and Fuller have accomplished had they been socially advantaged Anglicans? Further, when one takes into account the almost total lack of any educational background for Baptists such as these, with whom we traverse a whole century, we are astonished at their attainments. The only Hebrew tutor known to Gill was a text book; no one ever stood over his shoulder to check his work. In spite of this, his skills in Semitics were truly superlative. Abraham Booth, in mid-century, worked at a loom to keep Elizabeth and the children, while teaching himself English grammar in his spare time. In spite of (or, perhaps, because of) this, his writings were second to none in both piety and scholarship.[9] Nevertheless, the sad fact remains that these great men were never permitted to enter either English university and therefore could never, for example, have been stimulated by the 'Holy Club' at Oxford. It might be said, of course, that, like Charles Haddon Spurgeon and many others, they were better off without such background preparation. Be that as it may, John Piggott's remark, published as far back as 1714, cuts to the quick:

> You must not expect that Preachers will drop down from Heaven, or spring out of the Earth; but due Care must be taken for the incouragement of humble men that have *real Gifts* and let such be train'd up in *useful Learning*, that they may be able to defend the Truths they preach.[10]

It might even be suggested that the Baptist high Calvinists, being in the main self-educated men who were never given a chance to pursue theological studies in a Scots or Dutch university or in an English Dissenting academy, arrived at their final interpretations of Calvinism prematurely.[11] It might well be that, without eighteenth-century versions of Priscilla and Aquila standing by, early misunderstandings tended to become ingrained in the alert minds of these men who, Apollos-like, were confessedly mighty in the Scriptures. Perhaps the enhanced social stability of the following century, unfortunately denied them in their day, would have done wonders for and have changed the story of early eighteenth-century English high Calvinism. On the other hand, these men fought their way single-handed to knowledge; most of us will never come near them. In 1754 the Anglican James Hervey, in a letter to the Particular Baptist John Collett Ryland, referred to John Brine and John Gill as 'those master builders in Israel', of whom 'we may say, in an inferior degree, what was said in the most exalted sense of their divine Lord, Isai. xi.3.'[12] Isaiah 11:3 predicts that the Messiah would be 'of quick understanding in the fear of the LORD'.

John Sutcliff, a man who was no believer in the needless multiplication of committee meetings,[13] went to the work of training others without waiting upon associations for approval or backup. After marrying in his early forties he obtained a home of his own in Olney High Street. Annexing the house next door, he turned it into an academy for missionary and ministerial students; until his death in 1814 he received and trained some thirty-two men.[14] In Yorkshire, too, John Fawcett saw the vision. 'The grand design we have in view is to furnish the churches of Christ with lively, zealous, judicious, disinterested ministers of the Word. We need not say how much they are at present wanted.' So he wrote in a circular letter to ministers and other people in June, 1773.[15]

Let's go back to a time before the 1690s, the decade in which John Gill was born and the 'Strict Baptists' appeared on a tiny Northamptonshire corner of the stage of history. Even then the question of training for the ministry was hotly debated. Thomas Collier, the West Country Baptist, argued in 1651 that

> ... it is the spirit of Antichrist that seeks after humane help to supply the room or want of this Spirit of Christ and having gotten it they grow proud of it, are self conceited in it, make it their idol and dare reproach the Spirit and power of the Lord and His saints.[16]

Not all agreed. The men who succeeded in convening that memorable first assembly in London in 1689 are surely to be applauded for their suggestion that they should concern themselves with giving 'fit and proper encouragement for the raising up an able and honourable ministry for the time to come'.[17] This, too, was the main concern of the Baptist Board of 1717, as it had been of Edward Terrill at Bristol. The leaders of the Particular Baptists in those crucial years were wise; they knew the importance of investment in ministerial preparation. Moreover, they were surely right to restrict funding to men of Calvinistic persuasion who proposed to serve in like-minded churches not incorporated in Arminian associations. The eighteenth century teaches us that Particular Baptists continue to require their own seminaries. It is not good enough for us to consign our hopeful young men to evangelical institutions committed to teaching self-defined fundamentals, during which formative period the students concerned might or might not learn something about Baptist principles. Failure to invest at this point will probably mean ministerial weakness in later years. Our fathers feared this three hundred years ago.

* * *

Thirty years or so earlier than the 1689 assembly Robert Steed and Abraham Cheare in Tiverton wrote about their situation as Baptists. They were acutely aware that the pro-Roman Catholic Charles Stuart would in all probability become Charles II, King of England. History records that this actually happened not long after. Steed, Cheare and many like them were anxious men:

> And at this day is there not to be observed and lamented, a spirit of giddiness taking great hold of men and things; so that the whole series of what of late dayes had on it the impression of Reformation, seeming as it were to labour and encline towards its ancient corruption? In which house of temptation we are indeed in expectation of greater tryals than these, and yet in the middest of them have this to be glad in our God for, that all along he hath not left us without several gracious testimonies of his converting and quickening presence.[18]

Nearly three hundred and fifty years have passed. It would seem that the present Prince of Wales is destined to succeed Queen Elizabeth as Charles III. What of the future, given the politics, both secular and ecclesiastical, of the age? Will there be a final, definitive inclination in England towards the 'ancient corruption' of Rome? It seems almost inconceivable that the papacy would not be involved significantly at the next coronation. Time will tell. One thing, of course, we know to be sure: our God has not yet left his people. Nor will he do so, whatever might happen.

NOTES AND REFERENCES

Abbreviations Used

Apology   Abraham Booth, *An Apology for the Baptists* (1778)

BAR, I, II, III, IV   John Rippon, *The Baptist Annual Register*, I (1790-3); II (1794-7); III (1798-1801); IV (1801-2)

Body, I, II   John Gill, *A Complete Body of Doctrinal and Practical Divinity: Or A System of Evangelical Truths, Deduced from the Sacred Scriptures*, New Edition, 2 vols (1839)

BQ   *Baptist Quarterly*

Brown   Raymond Brown, *The English Baptists of the 18th Century* (1986)

Cause, I, II   John Gill, *The Cause of God and Truth; In Four Parts. With a Vindication of Part IV. From the Cavils, Calumnies, and Defamations of Mr. Henry Heywood, &c*, New Edition, 2 vols (1814)

Crosby, I, II, III, IV   Tho. Crosby, *The History of the English Baptists, From The Reformation to the Beginning of the Reign of King George I*, 4 vols (1738-40; republished by Church History Research and Archives, Lafayette, Tenn., no date)

Gospel   Andrew Fuller, *The Gospel Worthy of All Acceptation; The Gospel Its Own Witness* (Evansville, Ind., 1961; reprint of the second edition, 1801)

HEB, I, II, III, IV   Joseph Ivimey, *A History of the English Baptists*, 4 vols
                         (1811-30)

Sermons, I, II, III   John Gill, *Sermons and Tracts*, New Edition, 3 vols
                         (1814-15)

TBHS   *Transactions of the Baptist Historical Society*

Underwood   A.C. Underwood, *A History of the English Baptists*
                         (1947)

Watts   Michael R. Watts, *The Dissenters: From the Reforma-
                         tion to the French Revolution* (Oxford, 1978)

Where no place of publication is given, London should be assumed.

Introduction

1 *The Baptist Union: A Short History*, second edition (1964), p. 127.
2 *The Sword and the Trowel* (1887), iiif.
3 Quoted by Iain H. Murray, *The Forgotten Spurgeon*, second edition (1973), p. 163.
4 *A Manual of Faith and Practice: Designed for Young and Enquiring Christians* (1887), Preface, i.
5 *Ibid.*, Preface, iii.
6 *Ibid.*, p. 204.
7 In a personal letter received in 1989 by a member of the Tabernacle Baptist Church, Wellingborough, Northants.
8 W.T. Selley, *England in the Eighteenth Century, 1689-1815*, third edition (1962), p. 242.
9 *Into Battle: Speeches by the Right Hon. Winston S. Churchill, C.H., M.P.*, compiled by Randolph S. Churchill, M.P., eleventh edition (1945), p. 234.
10 K.H.D. Haley, 'The Political Context of Monmouth's Rebellion', in *The Monmouth Rising: Aspects of the 1685 Rebellion in the West Country,* edited by Ivan Roots (Exeter, 1986), pp. 17-30 (pp. 17f.).
11 See p. 129.
12 See p. 213.
13 Quoted in the *Wellingborough and Rushden Mercury and Herald,* 9 June 1989, p. 4.
14 See p. 77.
15 See p. 117.
16 *Documents of the Christian Church,* edited by Henry Bettenson, The World's Classics, 495 (1959), pp. 374-6.

I The English Particular Baptists: A Separate Denomination

1 T.B. Macaulay, *History of England*, 5 vols (London, 1848-61; reprinted London, 1967), II, 253-307.
2 *English Historical Documents*, general editor David C. Douglas, 12 vols (1953-), VIII, 424; Crosby, I, vii; III, xiii.
3 Gilbert Burnet, *A Pastoral Letter Writ by the Right Reverend Father in God Gilbert, Lord Bishop of Sarum* (1689), pp. 21f.; *An Account of the Reasons of the Nobility and Gentry's Invitation to His Highness the Prince of Orange into England. Being a Memorial from the English Protestants Concerning their Grievances* (1688), p. 1.
4 Gilbert Burnet, *A Sermon Preached in the Chappel of St. James before His Highness the Prince of Orange, the 23rd of December, 1688* (1689), p. 28.

5   D.B. Murray, 'The Seventeenth and Eighteenth Centuries', in *The Baptists in Scotland: A History*, edited by D.W. Bebbington (Glasgow, 1988), pp. 9-25 (p. 13).

6   *HEB*, I, 145f.; see Underwood, pp. 57-9.

7   *Ibid.*, p. 182.

8   *HEB*, III, 301-3.

9   *Ibid.*, I, 140.

10   Underwood, p. 45.

11   I, 173; Alfred W. Light, *Bunhill Fields* (1913), pp. 117-22.

12   John Ryland, *The Work of Faith, the Labour of Love, and the Patience of Hope, illustrated; In the Life and Death of the Rev. Andrew Fuller*, second edition (1818), p. 3.

13   Crosby, III, 271f.

14   *HEB*, III, 418f.; B.R. White, 'Thomas Crosby, Baptist Historian: (I) The First Forty Years 1683-1723; (II) Later Years', *BQ*, XXI (1965), 154-68; 219-34 (p. 219). See p. 35.

15   See p. 50.

16   So, B.R. White, 'Thomas Crosby, Baptist Historian', p. 231; *Baptist Bibliography*, 2 volumes (1916-22), I, 160.

17   See p. 47.

18   *HEB*, IV, 200; 'Salters' Hall 1719 and the Baptists', *TBHS*, V (1916-17), 172-89 (pp. 173f.).

19   *Actual Justification Rightly Stated. Containing a True Narrative of Sad Schism made in a Church of Christ at Kilby in Leicester-Shire* (1696), p. 14; John Ryland, *A Funeral Sermon Occasioned by the Death of the Rev. Robert Hall, sen.* (no date), p. 54; A. Betteridge, 'Early Baptists in Leicestershire and Rutland (4)', *BQ*, XXVI (1976), 209-23 (pp. 215f.). The 1696 publication appears to have been written by Henry Coleman.

20   Shem Evans, *Memoir of the late Mr. William Bassett of Countesthorpe: Together with the Improved Edition of Mr. Bassett's 'History of the Baptist Church at Arnesby'* (Leicester, 1862), p. 7.

21   See p. 49.

22   David Bogue and James Bennett, *History of Dissenters, from the Revolution in 1688, to the Year 1808*, 4 vols (1808), III, 332f.

II From Repression to Protection: Before and After the Revolution of 1688

1   Crosby, I, 147f.

2   *Ibid.*, 148f. Daniel Neal, *The History of the Puritans or Protestant Non- Conformists*, second edition, corrected, 2 vols (1754), II, 110, gave the date of secession as about 1638.

3   *HEB*, I, 138.
4   Crosby, I, 148f.; *HEB* I, 138f.
5   *Ibid.*, III, 294.
6   B.R. White, *The English Separatist Tradition from the Marian Martyrs to the Pilgrim Fathers* (Oxford, 1971), p. 167.
7   *HEB*, I, 176.
8   *Ibid.*, 175.
9   *A Confession of Faith of seven Congregations or Churches of Christ in London, which are commonly (but unjustly) called Anabaptists* (1646, reprinted 1809), p. 28; Crosby, I, Appendix, pp. 20f.
10 *The Confession of Faith of those Churches, which are commonly (though falsly) called Anabaptists* (1644), Article 33.
11 *HEB*, I., 195.
12 Watts, p. 106.
13 *The History of the Puritans or Protestant Non-Conformists*, II, 110,112.
14 *HEB*, I, 239-45.
15 *Ibid.*, 247.
16 Underwood, p. 85; Watts, p. 160.
17 Watts, pp. 161, 219.
18 *HEB*, I, 329.
19 Watts, p. 135.
20 *Ibid.*, p. 223.
21 *HEB*, I, 312; Daniel Neal, *The History of the Puritans or Protestant Non-Conformists*, II, 592f.
22 D. Lindsay Keir, *The Constitutional History of Modern Britain 1485-1937*, third edition, revised (1946), p. 241.
23 See D.C. Sparkes, 'The Test Act of 1673 and Its Aftermath', *BQ*, XXV (1973), 74-85.
24 Watts, p. 80.
25 *HEB*, III, 239.
26 D. Lindsay Keir, *Constitutional History*, p. 431.
27 Crosby, II, 294-312; *HEB*, I, 388-95.
28 Watts, p. 205.
29 See p. 79.
30 *A Vindication of the Primitive Church, and Diocesan Episcopacy; In Answer to Mr. Baxter's Church History of Bishops, and their Councils Abridged* (1682), p. 303.
31 Crosby, II, 312.
32 *HEB*, I, 421.
33 Crosby, II, 344.
34 *Ibid.*, 317.
35 *A Confession of Faith, put forth by the Elders and Brethren of many Congregations of Christians, (Baptized upon Profession of their Faith), in London and the Country* (1689, reprinted 1809), v.

36   Discussed in detail by William L. Lumpkin, *Baptist Confessions of Faith*, revised edition (Valley Forge, 1979), pp. 344f.
37   *HEB*, I, 403.
38   *Ibid.*, 403f.
39   *Ibid.*, III, 295.
40   *Ibid.*, I, 433f.
41   *Ibid.*, 442.
42   *Ibid.*, 451.
43   *Ibid.*, 452.
44   *Ibid.*, 455.
45   *Ibid.*, 470.
46   *Ibid.*, 471.
47   *Ibid.*, 470; III, 506.
48   *Ibid.*, III, 507.
49   *Ibid.*, 498f. See p. 103.
50   See p. 162.
51   *HEB*, III, 507.
52   Tho. Bennett, *A Discourse of Schism*, second edition (Cambridge, 1702), p. 103.
53   *A Treatise on Various Subjects* (no date), p. 174.
54   Watts, pp. 509f.
55   *The Correspondence and Diary of Philip Doddridge*, edited by J.D. Humphreys, 5 vols (London, 1830-1), III, 127-9, 139f.; Job Orton, *Memoirs of the Life, Character and Writings of the late Reverend Philip Doddridge, D.D. of Northampton* (1766), pp. 250f.
56   *Ibid.*, p. 252.
57   Not to be confused with the mixed-communion Pinners' Hall church; see *HEB*, II, 485; III, 373-407.
58   Crosby, III, 278f.
59   *HEB*, IV, 452-8.
60   Dr Williams's Library Funeral Sermons, 1799-1820, II, 45.
61   *HEB*, IV, 457.
62   So, Samuel Palmer, *A Vindication of the Learning, Loyalty, Morals, and most Christian Behaviour of the Dissenters toward the Church of England. In Answer to Mr. Wesley's Defence of his Letter concerning the Dissenters Education* (1705), p. 93.
63   *A Collection of Poems For and Against Dr. Sacheverell and on other Affairs of State; most of them never before Printed*, no author (1710), part 2, pp. 32f.
64   *Ibid.*, part 4, p. 3.
65   Daniel Defoe, *A true Collection of the Writings of the Author of the True Born English-man* (1703), p. 419.
66   *Ibid.*, p. 428.

67 Herbert S. Skeats and Charles S. Miall, *History of the Free Churches of England 1688-1891* (1891), p. 168.
68 *A Defence of the private Academies and Schools of the Protestant Dissenters, against the Misrepresentations of them, as being dangerous to Church and State*, no author (1714), pp. 2f.
69 *Ibid.*, p. 12.
70 *A Caveat Against the New Sect of Anabaptists Lately Sprung up at Exon* (1714), pp. 13f., 18.
71 Lord Hardwicke's Marriage Act, 1753. *English Historical Documents*, X, 242-7.
72 *HEB*, III, 589, note.
73 *English Historical Documents*, X, 397.
74 *HEB*, III, 282.
75 *Calendar of State Papers, Domestic Series, of the Reign of William and Mary. 13th Feb. 1689 -April 1690*, edited by William John Hardy, F.S.A. (1895), p. 332.
76 Watts, p. 486.

III The Early 1700s

1 *HEB*, I, 478.
2 According to the pamphlet produced by the Assembly; *HEB*, I, 480f.
3 Brown, p. 34.
4 Crosby, III, 246-58; *HEB*, I, 500.
5 R. Hayden, 'The Particular Baptist Confession 1689 and Baptists Today', *BQ*, XXXII (1988), 403-17 (p. 405).
6 Crosby, IV, 296f.
7 *HEB*, I, 548.
8 *Ibid.*, IV, 269.
9 *BAR*, I, 426.
10 K.W. Clements, 'The Significance of 1679', *BQ*, XXVIII (1979), 2-6 (pp. 2-4).
11 *HEB*, III, 542-5.
12 *Ibid.*, 553.
13 *Ibid.*, 548.
14 H. Foreman, 'Baptist Provision for Ministerial Education in the 18th Century', *BQ*, XXVII (1978), 358-69 (p. 360).
15 *HEB*, III, 33; H. Foreman, 'Baptist Provision', pp. 362f.
16 *HEB*, III, 31f.
17 H. Foreman, 'Baptist Provision', pp. 362f.; 366f.
18 Brown, p. 40.
19 See p. 153.
20 Skeats & Miall, *History*, p. 219; Light, *Bunhill Fields*, p. 193.

21   *HEB*, III, 105.
22   *Ibid.*, 251; Walter Wilson, *The History and Antiquities of Dissenting Churches and Meeting Houses, in London, Westminster, and Southwark; including the Lives of their Ministers, from the Rise of Nonconformity to the Present Time*, 4 vols (1808-14), II, 597.
23   *Rabshakeh's Retreat. A Sermon Preach'd in Little-Wild Street, December 18, 1745. Being the day appointed for a general FAST, on occasion of the present Rebellion*, second edition (1745), p. 39.
24   *HEB*, III, 251f.
25   Dr Williams's Library Funeral Sermons, 1799-1820, VIII, 32
26   *HEB*, II, 451-64; III, 564-91.
27   Dr Williams's Library Funeral Sermons, 1663-1706, XV, 39.
28   *Ibid.*, 1713-15, p. 54.
29   *HEB*, III, 566.
30   *Ibid.*, 568-72.
31   *Ibid.*, 579.
32   *Ibid.*, 593.
33   *Ibid.*, 601.
34   *Ibid.*
35   *Ibid.*, 609, note.
36   *Ibid.*, 161.
37   *Ibid.*, 160-6; *An Impartial State of the Late Differences Amongst the Protestant Dissenting Ministers at Salters-Hall* (1719), p. 5.
38   *Christ the Centre, being the Inaugural Address of the Rev. F.W. Gotch, LL.D., Chairman, at the Autumnal Meeting of the Baptist Union, October 14, 1868* (1868), p. 14.
39   Watts, p. 376; *HEB*, III, 162.
40   Watts, p. 376.
41   *HEB*, III, 166-9.
42   *Ibid.*, I, 534f.
43   W.T. Whitley, *A History of British Baptists*, second edition (1932), p. 215.
44   Watts, pp. 269-74.
45   *HEB*, III, 52.
46   Brown, p. 41.
47   Crosby, IV, 163.
48   *HEB*, III, 136.
49   W.T. Whitley, *The Baptists of London 1612-1928* (no date), pp. 15f.; Crosby, III, 164-8.
50   Wilson, *The History and Antiquities of Dissenting Churches*, II, 254.
51   'The Hollis Family and Pinner's Hall', *BQ*, I (1922-3), 78-81 (p. 80).
52   *HEB*, III, 136f.
53   *Ibid.*, 137.
54   *Ibid.*, 138.

55 *Records of the Churches of Christ, Gathered at Fenstanton, Warboys, and Hexham. 1644-1720,* edited by E.B. Underhill (1854), p. 264.
56 *HEB*, III, 150-60.
57 Crosby, IV, 199f.
58 *HEB*, III, 156f.
59 *Ibid.*, 152.
60 *Ibid.*, 159, note.
61 M.D. MacDonald, 'London Calvinistic Baptists 1689-1727: Tensions within a Dissenting community under Toleration' (unpublished D. Phil. dissertation, University of Oxford, 1982), p. 282.
62 Crosby, IV, 350-62; *HEB*, III, 152f.
63 M.D. MacDonald, 'London Calvinistic Baptists', p. 261.
64 *Ibid.*, p. 282.
65 *HEB*, III, 154.
66 *Ibid.*, 208.
67 *Ibid.*, 282f.
68 *Ibid.*, 283.
69 John Ryland, *A Funeral Sermon Occasioned by the Death of the Rev. Robert Hall, sen.*, p. 53; Watts, p. 330.
70 John Ryland, *A Funeral Sermon Occasioned by the Death of the Rev. Robert Hall, sen.*, p. 63; H. Foreman, 'Baptist Provision', p. 359.
71 John Ryland, *A Funeral Sermon Occasioned by the Death of the Rev. Robert Hall, sen.*, pp. 63f.; *BAR*, I, 231f.
72 Carlton Baptist Meeting, First Church Book, 29 January 1732; *BAR*, I, 336.
73 'A Call to the Pastorate, Abingdon', *TBHS*, VI (1918-19), 250.
74 *English Historical Documents*, X, 396.
75 Robert Steed and Abraham Cheare, *A Plain Discovery of the Unrighteous Judge and False Accuser. Wherein is soberly, and in the fear of the Lord brought to light, and tendered to the examination of the Upright in Heart, the Spirit of that Pamphlet, intituled, The Leper Cleansed: Published by Richard Bellamy of Tiverton* (1658), p. 42.
76 M.D. MacDonald, 'London Calvinistic Baptists', p. 64.
77 *Ibid.*, p. 62.
78 *A Testimony against Perriwigs and Perriwig-Making and Playing on Instruments of Musick among Christians, or any other in the days of the Gospel* (Northampton, 1677, reprinted 1708), p. 8.
79 William Walker and others, *A True Representation of the Case of Church of Christ at Olney*, an unpublished, undated document retained by the Olney Baptist Church, p. 10.
80 *Ibid.*, p. 3.
81 Benjamin Keach, *The Articles of Faith of the Church of Christ, or Congregation meeting at Horsley-down, Benjamin Keach, Pastor,*

As asserted this 10th of the 6th Month, 1697 (1697), dedicatory epistle.

82 Crosby, IV, 301.

83 John Rippon, *A Brief Memoir of the Life and Writings of the Late Rev. John Gill, D.D.* (1838), pp. 123f.

84 Watts, p. 348.

85 *HEB*, III, 188.

86 *Ibid.*

87 M.D. MacDonald, 'London Calvinistic Baptists', p. 108.

88 So, Brown, p. 79.

89 See *Selection from Letters by Mrs. Anne Dutton*, compiled by J. Knight (1884); Ann Dutton, *Thoughts on the Lord's Supper* (1746-8), p. 51.

90 J.C. Whitebrook, 'The Life and Works of Mrs. Ann Dutton', *TBHS*, VII (1920-1), 129-46 (pp. 136, 140).

91 *HEB*, III, 277.

92 *Ibid.*, IV, 461-9.

93 William Newman, *Rylandiana: Reminiscences relating to the Rev. John Ryland, A.M. of Northampton, Father of the Late Rev. Dr. Ryland, of Bristol* (1835), p. 3.

94 H. Wheeler Robinson, 'A Baptist Student — John Collett Ryland', *BQ*, III (1926-7), 25-33 (p. 25).

95 *Sermons*, 8 vols (1807-20), VIII, 54.

96 Benjamin Beddome, *A Scriptural Exposition of the Baptist Catechism By Way of Question and Answer* (1752), p. 165.

97 B.R. White, 'Open and Closed Membership among English and Welsh Baptists', *BQ*, XXIV (1972), 330-4, 341 (p. 332).

98 *Sermons*, III, 553; Light, *Bunhill Fields*, p. 247.

99 *HEB*, III, 221-8.

100 Cited by D.C. Sparkes, 'The Test Act of 1673 and Its Aftermath', 79.

101 *HEB*, III, 231.

102 *Ibid.*, 233.

103 C.B. Jewson, 'St. Mary's, Norwich', IV, *BQ*, X (1940-1), 282-8 (p. 287).

104 *HEB*, III, 416-30.

105 Brown, p. 44.

106 S.J. Price, 'Repairing a Meeting-house in 1720', *BQ*, V (1930-1), 28f.

107 B.R. White, 'John Gill in London, 1719-1729: A Biographical Fragment', *BQ*, XXII (1967), 72-91.

108 S.J. Price, 'Sidelights from an old Minute Book', *BQ*, V (1930-1), 86-96, (p. 90).

109 *HEB*, III, 427.

110 *Zeal for the Church: Or, The Lamentation of the Cl—rgy: Occasioned by the Reverend Mr. Whitefield's Return to England. In a Poem Humbly Offer'd to the Consideration of the Judicious* (1741), p. 3.
111 *George Whitefield's Letters 1734-42*, edited by S.M. Houghton (Edinburgh, 1976), pp. 393f.
112 *Ibid.*, p. 496.
113 To the Revd. Nathaniel Wood, 10 September 1741, from *The Correspondence and Diary of Philip Doddridge*, IV, 56.
114 Geoffrey F. Nuttall, *Howell Harris 1714-1773 - The Last Enthusiast* (Cardiff. 1965), p. 38.
115 *Ibid.*, p. 32.
116 *Rylandiana*, pp. 10f.
117 Dr Williams's Library Funeral Sermons, 1799-1820, V, 25.
118 W. Newman, *Rylandiana*, p. 9.
119 H. Wheeler Robinson, 'A Baptist Student — John Collett Ryland', p. 32.
120 Dr Williams's Library Funeral Sermons, 1799-1820, V, 48.
121 *Remarks on the Christian Minister's Reasons for Administering Baptism by Sprinkling or Pouring of Water and An Answer to The Christian Minister's Reasons for Baptizing Infants* (1772), xv.
122 *BAR*, IV, 650.
123 *Ibid.*, 651.
124 Skeats & Miall, *History*, p. 359.
125 *HEB*, III, 278f.
126 *Ibid.*, IV, 13, 21.
127 *Ibid.*, 21f.
128 *Ibid.*, III, 195.
129 *Ibid.*, 279.

IV 'Strict Baptist' Origins

1 Norman Glass, *The Early History of the Independent Church at Rothwell, alias Rowell, in Northamptonshire* (1871), p. 32.
2 *Ibid.*, p. 51.
3 *Album of the Northamptonshire Congregational Churches*, edited by T. Stephens (Wellingborough, 1894), p. 47.
4 *An Account of the Doctrine and Discipline of Mr. Richard Davis, of Rothwell, in the County of Northampton, And those of his Separation* (1700), p. 22.
5 *Ibid.*, i.f.
6 *Ibid.*, p. 22.
7 *Ibid.*, p. 21.

8   See p. 153.
9   See p. 112.
10   *An Account of the Doctrine and Discipline of Mr. Richard Davis*, p. 22.
11   *A Sermon Concerning the Ends, and Mode, and Subjects of Baptism* (1713), p. 14.
12   Rothwell United Reformed Church, First Church Book, Articles of Faith.
13   Rothwell United Reformed Church, Second Church Book, p. 84.
14   W.A. Wicks, *Concise History of the Baptist Church, Walgrave* (Northampton, 1892), p. 49.
15   Rothwell United Reformed Church, Second Church Book, pp. 90f., 97; Rothwell First Church Book, pp. 150, 155.
16   See p. 93.
17   *The House of God Opened, and His Table Free for Baptists and Paedobaptists who are Saints and Faithful in Christ* (1777), i.
18   *Apology*, p. 138.
19   *Ibid.*, p. 140.
20   *Ibid.*, p. 142.
21   See p. 153.
22   Thomas Bradbury, *The Duty and Doctrine of Baptism. In Thirteen Sermons* (1749), p. 39.
23   See p. 148.
24   John Brine, *The Baptists vindicated from some Groundless Charges Brought against them by Mr. Eltringham, In a Pamphlet, intitled, The Baptist against the Baptist, &c.* (1756), p. 4. See Fredk. Wm. Bull, *A Sketch of the History of the Town of Kettering* (Kettering, 1891), pp. 107f.
25   *The Baptists vindicated*, title page.
26   *The Doctrine of Believer's Baptism by Immersion for Justification, Exploded, and proved to be Antiscriptural*, pp. 11f.
27   *A Sermon Preached at the Baptism of Several Persons in Barbican, November 2, 1750*, second edition (1751), p. 36.
28   *The Doctrine of Believer's Baptism by Immersion for Justification Exploded*, p. 9.
29   William Eltringham, *The Baptist against the Baptist: Or, a Display of Antipaedo-Baptist Self-Inconsistency; In Answer to Several Letters from a Baptist-Brother. To which is added, A Reply to a Letter subscribed J.W. written by way of reproof to Me, and in defence of Dr. Gill* (1755), p. 25.
30   *Ibid.*, pp. 24, 32.
31   See p. 91.
32   *The Baptist against the Baptist*, p. 32.
33   *The Baptists vindicated*, p. 5.
34   *Ibid.*, p. 7.

35 *Ibid.*, p. 9.
36 John Bunyan, *Peacable Principles and true: Or, a brief Answer to Mr. Danvers and Mr. Paul's Books against my Confession of Faith, and Differences in Judgment about Baptism no Bar to Communion. Wherein their Scriptureless Notions are overthrown, and my peacable Principles still maintained, in The Works of that Eminent Servant of Christ, Mr. John Bunyan*, revised by Samuel Wilson, second edition, 2 vols (1736-7), II, 102-11 (p. 104).
37 *A Confession of my Faith, and a Reason of my Practice: Or, With who, and who not, I can hold Church-Fellowship, or the Communion of Saints, in The Works of that Eminent Servant of Christ, Mr. John Bunyan*, II, 47-71 (p. 58).
38 *Ibid.*, p. 56.
39 John Bunyan, *Peacable Principles*, p. 110.
40 John Bunyan, *Differences in Judgment About Water-Baptism, No Bar to Communion: OR, To Communicate with Saints, as Saints, proved lawful* (1673), p. 41.
41 *A Defence of a Book intitled, The Ancient Mode of Baptizing, by Immersion, Plunging, or Dipping in Water, etc. Against Mr. Matthias Maurice's Reply, call'd Plunging into Water no Scriptural Mode of Baptizing &c.* (1727), p. 3.
42 *The Olney Baptist Meeting*, an anonymous, undated, typed history of Olney Baptist Church retained at that church, p. 223.
43 *The Manner of Baptizing with Water Cleared up from the Word of God and Right Reason; In a Plain free Debate upon that Subject between Mr. J.P. and Mr. B.W. June 6. 1726* (1726), p. 48.
44 See p. 93.
45 W.T. Whitley, *Baptist Bibliography*, I, 152.
46 *HEB*, III, 477f.
47 *Ibid.*, 472.
48 Samuel Halkett and John Laing, *A Dictionary of the Anonymous and Pseudonymous Literature of Great Britain*, 4 vols (Edinburgh, 1882-8), do not refer to *The Manner of Baptizing*.
49 *HEB*, III, 465f.
50 *A Defence of a Book intitled The Ancient Mode of Baptizing*, p. 3.
51 Benjamin Wallin, *The Folly of Neglecting Divine Institutions. An Earnest Address to the Christian, Who continues to Refrain from the Appointments of the Gospel*, second edition (1758), v.
52 *Ibid.*, ix.
53 Benjamin Wallin, *The Universal Concern of Saints in Communion* (1762), p. 3.
54 *HEB*, III, 453. Whitley, *Baptist Bibliography*, I, 152, claims that Gill was responding to Maurice.
55 Norman Glass, *The Independent Church at Rothwell*, pp. 143f.

56   *Plunging into Water No Scriptural Mode of Baptizing*, pp. 5f.
57   *HEB*, IV, 205, 210; Wilson, *The History and Antiquities of Dissent-ing Churches*, III, 249, 254.
58   See p. 23; *HEB*, IV, 205-19, *passim*.
59   Wilson, *The History and Antiquities of Dissenting Churches*, III, 252.
60   *HEB*, IV, 205.
61   *A Farther Defence of Two Discourses relating to Positive Institu-tions: In answer to the Rev Mr. Caleb Fleming's Vindication of the Appendix to the Plea for Infants* (1746), p. 39.
62   See p. 88.
63   *HEB*, IV, 35.

V   Restricted-Communion Baptists and Controversy about Communion in the Late 1600s

1   B.R. White, 'Open and Closed Membership among English and Welsh Baptists', p. 330.
2   *Apology*, p. 25.
3   Lumpkin, p. 101.
4   *Ibid.*, p. 152.
5   *The Confession of Faith of those Churches, which are commonly (though falsly) called Anabaptists*, Article 33.
6   Lumpkin, pp. 209f.
7   *Ibid.*, p. 237; Underwood, p. 103.
8   B.R. White, 'Open and Closed Membership among English and Welsh Baptists', p. 332.
9   Lumpkin, p. 321.
10   *HEB*, I, 490.
11   *A Solemn Call, or a Discourse concerning Baptism* (1690).
12   *HEB*, I, 523; Carlton Baptist Meeting, First Church Book, p. 19.
13   Watts, p. 165.
14   *The Heavenly Footman or a Description of the Man that gets to Heaven* (1928 reprint of the 1860 edition), p. 10; See J.D. Ban, 'Was John Bunyan a Baptist? A Case-Study in Historiography', *BQ*, XXX (1984), 367-76 (p. 375).
15   *Peacable Principles*, p. 103.
16   Identified explicitly as such by Bunyan, *Peacable Principles*, p. 110.
17   *Differences in Judgment About Water-Baptism*, p. 97.
18   *The Pilgrim's Progress*, impression of the eleventh edition, 1688 (1928), p. 15.
19   *Grace Abounding to the Chief of Sinners*, twentieth-century revision of the eighth edition, 1688 (no date), pp. 155f.
20   *HEB*, II, 24, 36, note

21 *Ibid.*, 416-30, *passim*; 420.
22 *Differences in Judgment about Water-Baptism*, p. 121.
23 *Ibid.*, p. 3
24 *Ibid.*, p. 70.
25 *Ibid.*, p. 5.
26 *Ibid.*, p. 99.
27 *Ibid.*, p. 97.
28 *Ibid.*, p. 13.
29 *Ibid.*, pp. 50, 87.
30 *Ibid.*, pp. 13, 77.
31 *Ibid.*, p. 21.
32 *Ibid.*, p. 22.
33 *Ibid.*, p. 24.
34 *Ibid.*, pp. 25, 41.
35 *Ibid.*, pp. 36, 72.
36 *Ibid.*, p. 48.
37 *Ibid.*, pp. 36, 66f.
38 *Ibid.*, p. 41.
39 *Ibid.*, pp. 46-8.
40 *Ibid.*, pp. 50f., 90.
41 *Ibid.*, pp. 52, 55, 87.
42 *Ibid.*, p. 73.
43 *Ibid.*, pp. 80f.
44 *Ibid.*, pp. 82-4.
45 Crosby, III, 90.
46 Henry Danvers, *A Treatise of Baptism. Wherein That of Believers and that of Infants is examined by the Scriptures*, second edition (1674), p. 36.
47 Danvers, *A Treatise of Baptism* (1673), p. 42.
48 *Ibid.*, p. 43.
49 *Ibid.*, p. 48.
50 *Ibid.*, pp. 48f.
51 *Ibid.*, pp. 49, 51.
52 In the view of G.E. Lane, *Henry Danvers: Contender for Religious Liberty* (Ealing, 1972), pp. 51f.
53 This is not the full title. The cover page of the copy available to the writer has been defaced; a single word falling between 'Touching' and '*Communion*' remains illegible.
54 Crosby, III, 6; *HEB*, III, 315.
55 *Some Serious Reflections*, Preface to the Reader.
56 *Ibid.*
57 *Ibid.*
58 *Ibid.*, pp. 3f.
59 *Ibid.*, pp. 5f.; 56.

60   *Ibid.*, pp. 9f.; 26.
61   *Ibid.*, pp. 10f.; 23f.
62   *Ibid.*, pp. 13-15.
63   *Ibid.*, pp. 17-19.
64   *Ibid.*, p. 19.
65   *Ibid.*, pp. 20f.
66   *Ibid.*, pp. 21f.
67   *Ibid.*, p. 23.
68   *Ibid.*, pp. 29-32.
69   *Ibid.*, pp. 46-8.
70   *Ibid.*, pp. 48f.
71   *Ibid.*, pp. 51f.
72   *Ibid.*, p. 54.
73   *Ibid.*, p. 55.
74   *Ibid.*, p. 56.
75   *Ibid.*, p. 58.
76   *Ibid.*, p. 60.
77   *HEB*, III, 312.
78   *A Sober Discourse of Right to Church Communion* (1681), pp. 162f.
79   *Ibid.*, p. 161.
80   *Ibid.*, pp. 3-9.
81   *Ibid.*, p. 47.
82   *Ibid.*, pp. 64f.
83   *Ibid.*, pp. 88f.
84   *Ibid.*, p. 120.
85   *Ibid.*
86   *Ibid.*, p. 152.
87   *Ibid.*, p. 154.
88   R.W. Oliver, 'John Collett Ryland, Daniel Turner and Robert
      Robinson and the Communion Controversy, 1772-1781', *BQ*, XXIX
      (1981), 77-9.
89   *HEB*, III, 373.
90   Crosby, III, 45.
91   *Ibid.*, 45-7.

VI   The Communion Controversy during the 1700s

1   See pp. 79-82. A. Chamberlain's booklet, *A Notable Rothwell Family*
     (Rothwell, Northamptonshire, no date), p. 4, provides information
     about John Cogan.
2   See p. 162.
3   *The History and Antiquities of Dissenting Churches*, I, 532. Brine's
     sermon was *The Knowledge of Future Glory: The Support of the*

Saints, in present Troubles. A Sermon, Occasioned by the Death of the Reverend and Learned Mr. Clendon Daukes (1759).

4   *Some Just and Necessary Remarks*, p. 40.
5   Wilson, *The History and Antiquities of Dissenting Churches*, I, 531.
6   *Ibid.*, 532. See p.163.
7   See pp. 93-4.
8   *A Sermon Occasioned by the Death of Mrs. Rebekah Cox* (1769), p. 13, note.
9   *The Baptists Vindicated*, p. 9.
10 *Ibid.*, p. 10.
11 *HEB*, IV, 35f.
12 R.W. Oliver, 'John Collett Ryland, Daniel Turner and Robert Robinson and the Communion Controversy, 1772-1781'.
13 *Baptism a Divine Commandment to be Observed. Being a Sermon Preached at Barbican, Octob. 9, 1765. at the Baptism of the Reverend Mr. Robert Carmichael, Minister of the Gospel in Edinburgh* (1766), iiif.
14 *Ibid.*, iv.
15 *Infant Baptism, A Part and Pillar of Popery* (1766), p. 35.
16 *A Modest Plea for Free Communion at the Lord's Table; Particularly between the Baptists and the Paedobaptists. In a Letter to a Friend* (1772), p. 4.
17 *Ibid.*
18 *Ibid.*, p. 5.
19 *Ibid.*, pp. 5f.
20 *Ibid.*, pp. 6, 16.
21 *Ibid.*, pp. 7, 9.
22 *Ibid.*, pp. 7f.
23 *Ibid.*, pp. 8, 11.
24 *Ibid.*, p. 9.
25 *Ibid.*, pp. 11, 16; J.C. Ryland, *A Modest Plea for Free Communion at the Lord's Table; between True Believers of all Denominations: In a Letter to a Friend* (1772), pp. 2f.
26 Crosby, I, 288.
27 *Baptism a Term of Communion at the Lord's Supper*, second edition (Norwich, 1816), pp. 100f.
28 *Ibid.*, pp. 72f.
29 John Ryland, *Life and Death of the Rev. Andrew Fuller*, pp. 372-4; R. W. Oliver, 'The Emergence of a Strict and Particular Baptist Community among the English Calvinistic Baptists 1770-1850 (unpublished Ph.D. dissertation, London Bible College, 1986), pp. 52f.
30 *The House of God Opened*, i.
31 *Ibid.*, ii.
32 *Ibid.*, iii.

33   *Ibid.*
34   *Ibid.*, p. 1.
35   *Ibid.*, pp. 1f.
36   *Ibid.*, p. 2.
37   *Ibid.*
38   *Ibid.*, pp. 2f.
39   *Ibid.*, p. 3.
40   *Ibid.*, pp. 3f., 7.
41   *Ibid.*, p. 4.
42   *Ibid.*,
43   *Ibid.*, pp. 4-6, 22.
44   *Ibid.*, p. 6.
45   *Ibid.*, p. 7.
46   *Ibid.*, p. 8.
47   *Ibid.*
48   *Ibid.*, pp. 8f.
49   *Ibid.*, p. 9.
50   *Ibid.*, p. 10.
51   *Ibid.*, p. 11.
52   *Ibid.*, pp. 12f.
53   *Ibid.*, p. 14.
54   *Ibid.*, p. 16.
55   *Ibid.*, pp. 17-20.
56   *Free Communion an Innovation: Or, An Answer to Mr. John
     Brown's Pamphlet, Entitled, The House of God Opened and His
     Table Free, &c* (1778). A lecture given in 1917 by the Revd C.E.
     Charlesworth, of Luton, and published by the *Dunstable Borough
     Gazette*, 4 July 1917, refers to Buttfield as Butterfield, and gives the
     dates of his Thorn pastorate and decease.
57   *HEB*, IV, 32.
58   *Free Communion an Innovation*, pp. 1-9.
59   *Ibid.*, pp. 10f.
60   *Ibid.*, p. 13.
61   *Ibid.*, p. 14.
62   *Ibid.*, pp. 16-19, 18.
63   *Ibid.*, pp. 20f.
64   *Ibid.*, p. 22.
65   *Ibid.*, p. 23.
66   *Ibid.*, pp. 25, 32.
67   *Ibid.*, p. 26.
68   *Ibid.*, pp. 27, 31.
69   *Ibid.*, p. 37.
70   *Ibid.*, pp. 37-9.
71   *Ibid.*, p. 39.

72 *Ibid.*, pp. 40, 42.
73 *Ibid.*, pp. 43f.
74 *Ibid.*, p. 45.
75 *BAR*, IV, 770.
76 *A Candid Statement of the Reasons which induce the Baptists to differ in Opinion and Practice from so many of their Christian Brethren* (1814), x.
77 *Ibid.*, x-xi.
78 William Newman, *Rylandiana*, p. 7.
79 *Ibid.*, p. 11.
80 *HEB*, IV, 421.
81 *Ibid.*, 35.
82 See pp. 69-72.
83 *A Charge and Sermon, together with an Introductory Discourse and Confession of Faith, delivered at the Ordination of the Rev. Mr. Abraham Booth, Feb. 16, 1769, in Goodman's Fields (1769)*, pp. 22f.
84 *HEB*, IV, 36; *Apology*, p. 142.
85 *Apology*, preface.
86 *Ibid.*, p. 13.
87 *Ibid.*, p. 18.
88 *Ibid.*, p. 28.
89 *Ibid.*, pp. 31-3.
90 *Ibid.*, pp. 33-5.
91 *Ibid.*, pp. 35f.
92 *Ibid.*, p. 36.
93 *Ibid.*, pp. 38-49.
94 *Ibid.*, p. 50.
95 *Ibid.*, p. 55.
96 *Ibid.*, p. 57.
97 *Ibid.*, pp. 57-60.
98 *Ibid.*, p. 64.
99 *Ibid.*, pp. 64-9.
100 *Ibid.*, pp. 70f.
101 *Ibid.*, p. 146.
102 See p. 118. Sheila Mitchell, *Not Disobedient* (Leicester, 1984), p. 51.
103 See p. 118.

VII The Communion Controversy in the Early 1800s

1 *Open Communion Unscriptural; A Letter from the Late A. Fuller, of Kettering, (Dated Sept. 21, 1800,) to the Rev. W. Ward, Missionary at Serampore*, second edition (1824), p. 9.

2   Cited in Angus Library, Regent's Park College, Circular Letters 1766-94, p. 3.
3   *HEB*, IV, 333.
4   *Ibid.*, III, viii.
5   *Ibid.*, IV, v.
6   See p. 208.
7   'Life of the Rev. Robert Hall, D.D.', in *The Imperial Magazine*, XIV (no date), 195-219 (p. 210).
8   *Ibid., passim.* See also Sheila Mitchell, *Not Disobedient*, pp. 41-51.
9   Robert Hall, *Terms of Communion*, v.
10   *Ibid.*, iv.
11   *Ibid.*, pp. 1, 5.
12   *Ibid.*, p. 7.
13   *Ibid.*, p. 8.
14   *Ibid.*, pp. 9f.
15   *Ibid.*, pp. 13-41.
16   *Ibid.*, p. 39.
17   *Ibid.*, p. 41.
18   *Ibid.*, p. 42.
19   *Ibid.*, p. 44.
20   *Ibid.*, pp. 47, 48f.
21   *Ibid.*, p. 49.
22   *Ibid.*, p. 51.
23   *Ibid.*, pp. 53f.
24   *Ibid.*, p. 55.
25   *Ibid.*, p. 56.
26   *Ibid.*, pp. 60f.
27   *Ibid.*, p. 62.
28   *Ibid.*, p. 63.
29   *Ibid.*, pp. 65, 70, 72.
30   *Ibid.*, pp. 72f.
31   *Ibid.*, p. 74.
32   *Ibid.*, p. 75.
33   *Ibid.*, pp. 79f.
34   *Ibid.*, p. 81.
35   *Ibid.*, p. 83.
36   *Ibid.*
37   *Ibid.*, p. 85.
38   *Ibid.*, p. 87.
39   *Ibid.*, p. 89.
40   *Ibid.*, p. 90.
41   *Ibid.*, p. 91.
42   *Ibid.*, p. 92.
43   *Ibid.*, p. 94.

44 *Ibid.*, p. 111.
45 *Ibid.*, pp. 114f.
46 *Ibid.*
47 *Ibid.*, p. 116.
48 *Ibid.*, pp. 116f.
49 *Ibid.*, p. 120.
50 *Ibid.*, p. 121.
51 *Ibid.*, pp. 124f.
52 *Ibid.*, p. 127.
53 *Ibid.*, p. 129.
54 *Ibid.*, p. 131.
55 *Ibid.*, p. 133.
56 *Ibid.*, p. 134.
57 *Ibid.*, p. 137.
58 *Ibid.*, p. 140.
59 *Ibid.*, p. 143.
60 *Ibid.*, p. 148.
61 *Ibid.*, p. 150.
62 *Ibid.*, p. 152.
63 *Ibid.*, p. 155.
64 *Ibid.*, pp. 156, 159f.
65 *Ibid.*, pp. 164-6.
66 *Ibid.*, p. 169.
67 *Ibid.*, p. 174.
68 *Ibid.*, pp. 175f.
69 *Ibid.*, p. 179.
70 *Ibid.*, p. 183.
71 *Ibid.*, p. 186.
72 *Ibid.*, p. 189.
73 Skeats & Miall, *History*, p. 434.
74 *Baptism a Term of Communion*, iv.
75 *Ibid.*, p. 10.
76 *Ibid.*, pp. 1f.
77 *Ibid.*, p. 3.
78 *Ibid.*, p. 7.
79 *Ibid.*, p. 9.
80 *Ibid.*, pp. 11f., 16.
81 *Ibid.*, p. 17.
82 *Ibid.*, p. 20.
83 *Ibid.*, p. 24.
84 *Ibid.*, pp. 26, 30, 34.
85 *Ibid.*, pp. 36f., 39.
86 *Ibid.*, pp. 46, 49.
87 *Ibid.*, p. 54.

88 *Ibid.*, p. 55.
89 *Ibid.*, p. 56.
90 *Ibid.*, p. 58.
91 *Ibid.*, p. 64.
92 *Ibid.*, pp. 69f.
93 *Ibid.*, pp. 76f.
94 *Ibid.*, p. 78.
95 *Ibid.*, p. 85.
96 *Ibid.*, pp. 86, 88.
97 *Ibid.*, p. 89.
98 *Ibid.*, p. 91.
99 *Ibid.*, p. 95.
100 *Ibid.*, p. 99.
101 *Ibid.*, p. 100.
102 *Ibid.*, p. 114.
103 *Ibid.*, p. 108.
104 *Ibid.*, p. 118.
105 *Ibid.*, p. 119.
106 *Ibid.*, p. 122.
107 *Ibid.*
108 *Ibid.*, p. 128.
109 *Ibid.*, p. 131.
110 *Ibid.*, p. 139.
111 *Ibid.*, p. 142.
112 *Ibid.*, p. 146.
113 *Ibid.*, p. 153.
114 *Ibid.*
115 *Ibid.*, p. 156, citing from *The Confession of Faith, Agreed upon by the Assembly of Divines at Westminster, 1647* (Publication Committee of the Free Presbyterian Church of Scotland, 1958), p. 112.
116 *Baptism a Term of Communion*, p. 161.
117 *Ibid.*, p. 162.
118 *Ibid.*, p. 164.
119 *Ibid.*
120 *Ibid.*, p. 170.
121 *Ibid.*, p. 175.
122 *Ibid.*, p. 177.
123 *A Reply to the Rev. Joseph Kinghorn: Being A Further Vindication of the Practice of Free Communion* (Leicester, 1818), xiii.
124 *Ibid.*, pp. 17f.
125 *Ibid.*, p. 43.
126 *Ibid.*, p. 58.
127 To this he devotes a full chapter, *ibid.*, pp. 60-94.
128 *Ibid.*, pp. 74, 79, 81.

129 *Ibid.*, p. 87.
130 *Ibid.*, pp. 91-3.
131 *Ibid.*, p. 97.
132 *Ibid.*, p. 98.
133 *Ibid.*, p. 99.
134 *Ibid.*, p. 120.
135 *Ibid.*, pp. 109f.
136 *Ibid.*, p. 122.
137 *Ibid.*, pp. 131-5.
138 *Ibid.*, p. 145.
139 *Ibid.*, p. 149.
140 *Ibid.*, p. 190.
141 *Ibid.*, p. 201.
142 *Ibid.*, p. 205.
143 *Ibid.*, p. 198.
144 *Ibid.*, pp. 208f.
145 *Ibid.*, pp. 216-47, 219.
146 *Ibid.*, pp. 234, 240, 243, 246.
147 *Ibid.*, pp. 251, 261.
148 *Ibid.*, p. 255.
149 *Ibid.*, pp. 274, 279.
150 The date of Hall's disclosure was 1826, some five years before he died. See *The Works of Robert Hall*, A.M., 6 vols. second edition (1832-3), III, 411.
151 *A Reply to the Rev. Joseph Kinghorn*, p. 280.
152 *A Defence of "Baptism a Term of Communion". In Answer to the Rev. Robert Hall's Reply* (Norwich, 1820), p. 3.
153 *Ibid.*, p. 35.
154 *Ibid.*, p. 59.
155 *Ibid.*, p. 146.
156 *Ibid.*, p. 186.
157 *Ibid.*, pp. 189, 194-8.
158 *Ibid.*, pp. 201, 206.
159 See Noel Weeks, *The Sufficiency of Scripture* (Edinburgh, 1988), p. 12.

VIII   High Calvinism and the Particular Baptists

1 John Ryland, *The Life and Death of the Rev. Andrew Fuller*, p. 369.
2 *The Works of Augustus M. Toplady, A.B.*, New Edition, 6 vols (1825), III, 36f.
3 *Memoirs of the Life and Writings of Isaac Watts, D.D. with Extracts from his Correspondence*, no author (1806), p. 114.

4   O.C. Robison, 'The Legacy of John Gill', *BQ*, XXIV (1971), 111-25 (pp. 112f.).
5   Robert Hall, *Help to Zion's Travellers: Being an Attempt to remove Various Stumbling Blocks out of the Way, relating to Doctrinal, Experimental, and Practical Religion*, second edition (1807), ix.
6   *HEB*, III, 449, note.
7   Lewis Wayman, *A Further Enquiry after Truth* (1738), p. 54.
8   *Ibid.*, p. 96.
9   John Brine, *A Sermon Preach'd at the Ordination of the Revd Mr John Ryland, on the 26th of July, 1750* (no date), pp. 26, 30.
10 John Brine, *The Certain Efficacy of the Death of Christ, Asserted (1743)*, p. 211.
11 The late king was George I, 1714-27; *HEB*, III, 259f.
12 *Ibid.*, I, 418; III, 260.
13 *Christ Alone Exalted in the Perfection and Encouragement of the Saints, Notwithstanding Sins and Trials*, seventh edition, 2 vols (1832), I, 148.
14 *Sermons*, III, p. 10.
15 *The Sword and the Trowel* (March, 1887), pp. 123f.
16 *HEB*, III, 449, note.
17 See p. 69.
18 *An Account of the Doctrine and Discipline of Mr. Richard Davis*, p. 22.
19 Richard Davis, *Faith the Grand Evidence Of Our Interest in Christ: Or The Nature of Faith and Salvation open'd, from John vi. 40* (1704), pp. 85f.
20 G.F. Nuttall, 'Northamptonshire and *The Modern Question*, A Turning Point in Eighteenth-Century Dissent', *Journal of Theological Studies*, New Series, XVI (1965), 101-23 (p. 108), citing from R.T. Jenkins in *Y Cofiador rhifyn* 12 (Mawrth, 1935), p. 11.
21 *HEB*, III, 363.
22 *Ibid.*, 262.
23 *Divine Energy: Or the Efficacious Operations of the Spirit of God upon the Soul of Man, in his Effectual Calling and Conversion, Stated, Proved and Vindicated*, third edition (1815), p. 62.
24 *Ibid.*, p. 245.
25 *HEB*, III, 264.
26 *Ibid.*, 267.
27 G. Nuttall, *Calendar of the Correspondence of Philip Doddridge DD (1702-1751)* (1979), p. 41.
28 Matthias Maurice, *The Tribes of the Lord appearing before him: Or, Families in Publick Worship. A Sermon Preach'd At the opening of the New Meeting-House, at Rowel, November 9, 1735* (1736), p. 54, note.

29 *A Modern Question Modestly Answer'd* (1737), p. 4; *HEB*, III, 270, note.
30 *HEB*, III, 270, note.
31 *Ibid.*
32 Matthias Maurice, *The Modern Question Affirm'd and Prov'd: Viz. That the Eternal God does by his Word make it the Duty of poor unconverted Sinners, who hear the Gospel preach'd or publish'd, to believe in Jesus Christ* (1739), ivf.
33 *HEB*, III, 271, note.
34 *A Dialogue between Christophilus, Philalethes, and Philagathus. Wherein is contained an Answer to Mr. Alvery Jackson's Question Answered* (1753), p. 42.
35 *Some Mistakes in a Book of Mr. Johnson's of Liverpool, Intitled, The Faith of God's Elect, etc. Noted and Rectified* (1755), p. 33.
36 *Grace, proved to be at the Sovereign Disposal of God: In a Discourse Preached June 19, 1760* (1760), p. 15.
37 *HEB*, III, 430-61, *passim*.
38 John Gill, *A Sermon on the Knowledge of Christ ... to which is appended ... a Baptismal Hymn* (1846), p. 29.
39 *HEB*, III, 272.
40 *Ibid.*, 446.
41 *The Works of Robert Hall*, VI, 125.
42 So, Thomas J. Nettles, *By His Grace and for His Glory* (Grand Rapids, Mich., 1986), p. 88.
43 *HEB*, III, 460.
44 *Ibid.*, 461.
45 See p. 43; George Whitefield, *Fifteen Sermons Preached on Various Important Subjects* (New York, 1794), pp. 52f.
46 *Some Account of the Life and Writings of the Rev. John Martin, Pastor of the Church, Meeting in Store Street, Bedford Square* (1797), p. 43.
47 *Ibid.*, p. 44.
48 *HEB*, III, 176, note.
49 *Ibid.*, 451, note.
50 *Ibid.*
51 *Brief Memoir*, p. 118.
52 *HEB*, III, 455, 458.
53 John Wesley, *Works*, 14 vols, third edition (1829), VII, 373-86. The excerpt from Toplady's diary is cited by Light, *Bunhill Fields*, p. 126.
54 *George Whitefield's Letters 1734-42*, p. 189. See Gordon Rupp, *Religion in England 1689-1791* (Oxford, 1986), p. 371.
55 *The Doctrine of Predestination Stated, and Set in the Scripture Light in Opposition to Mr. Wesley's Predestination calmly Considered*, from *Sermons*, III, 100-32 (p. 120).

56   *The Doctrine of Predestination*, pp. 109f.
57   So, Nettles, *By His Grace*, p. 84.
58   *Ibid.*, p. 87.
59   *HEB*, III, 273.
60   As is suggested by Nettles, *By His Grace*, p. 95.
61   See p. 165.
62   *HEB*, III, 269.
63   *Ibid.*, 368.
64   John Martin, *Life and Writings*, p. 44.
65   *HEB*, III, 264f.
66   *Ibid.*, 372.
67   *The certain Efficacy*, p. 98.
68   *Ibid.*, p. 129.
69   E.A. Payne, 'Abraham Booth and some of his Descendants', *BQ*,
      XVI (1955-6), 196-9 (p. 196).
70   *HEB*, III, 482, citing a funeral sermon for Benjamin Wallin, 1782.
71   *Glad Tidings to Perishing Sinners, or, The Genuine Gospel, A
      Complete Warrant for the Ungodly to believe in Jesus*, fifth edition
      (1825), p. 113.
72   John Ryland, *The Life and Death of the Rev. Andrew Fuller*, p. 256.
73   *Ibid.*
74   *Glad Tidings to Perishing Sinners*, pp. 115f.
75   *HEB*, III, 273, 368-70.
76   *The Doctrine of Predestination*, p. 118.
77   *Ibid.*
78   *Ibid.*, p. 107.
79   *Gospel*, p. 36.
80   See p. 97; Wilson,*The History and Antiquities of Dissenting
      Churches*, I, 531.
81   *Ibid.*, I, 526-32; *HEB*, III, 499, 504. See p. 14.
82   Wilson, *The History and Antiquities of Dissenting Churches*, I, 439-
      54; *HEB*, III, 327-30.
83   Wilson, *The History and Antiquities of Dissenting Churches*, I, 532;
      HEB, III, 504. Wilson and Ivimey mention 1751 and 1761 respec-
      tively.
84   John Brine, *The Knowledge of Future Glory: The Support of the
      Saints, in present Troubles. A Sermon, Occasioned by the Death of
      the Reverend and Learned Mr. Clendon Daukes*, p. 29.
85   *HEB*, III, 505.
86   *Ibid.*, 507f.
87   *Ibid.*, 513, 517.
88   *Ibid.*, 515.
89   *Ibid.*, 518.
90   *Ibid.*, 518f.

IX John Gill and Faith

1   *Cause*, I, 274.
2   *Ibid.*, 106.
3   *Ibid.*, 96f.
4   *Ibid.*, 98.
5   *Ibid.*
6   *Ibid.*, 100f.; cf. II, 21f.
7   *Ibid.*, I, 73.
8   *Ibid.*, 76.
9   *Ibid.*
10 *Ibid.*, 106.
11 *Ibid.*
12 *Ibid.*, 107.
13 *Ibid.*, 109.
14 *Ibid.*, II, 65.
15 *Ibid.*, I, 109.
16 *Ibid.*, II, 21f., 186f.
17 *Ibid.*, 186.
18 *Ibid.*, 65.
19 *Ibid.*, I, 322f.
20 *Ibid.*, II, 30.
21 *Ibid.*, 55.
22 *Ibid.*, 54.
23 *Ibid.*, 48.
24 *Ibid.*
25 *Ibid.*

X John Gill and Eternal Justification

1   *Sermons*, II, 455-508.
2   *Ibid.*, 483.
3   *Ibid.*, 457.
4   *Ibid.*, 459.
5   *Ibid.*, 478.
6   *Ibid.*, 460.
7   *Ibid.*, 491.
8   *Ibid.*, 491f.
9   *Ibid.*; cf. Body, I, 292.
10 *Sermons*, II, 500.
11 *Body*, I, 294. Gill does not deploy Romans 8:1 in his important sermon about justification, *Sermons*, II, 455-508. Was he unsure of his exposition?
12 *Body*, I, 296; cf. *Sermons*, II, 489f.

13   *Body*, I, 293; *Sermons*, II, 491.
14   William Hendriksen, *New Testament Commentary: I & II Timothy & Titus* (Edinburgh, 1976), p. 260.
15   *Sermons*, II, 502.
16   *Body*, I, 535; *Cause*, I, 106.
17   *Sermons*, II, 500f.
18   *A Defence of the Doctrine of Eternal Justification*, p. 78.
19   *Gospel*, p. 55.
20   *Body*, I, 299; cf. *Sermons*, II, 501; III, 41f.
21   *Body*, II, 53; cf. *Sermons*, III, 417.
22   *Sermons*, III, 417, 420.
23   John Murray, *Redemption - Accomplished and Applied* (Edinburgh, 1979), p. 40.
24   So, C.H. Dodd. See Leon Morris, *The Apostolic Preaching of the Cross*, third edition (1972), pp. 148.
25   *The Child's Delight: Or Instructions for Children and Youth* (no date), p. 32.
26   *A Medium between two Extremes* (1698), iii.
27   *Ibid.*
28   *Ibid.*, pp. 21f.
29   Crosby, IV, 393f.
30   Herman Witsius, *The Oeconomy of the Covenants between God and Man. Comprehending a Complete Body of Divinity*, 3 vols, second edition, translated into English from Latin (London, 1775), II, 120f.
31   John Ryland, *The Life and Death of the Rev. Andrew Fuller*, p. 68.
32   *HEB*, III, 438f.

XI   John Gill and the Message of the Gospel

1   *Body*, II, 123; cf. 671.
2   *Cause*, II, 47.
3   *Body*, II, 124.
4   *Sermons*, II, 126.
5   *Ibid.*, 414; cf. *Cause*, II, 49.
6   *Sermons*, II, 462.
7   *New Testament Exposition*, II, 3.
8   *Cause*, I, 51.
9   *Ibid.*, 307.
10   *Ibid.*, 396.
11   *Body*, I, 172.
12   *Cause*, I, 350.
13   *Ibid.*, 118.
14   *Body*, II, 668.

15   *Ibid.*, 60f.
16   *Oeconomy*, I, 393.
17   *Ibid.*
18   *Body*, II, 635.
19   *Gospel*, p. 32.

XII   Andrew Fuller, Calvinism and High Calvinism

1   John Ryland, *The Life and Death of the Rev. Andrew Fuller*, pp. 269, 295, 383.
2   *Album of the Northamptonshire Congregational Churches*, p. 42; cf. *HEB*, IV, 528f.
3   *Ibid.*, note.
4   *HEB*, IV, 528f.
5   *Gospel*, p. 12.
6   *Ibid.*
7   *Ibid.*, p. 9.
8   *Ibid.*, p. 10.
9   *Ibid.*, p. 12
10   *Ibid.*, p. 13.
11   *Ibid.*
12   *Ibid.*, p. 16.
13   *Ibid.*, p. 14.
14   *Ibid.*, p. 20.
15   *Ibid.*, p. 21.
16   *Ibid.*, p. 22.
17   *Ibid.*, p. 23.
18   *Ibid.*
19   *Cause*, I, 59, 61, 339.
20   *Gospel*, p. 24.
21   The letter is undated in Ivimey's catalogue of Fuller's works; *HEB*, IV, 533, note.
22   *The Baptist Library: A Republication of Standard Baptist Works*, edited by C.G. Sommers, W. R. Williams and L.L. Hill, 3 vols (New York, 1843), III, 280.
23   *Gospel*, p. 26.
24   *Ibid.*, p. 29.
25   *Ibid.*, p. 31.
26   *Ibid.*, p. 32.
27   *Ibid.*, p. 33.
28   *Ibid.*, p. 34.
29   *Ibid.*, pp. 35f.
30   *Ibid.*, p. 36.

31 *Ibid.*, p. 37.
32 *Ibid.*, p. 38.
33 *Ibid.*, pp. 39f.
34 *Ibid.*, pp. 40-5.
35 *Ibid.*, p. 46.
36 *Body*, II, 368; *Cause*, I, 84, 106.
37 *Gospel*, p. 44.
38 *Ibid.*, p. 56.
39 *Ibid.*, p. 57.
40 *Ibid.*, p. 58.
41 *Ibid.*, p. 60.
42 *Ibid.*, p. 61.
43 *Ibid.*, p. 62.
44 *Ibid.*, p. 46.
45 *Ibid.*
46 *Ibid.*, p. 47.
47 *Ibid.*, pp. 48-51.
48 *Ibid.*, p. 53.
49 *Ibid.*
50 *Ibid.*, pp. 54, 169.
51 *The Works of the Rev. Andrew Fuller*, 8 vols (1824), IV, 124.
52 *Gospel*, p. 148, note.
53 *Ibid.*, pp. 168-74.
54 *Ibid.*, pp. 168f.
55 *Oeconomy*, I, 348.
56 *Ibid.*, 349f.
57 *Gospel*, pp. 54f.
58 *HEB*, IV, 88.
59 William Rushton, *A Defence of Particular Redemption, Wherein the Doctrine of Andrew Fuller relative to the Atonement of Christ is tried by the Word of God in Four Letters to a Baptist Minister* (Liverpool, 1831; reprinted by W.J. Berry, North Carolina, 1971), p. 19.
60 See p. 14.

XIII The Late 1700s

1 Carlton Baptist Meeting, First Church Book, November 1778.
2 *Works*, VII, 411.
3 *Ibid.*
4 Frank Baker, *William Grimshaw 1708-1763* (1963), p. 211.
5 Watts, p. 441; T.M. Bassett, *The Welsh Baptists* (Swansea, 1977), p. 95.

6   John Newton's Diary, 8 June 1774; 7 August 1776, as quoted in *The Olney Baptist Meeting*, pp. 95, 99.
7   *The New International Dictionary of the Christian Church*, general editor J.D. Douglas (Exeter, 1974), s.v. 'Simeon, Charles,' by P.S. Dawes, and 'Venn, Henry', by J.D. Douglas.
8   'A Letter from the Rev. Robert Hall, A.M., to the Rev. Charles Simeon, A.M. Vicar and Lecturer of Trinity Church, and Fellow of King's College, Cambridge', in *National Sins Considered, in Two Letters to the Rev. Thomas Robinson*, B. Flower (Cambridge, 1796), pp. 74, 79.
9   *HEB*, IV, 25.
10 *Ibid.*, 27-30.
11 *Ibid.*, 55-8.
12 *Ibid.*, 77.
13 *Ibid.*, 77-81.
14 *Ibid.*, 38f.
15 *Ibid.*, 39.
16 *BAR*, I, 56; cf. *HEB*, IV, 62.
17 *HEB*, IV, 74; *BAR*, III, 40-2.
18 Angus Library, Regent's Park College, Oxford, Circular Letters, 1766-94; Northamptonshire Association Minutes, 1790, p. 9.
19 *Ibid.*
20 Angus Library, Regent's Park College, Oxford, Circular Letters, 1766-94, *passim.*
21 *HEB*, IV, 41.
22 *Ibid.*
23 Robert Hall, *Help to Zion's Travellers*, pp. 103f.
24 *Northampton Association Letter*, 1781, p. 11, note.
25 Robert Hall, *Help to Zion's Travellers*, vi.
26 See Iain H. Murray, *Jonathan Edwards: A New Biography* (Edinburgh. 1987), pp. 313-29.
27 *Baptism a Term of Communion*, p. 109.
28 Watts, pp. 458f.
29 Underwood, p. 164.
30 John Martin, *Life and Writings*, pp. 118f.
31 *Ibid.*
32 According to Underwood, p. 164.
33 *Ibid.*
34 *Works*, IV, 196, footnote.
35 Watts, p. 459.
36 G.W. Hughes, 'Robert Hall of Arnesby, 1728-1791', *BQ*, X (1940-1), 444-7 (pp. 445f.).
37 *HEB*, IV, 76.
38 *Ibid.*, 50f.

39   *On Terms of Communion*, ix.
40   Angus Library, Regent's Park College, Oxford, Circular Letters, 1766-94, pp. 4f.
41   W. Taylor Bowie, 'William Carey', *BQ*, VII (1934-5), 167-74 (p. 172).
42   Olney Baptist Church, First Church Book, 1752-1854, pp. 51-9.
43   *HEB*, IV, 65f.
44   Angus Library, Regent's Park College, Circular Letters, 1766-94, p. 8.
45   John Ryland, *The Life and Death of the Rev. Andrew Fuller*, pp. 355f.
46   Sheila Mitchell, *Not Disobedient*, p. 28.
47   *HEB*, IV, 67.
48   *The Olney Baptist Meeting*, p. 153.
49   Northamptonshire Association Letter, 1786, p. 10, note.
50   *HEB*, IV, 68, 70.
51   *HEB*, IV, 375.
52   *Gospel*, p. 22.
53   James Dore and John Rippon, *A Sermon, Occasioned by the Death of the Rev. Abraham Booth ... and a Short Memoir of the Deceased* (no date); *Memoir*, p. 63.
54   Murray, *The Forgotten Spurgeon*, p. 58.

Conclusion

1   *A Manual of Faith and Practice*, i.
2   *Ibid.*, p. 238.
3   *Apology*, p. 140.
4   *Ibid.*, p. 146.
5   For example, *Differences in Judgment About Water-Baptism*, p. 3.
6   See p. 90; *HEB*, I, 523.
7   Over, Cambridgeshire, Baptist Church, First Church Book, pp. 4f.; T. Ladson, *Grace and Providence in Robes of Glory* (1822), pp. 64f.; *London Christian Instructor*, II (1819), pp. 697f.
8   C.B. Jewson, 'St. Mary's, Norwich', V, *BQ*, X (1940-1), 340-6 (p. 345).
9   *HEB*, IV, 364-79, *passim*.
10   *Eleven Sermons* (1714), p. 239.
11   Peter Toon, *Hyper-Calvinism in English Nonconformity 1689-1765* (1967), pp. 147f.
12   John Ryland, *The Character of the Rev. James Hervey, A.M. Late Rector of Weston Favell, in Northamptonshire, Considered* (no date), pp. 14f.

13   According to James Culross and John Taylor, *Founders and Pioneers of Modern Missions* (Northampton, 1899), p. 38.
14   K.W.H. Howard, 'John Sutcliff of Olney', *BQ*, XIV (1951-2), 304-9 (pp. 308f.).
15   *An Account of the Life, Ministry, and Writings of the late Rev. John Fawcett, D.D.* (1818), pp. 176f.
16   Cited by Norman S. Moon, *Education for the Ministry: Bristol Baptist College 1679-1979* (Bristol, 1979), p. 2.
17   *HEB*, I, 479.
18   Robert Steed & Abraham Cheare, *A Plain Discovery*, p. 75.

BIBLIOGRAPHY OF WORKS CITED IN THE TEXT AND NOTES

Primary Sources

A Caveat Against the New Sect of Anabaptists Lately Sprung up at Exon (1714)

A Collection of Poems For and Against Dr. Sacheverell and On other Affairs of State; most of them never before Printed (1710)

A Confession of Faith of seven Congregations or Churches of Christ in London, which are commonly (but unjustly) called Anabaptists (1646, reprinted 1809)

A Confession of Faith, put forth by the Elders and Brethren of many Congregations of Christians, (Baptized upon Profession of their Faith), in London and the Country (1689, reprinted 1809)

A Defence of the private Academies and Schools of the Protestant Dissenters, against the Misrepresentations of them, as being dangerous to Church and State (1714)

An Account of the Doctrine and Discipline of Mr. Richard Davis, of Rothwell, in the County of Northampton, And those of his Separation. With the Canons of George Fox, appointed to be Read in the all the Quakers Meetings (1700)

An Account of the Life, Ministry, and Writings of the late Rev. John Fawcett, D.D. (1818)

An Account of the Reasons of the Nobility and Gentry's Invitation to His Highness the Prince of Orange into England. Being a Memorial from the English Protestants Concerning their Grievances (1688)

An Impartial State of the Late Differences Amongst the Protestant Dissenting Ministers at Salters-Hall (1719)

Beddome, Benjamin, *A Scriptural Exposition of the Baptist Catechism By Way of Question and Answer* (1752)

— *Collected Sermons*, 8 vols (1807-20)

Bennett, Tho., *A Discourse of Schism*, 2nd ed. (Cambridge, 1702)

Bogue, David, and James Bennett, *History of Dissenters, from the Revolution in 1688, to the Year 1808*, 4 vols (1808)

Booth, Abraham, *An Apology for the Baptists* (1778)

— *Glad Tidings to Perishing Sinners, or The Genuine Gospel, A Complete Warrant for the Ungodly to Believe in Jesus*, 5th ed. (1825)

Bradbury, Thomas, *The Duty and Doctrine of Baptism. In Thirteen Sermons* (1749)

Brine, John, *A Defence of the Doctrine of Eternal Justification* (1732)

— *The Certain Efficacy of the Death of Christ, Asserted* (1743)

— *A Dialogue between Christophilus, Philalethes, and Philagathus. Wherein is contained an Answer to Mr. Alvery Jackson's Question Answered* (1753)

— *Some Mistakes in a Book of Mr. Johnson's of Liverpool, Intitled, The Faith of God's Elect, etc. Noted and Rectified* (1755)

— *The Baptists vindicated from some Groundless Charges Brought against them by Mr. Eltringham, In a Pamphlet, intitled, The Baptist against the Baptist, &c.* (1756)

— *The Knowledge of Future Glory: The Support of the Saints, in present Troubles. A Sermon, Occasioned by the Death of the Reverend and Learned Mr. Clendon Daukes* (1759)

— *Grace, proved to be at the Sovereign Disposal of God: In a Discourse Preached June 19, 1760* (1760)

— *A Sermon Preach'd at the Ordination of the Revd Mr John Ryland, on the 26th of July, 1750* (no date)

— *A Treatise on Various Subjects* (no date)

Brown, John, *The House of God Opened and His Table Free for Baptists and Paedo-baptists, who are Saints and Faithful in Christ* (1777)

Bunyan, John, *A Confession of my Faith, and a Reason of my Practice: Or, With who, and who not, I can hold Church-Fellowship, or the Communion of Saints, in The Works of that Eminent Servant of Christ, Mr. John Bunyan*, revised by Samuel Wilson, 2nd ed., 2 vols (1736-7), II, 47-71

— *Differences in Judgment About Water-Baptism, No Bar to Communion: OR, To Communicate with Saints, as Saints, proved lawful* (1673)

— *Grace Abounding to the Chief of Sinners*, 20th-century revision of the 8th ed., 1688 (no date)

— *Peacable Principles and true: Or, a brief Answer to Mr. Danvers and Mr. Paul's Books against my Confession of Faith, and Differences in Judgment about Baptism no Bar to Communion. Wherein their Scriptureless Notions are overthrown, and my peacable Principles still maintained, in The Works of that Eminent Servant of Christ, Mr. John Bunyan*, revised by Samuel Wilson, 2nd ed., 2 vols (1736-7), II, 102-11

— *The Heavenly Footman or a Description of the Man that gets to Heaven* (1928 reprint of the 1860 ed.)

— *The Pilgrim's Progress*, impression of the 11th ed., 1688 (1928)

Burnet, Gilbert, *A Pastoral Letter Writ by the Right Reverend Father in God Gilbert, Lord Bishop of Sarum* (1689)

— *A Sermon Preached in the Chappel of St. James before His Highness the Prince of Orange, the 23rd of December*, 1688 (1689)

Burroughs, Joseph, *A Farther Defence of Two Discourses relating to Positive Institutions: In answer to the Rev Mr. Caleb Fleming's Vindication of the Appendix to the Plea for Infants* (1746)

Buttfield, William, *Free Communion an Innovation: Or, An Answer to Mr. John Brown's Pamphlet, Entitled, The House of God Opened and His Table Free, &c* (1778)

Carey, Philip, *A Solemn Call, or a Discourse concerning Baptism* (1690)

Carlton, Bedfordshire, Baptist Meeting, First Church Book

Cogan, John, *Some Just and Necessary Remarks upon John Gill's Defence of Plunging: Or, The Scriptural Mode of Baptizing with Water maintained* (1727)

[Coleman, Henry], *Actual Justification Rightly Stated. Containing a True Narrative of a Sad Schism made in a Church of Christ at Kilby in Leicester-Shire* (1696)

Crisp, Tobias, *Christ Alone Exalted in the Perfection and Encouragement of the Saints, Notwithstanding Sins and Trials*, 7th ed., 2 vols (1832)

Crosby, Tho., *The History of the English Baptists, From The Reformation to the Beginning of the Reign of King George I*, 4 vols (1738-40; republished by Church History Research and Archives, Lafayette, Tenn., no date)

Danvers, Henry, *A Treatise of Baptism: Wherein That of Believers, and that of Infants, is examined by the Scriptures* (1673)

— *A Treatise of Baptism: Wherein That of Believers, and that of Infants, is examined by the Scriptures*, 2nd ed. (1674)

Davis, Richard, *Faith the Grand Evidence Of Our Interest in Christ: Or The Nature of Faith and Salvation open'd, from John vi.40* (1704)

Defoe, Daniel, *A true Collection of the Writings of the Author of the True Born English-man* (1703)

Dr Williams's Library Funeral Sermons, 1663-1706

— 1799-1820

Dore, James and John Rippon, *A Sermon, Occasioned by the Death of the Rev. Abraham Booth ... and a Short Memoir of the Deceased* (no date)

Dutton, Ann, *Thoughts on the Lord's Supper* (1746-8)

[Eltringham, William], *The Doctrine of Believer's Baptism by Immersion for Justification, Exploded, and proved to be Antiscriptural* (1754)

— *The Baptist against the Baptist: Or, a Display of Antipaedo-Baptist Self-Inconsistency; In Answer to Several Letters from a Baptist-Brother . To which is added, A Reply to a Letter subscribed J.W. written by way of reproof to Me, and in defence of Dr. Gill* (1755)

Fuller, Andrew, *Open Communion Unscriptural; A Letter from the Late A. Fuller, of Kettering, (Dated Sept. 21, 1800,) to the Rev. W. Ward, Missionary at Serampore,* 2nd ed. (1824)

— *The Gospel Worthy of All Acceptation; The Gospel Its Own Witness* (Evansville, Ind., 1961; reprint of the 2nd ed., 1801)

— *The Works of the Rev. Andrew Fuller,* 8 vols (1824)

Gill, John, *The Antient Mode of Baptizing, by Immersion, Plunging, or Dipping into Water; Maintain'd and Vindicated: Against the Cavils and Exceptions of the Author of a late Pamphlet, Entitled, The Manner of Baptizing with Water clear'd up from the Word of God and right Reason, &c. Together with some Remarks upon the Author's Reasons for the Practice of a free or mixt Communion in Churches* (1726)

— *A Defence of the Book intitled, The Ancient Mode of Baptizing, by Immersion, Plunging, or Dipping in Water, etc. Against Mr. Matthias Maurice's Reply, call'd Plunging into Water no Scriptural Mode of Baptizing &c.* (1727)

— *A Sermon Preached at the Baptism of Several Persons in Barbican, November 2, 1750,* 2nd ed. (1751)

— *Baptism a Divine Commandment to be Observed. Being a Sermon Preached at Barbican, Octob. 9, 1765. At the Baptism of the Reverend Mr. Robert Carmichael, Minister of the Gospel in Edinburgh* (1766)

— *Infant Baptism, a Part and Pillar of Popery* (1766)

— *The Cause of God and Truth; In Four Parts. With a Vindication of Part IV. From the Cavils, Calumnies, and Defamations of Mr. Henry Heywood, &c.,* New Edition, 2 vols (1814)

— *Sermons and Tracts,* New Edition, 3 vols (1814-15)

— *A Complete Body of Doctrinal and Practical Divinity: Or A System of Evangelical Truths, Deduced from the Sacred Scriptures,* New Edition, 2 vols (1839)

— *A Sermon on the Knowledge of Christ ... to which is appended ... a Baptismal Hymn* (1846)

—*An Exposition of the New Testament*, 2 vols (1853)

Gotch, F.W., *Christ the Centre, being the Inaugural Address of the Rev. F.W. Gotch, LL.D., Chairman, at the Autumnal Meeting of the Baptist Union, October 14, 1868* (1868)

Gurney, Thomas, *Zeal for the Church: Or, The Lamentation of the Cl—rgy: Occasioned by the Reverend Mr. Whitefield's Return to England. In a Poem Humbly Offer'd to the Consideration of the Judicious* (1741)

Hall, Robert, senior, *Help to Zion's Travellers: Being an Attempt to remove Various Stumbling Blocks out of the Way, relating to Doctrinal, Experimental, and Practical Religion*, 2nd ed. (1807)

Hall, Robert, junior, 'A Letter from the Rev. Robert Hall, A.M., to the Rev.Charles Simeon, A.M. Vicar and Lecturer of Trinity Church, and Fellow of King's College, Cambridge', in *National Sins Considered, in Two Letters to the Rev. Thomas Robinson*, B. Flower (Cambridge, 1796)

— *On Terms of Communion; with a Particular View to the Case of the Baptists and Paedobaptists* (Leicester, 1816)

— *A Reply to the Rev. Joseph Kinghorn: Being A Further Vindication of the Practice of Free Communion* (Leicester, 1818)

— *The Works of Robert Hall, A.M.*, 3rd ed., 6 vols (1832-3)

Ivimey, Joseph, *A History of the English Baptists*, 4 vols (1811-30)

Keach, Benjamin, *The Articles of Faith of the Church of Christ, or Congregation meeting at Horsley-down, Benjamin Keach, Pastor, As Asserted this 10th of the 6th Month, 1697* (1697)

— *A Medium between two Extremes* (1698)

— *The Child's Delight: Or Instruction for Children and Youth* (no date)

Kiffin, William, *Some Serious Reflections On that Part of John Bunion's Confession of Faith: touching Communion With Unbaptized Persons* (1673)

— *A Sober Discourse of Right to Church Communion* (1681)

Kinghorn, Joseph, *Baptism a Term of Communion at the Lord's Supper*, 2nd ed. (Norwich, 1816)

— *A Defence of "Baptism a Term of Communion". In Answer to the Rev. Robert Hall's Reply* (Norwich, 1820)

Ladson, T., *Grace and Providence in Robes of Glory* (1822)

'Life of the Rev. Robert Hall, D.D.', *The Imperial Magazine*, XIV (no date), 195-219

London Christian Instructor, II (1819)

Martin, John, *Some Account of the Life and Writings of the Rev. John Martin, Pastor of the Church, Meeting in Store Street, Bedford Square* (1797)

Maurice, Matthias, *A Vindication of the Primitive Church, and Diocesan Episcopacy; In Answer to Mr. Baxter's Church History of Bishops, and their Councils Abridged* (1682)

[Maurice, Matthias], *The Manner of Baptizing with Water Cleared up from the Word of God and Right Reason; In a Plain free Debate upon that Subject between Mr. J.P. and Mr. B.W. June 6. 1726* (1726)

— *Plunging into Water No Scriptural Mode of Baptizing: Or, Mr. Gill fairly answered, and Baptizing with Water defended* (1727)

— *The Tribes of the Lord appearing before him: Or, Families in Publick Worship. A Sermon Preach'd At the opening of the New Meeting-House, at Rowel, November 9, 1735* (1736)

— *A Modern Question Modestly Answer'd* (1737)

— *The Modern Question Affirm'd and Prov'd: Viz. That the Eternal God does by his Word make it the Duty of poor unconverted Sinners, who hear the Gospel preach'd or publish'd, to believe in Jesus Christ* (1739)

Mayo, Daniel, *A Sermon Concerning the Ends, and Mode, and Subjects of Baptism* (1713)

Memoirs of the Life and Writings of Isaac Watts, D.D. with Extracts from his Correspondence (1806)

Mulliner, John, *A Testimony against Perriwigs and Perriwig-Making and Playing on Instruments of Musick among Christians, or any other in the days of the Gospel* (Northampton, 1677; reprinted 1708)

Neal, Daniel, *The History of the Puritans or Protestant Non-Conformists*, 2nd ed., corrected, 2 vols (1754)

Newman, William, *Rylandiana: Reminiscences relating to the Rev. John Ryland, A.M. of Northampton, Father of the Late Rev. Dr. Ryland,of Bristol* (1835)

Newton, John, *Diary*, as quoted in *The Olney Baptist Meeting*, an anonymous, undated, typed history of Olney Baptist Church, Bucks, retained at Olney.

Olney, Buckinghamshire, Baptist Church, First Church Book, 1752-1854

Orton, Job, *Memoirs of the Life, Character and Writings of the late Reverend Philip Doddridge, D.D. of Northampton* (1766)

Over, Cambridgeshire, Baptist Church, First Church Book

Palmer, Samuel, *A Vindication of the Learning, Loyalty, Morals, and most Christian Behaviour of the Dissenters toward the Church of England. In Answer to Mr. Wesley's Defence of his Letter concerning the Dissenters Education* (1705)

Piggott, John, *Eleven Sermons* (1714)

Rippon, John, *The Baptist Annual Register*, I (1790-3); II (1794-7); III (1798-1801); IV (1801-2)

—*A Brief Memoir of the Life and Writings of the Late Rev. John Gill, D.D.* (1838)

Rothwell, Northamptonshire, United Reformed Church, First Church Book

— Second Church Book

Rushton, William, *A Defence of Particular Redemption, Wherein the Doctrine of Andrew Fuller relative to the Atonement of Christ is tried by the Word of God in Four Letters to a Baptist Minister* (Liverpool, 1831; reprinted by W.J. Berry, North Carolina, 1971)

Ryland, John, *A Funeral Sermon Occasioned by the Death of the Rev. Robert Hall, sen.* (no date)

— *The Character of the Rev. James Hervey, A.M. Late Rector of Weston Favell, in Northamptonshire, Considered* (no date)

— *A Candid Statement of the Reasons which induce the Baptists to differ in Opinion and Practice from so many of their Christian Brethren* (1814)

— *The Work of Faith, the Labour of Love, and the Patience of Hope, illustrated; In the Life and Death of the Rev. Andrew Fuller*, 2nd ed. (1818)

Ryland, John Collett, *A Modest Plea for Free Communion at the Lord's Table; between True Believers of all Denominations: In a Letter to a Friend* (1772)

Skepp, John, *Divine Energy: or the Efficacious Operations of the Spirit of God upon the Soul of Man, in his Effectual Calling and Conversion, Stated, Proved and Vindicated*, 3rd ed. (1815)

Steed, Robert, and Abraham Cheare, *A Plain Discovery Of the Unrighteous Judge and False Accuser. Wherein is soberly, and in the fear of the Lord brought to light, and tendered to the examination of the Upright in Heart, the Spirit of that Pamphlet, intituled, The Leper Cleansed: Published by Richard Bellamy of Tiverton* (1658)

Stennett, Joseph, *Rabshakeh's Retreat. A Sermon Preach'd in Little-Wild Street, December 18, 1745. Being the day appointed for a general Fast, on occasion of the present Rebellion*, 2nd ed. (1745)

Stennett, Samuel, *Remarks on the Christian Minister's Reasons for Administering Baptism by Sprinkling or Pouring of Water and An Answer to The Christian Minister's Reasons for Baptizing Infants* (1772)

Sutcliff, John, *Northamptonshire Particular Baptist Association Letter*, 1786, in Angus Library Circular Letters, 1766-94

The Baptist Library: A Republication of Standard Baptist Works, edited by C.G. Sommers, W. R. Williams and L.L. Hill, 3 vols (New York, 1843)

The Confession of Faith, Agreed upon by the Assembly of Divines at Westminster, 1647 (Publication Committee of the Free Presbyterian Church of Scotland, 1958)

The Confession of Faith of those Churches, which are commonly (though falsly) called Anabaptists (1644)

The Correspondence and Diary of Philip Doddridge, edited by J.D. Humphreys, 5 vols (1830-1)

The Sword and the Trowel, edited by Charles Haddon Spurgeon (1887)

Toplady, Augustus M., *The Works of Augustus M. Toplady, A.B.*, New Edition, 6 vols (1825)

Turner, Daniel, *A Modest Plea for Free Communion at the Lord's Table; Particularly between the Baptists and the Paedobaptists. In a Letter to a Friend* (1772)

Walker, William, and others, *A True Representation of the Case of the Church of Christ at Olney*, an unpublished, undated document retained by Olney Baptist Church

Wallin, Benjamin, *The Folly of Neglecting Divine Institutions. An Earnest Address to the Christian, Who continues to Refrain from the Appointments of the Gospel*, 2nd ed. (1758)

— *The Universal Concern of Saints in Communion* (1762)

— *A Sermon Occasioned by the Death of Mrs. Rebekah Cox* (1769)

— Samuel Stennett and Abraham Booth, *A Charge and Sermon, together with an Introductory Discourse and Confession of Faith, delivered at the Ordination of the Rev. Mr. Abraham Booth, Feb. 16, 1769, in Goodman's Fields* (1769)

Wayman, Lewis, *A Further Enquiry after Truth* (1738)

Wesley, John, *The Works of the Rev. J. Wesley, A.M.*, 3rd ed., 14 vols (1829)

Whitefield, George, *Fifteen Sermons Preached on Various Important Subjects* (New York, 1794)

Witsius, Herman, *The Oeconomy of the Covenants between God and Man, Comprehending a Complete Body of Divinity*, English translation from Latin, 2nd ed., 3 vols (1775)

Secondary Sources and Other Material

'A Call to the Pastorate, Abingdon', *TBHS*, VI (1918-19), 250

Album of the Northamptonshire Congregational Churches, edited by T. Stephens (Wellingborough, 1894)

Baker, Frank, *William Grimshaw 1708-1763* (1963)

Ban, J.D., 'Was John Bunyan a Baptist? A Case-Study in Historiography', *BQ*, XXX (1984), 367-76

Bassett, T.M., *The Welsh Baptists* (Swansea, 1977)

Betteridge, Alan, 'Early Baptists in Leicestershire and Rutland (4)', *BQ*, XXVI (1976), 209-23

Brown, Raymond, *The English Baptists of the Eighteenth Century* (1986)

Bull, Fredk. Wm., *A Sketch of the History of the Town of Kettering* (Kettering, 1891)

Calendar of State Papers, Domestic Series, of the Reign of William and Mary. 13th Feb. 1689 - April 1690, edited by William John Hardy, F.S.A. (1895)

Chamberlain, A., *A Notable Rothwell Family* (Rothwell, Northamptonshire, no date)

Clements, K.W., 'The Significance of 1679', *BQ*, XXVIII (1979), 2-6

Culross, James, and John Taylor, *Founders and Pioneers of Modern Missions* (Northampton, 1899)

Documents of the Christian Church, edited by Henry Bettenson, The World's Classics, 495 (1959)

Dunstable Borough Gazette, 4 July 1917

English Historical Documents, general editor David C. Douglas, 12 vols (1953-)

Evans, Shem, *Memoir of the late Mr. William Bassett of Countesthorpe: Together with the Improved Edition of Mr. Bassett's 'History of the Baptist Church at Arnesby'* (Leicester, 1862)

Foreman, H., 'Baptist Provision for Ministerial Education in the 18th Century', *BQ*, XXVII (1978), 358-69

George Whitefield's Letters, 1734-42, edited by S.M. Houghton (Edinburgh, 1976)

Glass, Norman, *The Early History of the Independent Church at Rothwell, alias Rowell, in Northamptonshire* (1871)

Haley, K.H.D., 'The Political Context of Monmouth's Rebellion', in *The Monmouth Rising: Aspects of the 1685 Rebellion in the West Country*, edited by Ivan Roots (Exeter, 1986), pp. 17-30

Halkett, Samuel, and John Laing, *A Dictionary of the Anonymous and Pseudonymous Literature of Great Britain*, 4 vols (Edinburgh, 1882-8)

Hayden, R., 'The Particular Baptist Confession 1689 and Baptists Today', *BQ*, XXXII (1988), 403-17

Hendriksen, William, *New Testament Commentary: I & II Timothy & Titus* (Edinburgh, 1976)

Howard, K.W.H., 'John Sutcliff of Olney', *BQ*, XIV (1951-2), 304-9

Hughes, G.W., 'Robert Hall of Arnesby, 1728-1791', *BQ*, X (1940-1), 444-7

Into Battle: Speeches by the Right Hon. Winston S. Churchill, C.H., M.P., compiled by Randolph S. Churchill, M.P., 11th ed. (1945)

Jewson, C.B., 'St. Mary's, Norwich', IV, *BQ*, X (1940-1), 282-8; V, 340-6

Lane, G.E., *Henry Danvers: Contender for Religious Liberty* (Ealing, 1972)

Light, Alfred W., *Bunhill Fields* (1913)

Lindsay Keir, D., *The Constitutional History of Modern Britain 1485-1937*, 3rd. ed., revised (1946)

Lumpkin, William L., *Baptist Confessions of Faith*, revised edition (Valley Forge, 1969)

Macaulay, T.B., *History of England*, 5 vols (1848-61; reprinted 1967)

MacDonald, M.D., 'London Calvinistic Baptists 1689-1727: Tensions within a Dissenting community under Toleration' (unpublished D. Phil. dissertation, University of Oxford, 1982)

Mitchell, Sheila, *Not Disobedient* (Leicester, 1984)

Moon, Norman S., *Education for the Ministry: Bristol Baptist College 1679-1979* (Bristol, 1979)

Morris, Leon, *The Apostolic Preaching of the Cross*, 3rd ed. (1972)

Murray, D.B., 'The Seventeenth and Eighteenth Centuries', in *The Baptists in Scotland: A History*, edited by D.W. Bebbington (Glasgow, 1988), pp. 9-25

Murray, Iain H.,*The Forgotten Spurgeon*, 2nd ed. (1973)

— *Jonathan Edwards: A New Biography* (Edinburgh, 1987)

Nettles, Thomas J.,*By His Grace and for His Glory* (Grand Rapids, Mich., 1986)

Nuttall, Geoffrey F., *Howell Harris 1714-1773: The Last Enthusiast* (Cardiff, 1965)

— 'Northamptonshire and *The Modern Question*: A Turning-Point in Eighteenth Century Dissent', *Journal of Theological Studies*, New Series XVI (1965), 101-23

— *Calendar of the Correspondence of Philip Doddridge DD (1702-1751)* (1979)

— 'Baptists and Independents in Olney to the Time of John Newton',*BQ*, XXX (1983), 26-37

Oliver, Robert W., 'John Collett Ryland, Daniel Turner and Robert Robinson and the Communion Controversy, 1772-1781', *BQ*, XXIX (1981), 77-9

— 'The Emergence of a Strict and Particular Baptist Community among the English Calvinistic Baptists 1770-1850' (unpublished Ph.D. dissertation, London Bible College, 1986)

Payne, Ernest A., 'Abraham Booth and some of his Descendants', *BQ*, XVI (1955-6), 196-9

— *The Baptist Union: A Short History*, 2nd ed. (1964)

Price, S.J., 'Repairing a Meeting-house in 1720', *BQ*, V (1930-1), 28f.

— 'Sidelights from an old Minute Book', *BQ*, V (1930-1), 86-96

Records of the Churches of Christ, Gathered at Fenstanton, Warboys, and Hexham. 1644-1720, edited by E.B. Underhill (1854)

Robison, O.C., 'The Legacy of John Gill', *BQ*, XXIV (1971), 111-25

Rupp, Gordon, *Religion in England 1689-1791* (Oxford, 1986)

'Salters' Hall 1719 and the Baptists', *TBHS*, V (1916-17), 172-89

Selection from Letters by Mrs. Anne Dutton, compiled by J. Knight (1884)

Selley, W.T., *England in the Eighteenth Century, 1689-1815*, 3rd ed. (1962)

Skeats, Herbert S., and Charles S. Miall, *History of the Free Churches of England 1688-1891* (1891)

Sparkes, D.C., 'The Test Act of 1673 and Its Aftermath', *BQ*, XXV (1973), 74-85

Styles, William Jeyes, *A Manual of Faith and Practice: Designed for Young and Enquiring Christians* (1887)

Taylor Bowie, W., 'William Carey', *BQ*, VII (1934-5), 167-74

'The Hollis Family and Pinners' Hall', *BQ*, I (1922-3), 78-81

The New International Dictionary of the Christian Church, edited by J.D. Douglas (Exeter, 1974)

The Olney Baptist Meeting, an anonymous, undated, typed history of Olney Baptist Church retained at Olney

Toon, Peter, *The Emergence of Hyper-Calvinism in English Nonconformity 1689-1765* (1967)

Underwood, A.C., *A History of the English Baptists* (1947)

Watts, Michael R., *The Dissenters: From the Reformation to the French Revolution* (Oxford, 1978)

Weeks, Noel, *The Sufficiency of Scripture* (Edinburgh, 1988)

Wellingborough and Rushden Mercury and Herald, 9 June 1989

Wheeler Robinson, H., 'A Baptist Student — John Collett Ryland', *BQ*, III (1926-7), 25-33

White, B.R., 'Thomas Crosby, Baptist Historian: (I) The First Forty Years 1683-1723; (II) Later Years', *BQ*, XXI (1965), 154-68; 219-34

— 'John Gill in London, 1719-1729: A Biographical Fragment', *BQ*, XXII (1967), 72-91

— *The English Separatist Tradition from the Marian Martyrs to the Pilgrim Fathers* (Oxford, 1971)

— 'Open and Closed Membership among English and Welsh Baptists', *BQ*, XXIV (1972), 330-4

Whitebrook, J.C., 'The Life and Works of Mrs. Ann Dutton', *TBHS*, VII, (1920-1), 129-46

Whitley, W.T., *Baptist Bibliography*, 2 vols (1916-22)

— *A History of British Baptists*, 2nd ed. (1932)

— *The Baptists of London 1612-1928* (no date)

Wicks, W.A., *Concise History of the Baptist Church, Walgrave* (Northampton, 1892)

Wilson, Walter, *The History and Antiquities of Dissenting Churches and Meeting Houses, in London, Westminster, and Southwark; including the Lives of their Ministers, from the Rise of Nonconformity to the Present Time*, 4 vols (1808-14)

INDEX OF SCRIPTURE PASSAGES

GENERAL INDEX